Ethelred L. (Ethelred Luke) Taunton

The English Black Monks

A Sketch of Their History from the Coming of St. Augustine to the Present Day

Ethelred L. (Ethelred Luke) Taunton

The English Black Monks
A Sketch of Their History from the Coming of St. Augustine to the Present Day

ISBN/EAN: 9783744659253

Printed in Europe, USA, Canada, Australia, Japan

Cover: Foto ©ninafisch / pixelio.de

More available books at **www.hansebooks.com**

THE
ENGLISH BLACK MONKS OF ST. BENEDICT

A SKETCH OF THEIR HISTORY FROM THE
COMING OF ST. AUGUSTINE TO
THE PRESENT DAY

BY THE
REV. ETHELRED L. TAUNTON

IN TWO VOLUMES
VOLUME THE SECOND

LONDON
JOHN C. NIMMO
NEW YORK: LONGMANS, GREEN, & CO.
MDCCCXCVII

CONTENTS

VOLUME THE SECOND

CHAPTER XI

THE BENEDICTINE MISSION

PAGES

The effect of the English dissensions upon the continent—The attitude of the heads of the seminaries and of the students—Repudiation of political motives by Campion and Parsons at the London conclave of 1581—The effect of the declaration on Dr. Allen and others—The dissensions with the jesuits responsible for the influx of students to the benedictine order—The beginning of the benedictine mission in Italy: the first missioners—The movement favoured by cardinal Allen: his later distrust of the jesuits: advice to the young men who wished to become monks—The difficulties they met with—Beginning of the movement in Spain—Mark Barkworth: he goes to Rome, but is sent to Valladolid: his desire to become a monk is apparently frustrated: he sets out on the mission: is hanged as a monk at Tyburn—The Spanish congregation—Other English students who took the benedictine habit: Bradshaw, Jones or Scudamore, John Roberts—Lewis Owen's *Running Register*: his account of Roberts trustworthy—Fresh efforts to gain the English mission for the monks—Efforts of the jesuits to stop the renewed influx to the benedictines—The nuncio interferes—Continued opposition—Effect of the Spanish climate on the English monks—The mission granted by the pope to English monks of the Spanish and Cassinese congregations—Arrival of the first missioners: their meeting with one of the old Westminster monks 1-24

CHAPTER XII

DOUAI AND DIEULEWARD

PAGES

Success of the Spanish missioners—The popularity and influence of Dom John Roberts, as witnessed by Lewis Owen—The necessity of an accessible benedictine foundation for training English subjects—Advantages of Douai urged by Doctor Gifford—Imprisonment and banishment of Roberts: he visits Douai and proceeds to Spain: arrives again in England: his second arrest and return to Spain: his benedictine foundation at Douai narrated by Owen: he again visits England—Dom Augustine Bradshaw appointed vicar over the Spanish congregation's missioners in England—Roberts again imprisoned and banished: he returns to Douai—Gunpowder plot—Weldon's account of the plot: its unreliability—Return of Roberts to England: he is again arrested—Philip Caverel, abbat of Arras, becomes benefactor to the Douai benedictines—Opposition of the English jesuits renewed: their efforts to frustrate the foundation at Douai—Intrigues in relation to the Douai secular college; their aim to lower the intellectual status of the clergy—Dom Bradshaw arrives at Douai: endeavours of the jesuits to eject the monks—Dr. Gifford's efforts on behalf of the benedictines: he obtains the church and cloister of Dieuleward for the Douai monks—Roberts arrives at Douai—Parsons' charges against the benedictines at Rome, and Dom Anselm Beech's defence—Roberts again visits England and is imprisoned: his escape—The occupation of Dieuleward commenced—The building of the monastery—Roberts's exertions in Spain on behalf of Douai: his success: he returns to England, is arrested, and executed—Building of Douai monastery commenced by Philip Caverel—Employments of the monks—Benefactions of abbat Philip Caverel: his character and work—Death of Parsons—The firm establishment of the Spanish fathers on the continent 25–69

CONTENTS

CHAPTER XIII

THE RENEWAL OF THE ENGLISH CONGREGATION

PAGES

Growth of the Spanish mission in England—Difficulties of the Italian fathers: their desire for union—Dom Sigebert Buckley: he supposed to be the sole survivor of the old English congregation—David Baker: his conversion and meeting with Buckley: his belief in Buckley's inheritance of the rights and privileges of the English congregation: his reception into the Italian congregation: his efforts to preserve the succession—Buckley again imprisoned: he aggregates two novices to the Westminster monastery and receives the profession of Baker—The direct succession secured—The testimony of Maihew—Death of Buckley—Documentary evidence of the aggregation of monks to Westminster by Buckley: his delegation of authority over the old English congregation to the Italian superior—Fresh efforts for a union of the English congregations—Proposed terms of the union—Objections of the Spanish fathers—Further negotiations—The objections of the Spanish congregation overruled—"The Union of the Four Articles"—The pope insists upon a union—Objections of the Italian fathers: they are left out of the union—Plans for the government of the missioners—Election of definitors—The problem before them—The Cassinese system rejected—The renewal to be a reality—The resolutions arrived at—The position of the new congregation—Objections to the confirmation of the union—The confirmation finally secured . . 70–100

CHAPTER XIV

DOM LEANDER AND HIS MISSION

Objects of Leander's visit to England—The oath of allegiance: its origin—Intrigues of the jesuits to secure a catholic succession—Gunpowder plot—The king's terror—The oath framed: its origin and bases—The pope's policy—Adverse representations—The pope's futile mission to the king—The oath declared unlawful to catholics—Attitude of the English catholics—The question of the appointment of bishops—Parsons' appointment of arch-priests to thwart the desire for bishops—Appointment of a bishop as ordinary of England and Scotland: his authority disputed by the jesuits: he is compelled to fly to France—The rival claims of the jesuits and the clergy—Cause of the bishop's exile—Accession of Urban VIII.: his conciliatory policy—Leander and his mission: his parentage and early life—Laud's desire for a reunion of England with Rome—The state of catholicism in England, 1632-6—Secretary Windebank's permission for Leander's return to England: precautions taken for his safety: his correspondence with Windebank: his report to cardinal Bentivoglio—Adverse opinions concerning Leander: his letter to Windebank on the subject: appointment as prefect of the benedictine English mission: his opinion of the oath and of the attitude necessary for Rome: his report on the state of the apostolical mission in England: he takes an oath of allegiance to the king: his mission not an official one—Gregorio Panzani joins him as accredited agent—Leander's letter to him in reference to his rumoured advocacy of the oath—Leander's instructions to an envoy concerning the hopes for reunion: his views and propositions: he falls ill: reconciles the clergy and regulars: begs the royal protection for his brethren—The envoy sent to Rome—The king's instructions to him—Death of Leander 101-161

CHAPTER XV

CHRONICLES OF THE CONGREGATION. II

The second general chapter of Douai—The union attacked by two Spanish monks: their ignorance of mediæval English monachism—Augustine Baker's knowledge on this point: his *Apostolatus benedictinorum in Anglia*: its permanent value—The English monks obtain the loan of German abbeys and also the gift of a college at Rome—The bull *Plantata in agro Dominico* of Urban VIII.: the rights and privileges conferred by it upon the English monks: the expectation upon which it was obtained—The existence of a duality of aim among the benedictines—A commission appointed by the chapter to report upon the congregation: the definitions arrived at—The propositions of D. Lawrence Reyner—The dependence of the congregation upon the Spanish general abolished—Gratitude of Charles II. to the monks: he secures a body of them for the chapel royal—The accession of James II.: he founds a royal monastery at St. James's palace—Other foundations—The check of the revolution—The appointment of vicars-apostolic by James, and the revival of the old questions of jurisdiction—Destruction of the new foundations in the revolution—The general chapter of 1697: its enactions abolished in 1717—The endeavour to establish schools in England—The hopes of reunion crushed by the accession of the House of Hanover—The Jansenist controversy—The *Commission des réguliers* of Louis XV.—The French Revolution—The benedictine fathers in 1794—The attack of bishop Baines on the canonical existence of the congregation in 1829—Opening of a general novitiate for the three existing monasteries in 1859—St. Michael's monastery, near Hereford—Recent papal decrees in the interests of the English congregation 162–189

CHAPTER XVI

ST. GREGORY'S MONASTERY

The resumption of its history from 1611—The men who presided over it—Efforts to secure a proper allowance for the new foundation—The paternal care of Caverel: he gives 2000 florins a year to the new monastery—Conditions of the foundation—The deed sanctioned by the pope—The ejection of the benedictines from the college of Marchienne, and their reception into the new college of St. Vedast's—The foundation of an English school at St. Gregory's—The martyrs belonging to the monastery—The coming of D. Augustine Baker: his work at Cambrai and Douai—The dispute with bishop Smith concerning jurisdiction—The position taken by D. Rudisind Barlow: his letter to the Propaganda: its results—Other visitors and postulants at Douai—The conversion of Charles II. by D. John Huddleston—D. Serenus Cressy—The visit of cardinal Howard to the monastery—The daily life at St. Gregory's up to the time of the revolution—Siege of Douai by

Louis XIV. in 1667—Siege by Marlborough in 1710—Prospects of an American settlement—Suppression of St. Gregory's during the French revolution—D. Brewer's history of the events—The appropriation to the nation of all English colleges—The list of the gregorian *familia* at the time of the revolution—The expulsion of the monks—Escape of part of the monks, and the prison life of the remnant—Doullens and Wisbeach—The fall of Robespierre, and their return to Douai—Condition of the town—They return to England and obtain shelter at Acton Burnell—Purchase of the Downside property—The installation—Affairs at Douai—Accession of Louis XVIII.—Return of the monastic property to the benedictines—A return to Douai decided upon, but afterwards abandoned—The settlement at Downside determined upon—Building commenced—The church opened by bishop Baines: his early life and ambitions: his endeavour to make a foundation at Prior Park: his question of the canonical rights of the benedictine congregation: his death—Benedictine missions in foreign countries—Founding of the college—The foundation-stone of the minster laid by archbishop Manning—Work of the monks—Position and aims of St. Gregory's . . 190–250

CHAPTER XVII

ST. LAWRENCE'S MONASTERY

The foundation of the monastery: its principal promoters—The "Union of the Four Articles"—D. Maihew comes to Dieuleward: the state of the monastery on his arrival: his efforts to obtain entire possession: he throws over the "Union of the Four Articles": holds a general chapter: the mission oath introduced by him—The strict observance of the house: its reputation and industrial establishments—The war of 1636: it is followed by pestilence—The martyrdom of D. Alban Roe—Effect of the disasters—Death of D. Cuthbert Horsley—His conduct of the house—Other deaths and disasters—Condition of the house before the French revolution—Trial of D. Anselm Bolton in England on a charge of high treason—First effects of the revolution—Departure of the community for England—Dangerous position of those who remained behind—The storm breaks—Escape of the prior—Shelter obtained at Acton Burnell—Movements of the community—Gift of a house at Ampleforth to D. Bolton by Miss Fairfax: he hands it over to the laurentians—Refounding of the monastery—Some of the men connected with Ampleforth—Present position of the monastery 251–277

CHAPTER XVIII

ST. EDMUND'S MONASTERY

Origin of the house—Arrival of the Dieuleward monks in Paris: their difficulties and failure to obtain a house by patronage—Beginnings of the monastery—The monks are ejected from the college of Marmontier, but get possession of La Celle—The monastery established by royal letters patent—The king's favours—Building of the church—The funeral obsequies of James II.—Inner history of the monastery—Notable visitors: St. Francis de Sales, Franklin, Dr. Johnson—The intellectual life of the house in the middle of the eighteenth century: its difficulties—State of the house before the revolution—The first effects as evidenced in letters from the prior and procurator—Destruction of the monastery—Efforts of the prior to recover possession of the property after the revolution—Opening of a college at Douai—Proposals at the chapter—Efforts to secure the re-establishment of St. Edmund's at Douai—The transfer of the monasteries sanctioned at Rome—The president's action—Opposition of bishop Baines and others—Intervention of Rome to annul hostilities—Subsequent progress of the college and monastery—Recent superiors—The service of St. Edmund to the English clergy 278–299

CHAPTER XIX

ST. MALO, LAMBSPRING, AND CAMBRAI

The foundation at St. Malo—Difficulties to be overcome—The church opened—Prior Gifford's part in the reform of Fontevraud by D. Bradshaw—A scheme of union proposed—Misgivings of the vicar: he is removed—Visit of Charles II. to the house at Clermont—Loss of the St. Malo house through the difficulties which beset the monks—The opportunity of settlement in German monasteries offered to the English monks—Weldon's mention of D. Placid Frere—Use made of the German houses—Lambspring the house of most service: its progress—D. Maurus Corker received by James II.: his connection with archbishop Plunket—D. Placid Francis and his connection with James's illegal proceedings at Cambridge—State of Lambspring at the close of the seventeenth century—The successors of abbat Corker and their work—Suppression of Lambspring by the Prussians in 1803—The effort to open houses for nuns—The first benedictine convents—D. Benet Jones or Price and his efforts to make a foundation for nuns—The little community settles at Cambrai—Foundation of the abbey—Arrival of D. Augustine Baker: his system of spirituality—The confessions of dame Helen More—D. Baker's letter to Sir R. Cotton—Growth of the community—Disasters caused by the civil war in England—Break-up of the community in the French revolution—Imprisonment and sufferings of the nuns—Their release and journey to London—Their movements in England—Final settlement at Stanbrook 300-323

CHAPTER XX

OTHER BENEDICTINE HOUSES, DENIZEN AND ALIEN

The abbey of the "Glorious Assumption of our Lady" at East Bergholt—The foundation of an English house proposed by Lady Mary Percy—She is joined by two English ladies—The foundation authorised by the pope—Dame Joanna Berkeley installed as abbess—The difficulties surrounding ladies who wished to leave England to join—Growth of the convent—Lady Mary Percy becomes abbess—Relations of the house with the jesuits—The English dissensions find their way into the community—The nuns compelled to leave Brussels by the revolution: they make their way to England: their poverty: their settlement at East Bergholt—Origin of the Ghent house—The futile endeavours of Ladies Lucy Knatchbull and Magdalen Digby to found a benedictine convent: they return to Brussels—The exertions of Fr. Norton, S.J.—The foundation effected at Ghent—Removal to a larger monastery—Charles II. visits the convent: his benefactions—Letters of Charles II. and James II. to the abbess—The nuns forced by the French revolution to return to England: their settlement at Oulton, near Stone—St. Scholastica's abbey at Teignmouth: it was the royal foundation made from Ghent at Dunkirk—Charles II.'s contributions to its foundation—Troubles of the early settlement: their escape to England and settlement at Teignmouth—The priory of our Lady of Good Hope and St. Benedict at Colwich: its foundation at Paris by dame Clementia Cary of Cambrai—Imprisonment of the nuns and their subsequent return to England—The convent of Princethorpe, near Rugby: their arrival from France in 1792 and settlement in England —The Belgian monastery in the Isle of Wight—Tenby and St. Mildred's Minster—French and Prussian settlements in England 324-348

INDEX 349-367

THE ENGLISH BLACK MONKS OF ST. BENEDICT

CHAPTER XI

THE BENEDICTINE MISSION

THE dissensions existing in England had their full effect on the seminaries abroad. Whatever the designs of the superiors may have been, the seminarists, as a body, had no inclination to become political agents for any one. As Mr. R. Simpson remarks: "There is no manner of doubt that the heads of the seminaries, Allen at Rheims and Agazzari at Rome, wished it to be so. But it was on this very point that so many divisions arose in these colleges. The great majority of students wished to be martyrs, not for a political plot, but for religion; they wished to be Christ's ministers, not Philip's soldiers. And they repudiated honestly and heartily all designs of political meddling. I have already related the acts of the conclave of priests which met in London in July 1581, when Campion and Parsons, in their own names and in those of all the priests who had come with them, solemnly declared that their coming was only apostolical—'To treat of religion in truth and simplicity, and to attend to the gaining of souls without any pretence or knowledge of matters of state.' ... When news of this reached Dr. Allen he seems to have been much disconcerted at it. ... The politicians who had sent them over for their own purposes were naturally disappointed when the priests renounced all political action. The queen and her council knew well that the missionaries were for the most part honest in their repudiation of interference in matters of state."[1]

One result of these domestic disturbances was to turn the minds of many students to other places where they might both continue their studies and, when on the mission, be able to keep clear of either of the contending parties. Their thoughts naturally turned towards that great order which had converted England, and which was so bound up with the glories of their church. The benedictines were

---

[1] R. Simpson, *Edmund Campion*, p. 330. One must judge of Allen and his political associates in a fair and impartial manner. Elizabeth's government was certainly tyrannical; and any one (it is presumed) with a sufficient probability of success can lawfully attempt to dethrone a tyrant and restore liberty to his country. Allen had as much right to invoke foreign aid as the protestants who called Dutch William to come and save them from the arbitrary proceedings of James II. Allen's attempt was a failure, and therefore it is called "Rebellion;" while the other was successful, so it is named the "Glorious Revolution." But by the year 1600 (and for some years earlier) it was clear enough what was the issue of the politics that had been pursued. *Væ Victis!*

men of peace too, and had an old tradition at their back; and, though ready to adapt themselves to new circumstances, were not lovers of novelty. Besides, there was nothing in the life of a monk to prevent him from taking up mission work in face of sufficient cause and when duly called upon; for had not they been the great missionaries of Europe?

The movement began first in Rome, and was led off by one Robert Sayer.[1] He had been a student at Cambridge, and on his conversion went to the English college at Rheims, and thence to Rome. In 1587 he went to Monte Cassino, and there took the holy habit, together with the name of Gregory. But he never saw his native country again, for he died in Venice, October 30, 1602, when on the threshold of the Promised Land. The next was Thomas Preston, a secular priest of middle age and a noted canonist. When he became a monk he was told by his novice-master: "You are not come hither to exercise your priestly function, that hath dignity

[1] D. Robert Sayer, as the first secular to begin the movement towards the benedictines, is of interest. He matriculated as a pensioner at Caius College, in the December of 1576. He must soon have shown his leanings towards catholicity; for when the time came for the B.A., the college authorities would not allow him to proceed: "1st, for that he by secret correspondence had laboured to pervert divers scholars, and some had perverted; 2nd, for that he had used divers allegations against divers points of Mr. Jewell's book; 3rd, for that he had been of great and familiar acquaintance with Fingelay, a pernicious papist; 4th, for that he had used to gather together papistical books and convey them secretly into the country" (Cooper's *Athenæ Cantab.*, vol. ii. pp. 334, 335). Leaving Caius he went to Peter House, and took his B.A. 1580-81.

or honour in it, but to become recollected, to know and humble yourself and cleanse your soul." Then followed Beech, known afterwards as D. Anselm of Manchester, who joined the benedictines at the abbey of St. Justina at Padua; D. Austin Smith, who became vicar-general to the abbat of Monte Cassino; one known as D. Rafael, who became procurator for his congregation at Rome; D. Richard Huddleston, D. Bernard Preston, also of Monte Cassino; D. Maurus Taylor of Venice, D. Anthony Martin of La Cava, and others.

The movement towards the old order was looked upon with favour by cardinal Allen. He towards the end of his life had lost conceit of his former friends and allies.[1] The young men who wanted to become monks found in him a faithful and kind friend, who used his influence to recommend them

---

[1] It is impossible any longer to deny the fact that cardinal Allen came at last in some measure to distrust his jesuit allies and to disapprove of their schemes. Charles Paget (Answer to Parsons' *Apologie*, p. 20) writes: "He began in his latter times to mislike yours and Fr. Parsons' violent humours in such sort, as if he had lived, he would have curbed you shorter for meddling either in matters of state or in the seminaries or missions of priests." Agazzari, rector of the English college, Rome, writes to Parsons (September 25, 1596): "Certainly, my father, it seems to me a great indication of the divine majesty, and a great and visible sign of God's love towards the company, this college, and the cause of England, that when human means fail, He almost miraculously interposes His divine hand. So long as Allen walked aright in this matter, in union with and fidelity to the company, as he could do, God preserved him, prospered and exalted him; but when he began to leave this path, in a moment the thread of his plans and life were cut short together." See *Historical Introduction to First and Second Diaries of the English College, Douai* (ed. Knox), pp. xcviii, xcix.

to various monasteries. In a beautiful letter (February 1594) to one of them,[1] he discloses his mind on the point as follows:—

"But that you might know how much I esteem your progress in that most holy state of life, which much more now in the Lord than ever in the world (though your remarkable talents ever rendered you very dear to me) I love you and embrace you. . . . Lastly, that I might communicate unto you the joy I have conceived of this most happy state of life, to which I apply the words of the Apostle—*I have no greater joy than to hear that my children walk in the truth* (2 St. John iv.). Wherefore I most highly congratulate your contempt of human affairs and fervour in pursuit of those of heaven; and that having escaped and overcome the most cruel and most turbulent movements of a worldly and secular life, you model and form yourself in such holy discipline; prudently preferring to the most turbulent business of the world the most holy leisure of a most ancient and most glorious religious state of life. For this most solid good and most saving advantage, I congratulate with you from the bottom of my heart, . . . neither is there

---

[1] Among the archives of the diocese of Westminster (vol. viii. n. 292) is an autograph memorial to the pope from Fr. Joseph Cresswell, S.J., dated April 20, 1596, in which the jesuit makes, on the authority of an unnamed priest, the statement that Anthony Martin, to whom Allen wrote, had been sent at the expense of the English Government to Italy to become a monk, and then to return to England to oppose the society. Containing such a preposterous charge, the memorial was not presented. See Knox's *Historical Introduction to the First and Second Douai Diaries*, p. lxxix.

anything more for you or me to crave from Christ our Sovereign Good who inspired you this, than that He will please of His infinite piety and goodness to assist you to the end of the work of your salvation which He has so happily begun; which He will not fail, if since you have put your hand to the plough of the Lord, you do not look back, but advance forward to the utmost you may be able, . . . if you cast out of your mind, what for your trial you have suffered in the world either from heretics or bad catholics or rivals or envious, and also pray for your persecutors. . . . Let others think and say what they list of this your most holy state of life, I would have you persuaded I most heartily espouse your affairs, and mightily like this resolution you have taken of engaging in religion, and hope that you are taken from this wicked world to contribute to the restoration of this most holy order which formerly so flourished in our country, and your pen and genius will render you an ornament thereof; and therefore so much the more profit you make in that most holy discipline, so much the more I shall love you, and you will have no occasion to repent you of this resolution."[1]

Reading the above, we can detect a tone of frustrated hopes on the part of the old champion of English catholicity; and at the same time a conviction that "the solid glory of Christ and His

[1] *Letters and Memorials of William cardinal Allen* (ed. Knox).

church" would be promoted by the recall of the first labourers in that vineyard. We also see a reference to the difficulties the young men met with in following their vocation. For, truth to tell, the movement was regarded with but little love by the superiors of the English college at Rome, who saw some of the best men removed from their influence. Allen had, indeed, retained them within bounds, but immediately after his death the opposition became pronounced.

While these men were being attracted to the Italian abbeys, a similar movement, due to like causes, began in Spain. We have more information regarding this latter, for it was on a larger scale, and had more influence on the subsequent history. It began in Valladolid, and the way was led by Mark Barkworth, *alias* Lambert. He had been a student at Douai for a year and a half, and when the plague broke out (in 1595) went with other students to Rome, where he stayed only a few months. There, of course, he would hear how and why many students had gone to the benedictines. He also felt himself called in the same path; but there were now difficulties in his way. The general chapter of the Cassinese congregation had in the previous year (1594) petitioned the holy see to grant their English subjects leave to go on the mission; but the petition had been vehemently opposed by those who were masters of the situation. A few months only had Barkworth been at Rome when he was hurried off to Valladolid. Probably he had given some signs of his inclination, and was sent off out of harm's way. He arrived at the English college at Valladolid with five companions on December 16, 1596. Great as his desire was to become a monk, it now seemed impossible; for he had to take the oath to go out on that mission which the holy see had just refused to grant to monks. He seems to have talked about the matter to his fellow-students, and made many think over the possibility of becoming benedictine missionaries after all. Barkworth was sent out, as a secular, on the mission in 1599, and on his way stopped at the monastery of our Lady at Yrache in Navarre, where, confiding his hopes and their frustration to the abbat, he was comforted by being told that he should not die without becoming a benedictine. Asking how this could be, the abbat said: "We will receive you now for then."[1] So the novice, received by anticipation of the hour of death, went on his way rejoicing; and two years afterwards (February 27, 1601) was hanged as a monk, in a benedictine habit and tonsure, at Tyburn.

At Valladolid, the famous monastery of San Benito, founded about 1390, was the central house of the Spanish congregation. The abbat of this house[2] was

---

[1] *Revue bénédictine* (1895), p. 366.
[2] Alexander VI. raised the house to the dignity of an abbey; and though the election was a purely domestic one, yet the abbat was the general, and visitor over the whole congregation. (See Helyot, *Histoire des Ordres Monastique*, tome vi. p. 237.)

ex officio general over the fifty houses which made up the congregation. He it was to whom the king had submitted the question of the foundation of the English seminary of Valladolid, and who had befriended Parsons when his project was opposed by the Irish.[1]

Now, at the secular seminary, one of the young Englishmen, named Bradshaw (*alias* White), was taken very ill in the winter of 1598, and vowed to God he would, if his life was spared, become a monk of St. Benedict's order. He recovered, and in his twenty-first year applied as a postulant at San Benito's, and was received. Not much opposition seems to have been made to his departure. In May 1599 he was sent to the abbey of San Martino, at Compostella, where he was clothed on the 26th of May, and took the name of Augustine, the apostle of England, whose feast was kept on that day.

One of the next to follow was a young Welshman, John Jones or Scudamore, an Oxford student. He had been converted in June 1596 by Fr. Gerard, S.J., at that time a prisoner in the Clink. A few months afterwards Fr. Gerard sent him into Spain, and, in his twenty-second year, he was admitted a seminarist at Valladolid, December 13, 1596. A story is told that one night at sea, when on his journey, in a dream he saw standing over him a venerable man, clad in black garments of a peculiar

---

[1] More's *Hist. Prov. Soc. Jesu*, p. 158.

shape. The vision spoke and told him not to fear, for all would be well with him. After his arrival in Valladolid, he happened one day to see in the street a figure clad in the dress he had seen in his dream. Seized by some uncontrollable impulse, he went and threw himself at the feet of the monk, the first he had ever seen, and determined there and then to become one.

His departure from the seminary seems to have been only one of several that took place under the following circumstances. Bradshaw's leaving had been a serious loss to the seminary, and alarmed the superiors. When a short time afterwards John Roberts,[1] another student, who up to this had concealed his desire of entering religion, and had lived a life hidden and peaceful, asked the fathers to recommend him also to the prior of San Benito, it was high time, they thought, to put a stop to this exodus. Here we begin to have more details of the story of John Roberts, and of the movement in Spain, for in the British Museum is a book entitled *"The Running Register: recording a True Relation of the States of the English Colledges, Seminaries, and Cloisters in all Forain Parts. Together with a Briefe and Compendious Discourse of the Lives, Practices, Coozenages, Impostures, and Deceits of*

---

[1] John Roberts had been at St. John's, Oxford, and then, in 1598, became a lawyer's clerk at Furnival's Inn. He was that same year converted at Paris; and then went to Valladolid, where he arrived on September 15.

all our *English Monks, Friers, Jesuits, and Seminarie Priests in generall. By Lewis Owen,* 1626." The author, as may easily be guessed, was one of those paid spies who, under pretence of conversion, penetrated our colleges abroad, and, on their apostacy, gave such information as they could to their masters at home. The State Paper offices abound with the reports of these agents, but their information may be commonly looked upon with suspicion. In this case, at least as far as it concerns John Roberts, the witness of Lewis Owen can be trusted, for his story is verified from other unimpeachable sources, and he speaks here with a peculiar authority. For not only was he himself at Valladolid (1605), but became brother-in-law to John Roberts by marrying his sister Blanche. Hence in his account will be noticed a certain sense of pride in telling the deeds of his brother-in-law, and an abstinence from the abuse he so freely flings upon all others.

Lewis Owen, then, shall tell us the story of John Roberts' entry into religion. He had gone off one morning to San Benito, and that same day his late superiors "(knowing full well *Roberts* to be a man of a turbulent spirit, and one that was like to cross them in their affairs here in England) repaired with all speed to the lord abbat of that abbey, and with open mouths exclaimed against *Roberts,* saying that he was a very deboyshed fellow; a common mover and breeder of debates in their college, a notorious drunkard, a prophane blasphemer and swearer, and withal one whom they suspected to be no good catholic, but rather a spy or an intelligencer sent thither out of England to discover the state of the college, and that they had given him sundry private corrections for many heinous crimes and offences not fit to be nominated.

"But, in the end, when they perceived that there was no hope of amendment in him, but rather that he grew daily to be worse and worse, they expulsed him out of their college, and gave him a sufficient *viaticum* to bring him to his country or some other part: protesting withal they did not speak this for any malice that they bare him; but because the lord abbat and the rest of those religious monks should not think hardly of them or any other English catholics, by reason of his lewd behaviour.

"The abbat having heard all they could say against *Roberts*, and believing all to be true that they reported, as soon as they were departed[1] he sent for *Roberts*, and privately related unto him all the whole discourse, and told him plainly he could

---

[1] D. Leander, in a manuscript preserved at Monte Cassino, says some four or five of them came to accuse the young man. "A short time after Brother Mervinia, *alias* Roberts, who up to this had concealed his desire of entering religion, and had lived a life hidden and peaceful, asked the fathers to recommend him also to the superior of Valladolid. Upon this they sent him off one morning very early from the college to the monastery, and later on in the day some four or five of them came also there, but instead of giving the recommendation charity demanded for all pilgrims, they began to charge him before the monks with so many grave accusations, that the prior (?) was completely changed from his intention of admitting him."

not entertain him any longer in the abbey, whereupon *Roberts*, being driven to such a *non-plus*, knew not what to say; but in the end he began to apologise for himself, and said that he was a gentleman, very well descended, and one that might have lived very well in his country, in good fashion and credit among his friends and neighbours; but his zeal to God's glory and the good of the catholic church had moved him to forsake his own native soil, and to come to Spain to study and take the holy order of priesthood and the habit of St. Benet, and not any particular profit of his own; and therefore he besought his lordship to conceive a charitable opinion of him until such time that he should purge and clear himself of those false accusations laid to his charge by his unkind countrymen the English jesuits; protesting withal that he was not such a man as they had reported him to be, neither had he ever received any correction, private or public, in the English college or elsewhere, for any offence whatsoever, or was ever expulsed out of the same, but came away from the college unknown to any of the jesuits or students, except to one or two of his chamber fellows, who were very desirous to be religious monks of St. Benet's order; and that he was certainly persuaded in his conscience that Father Parsons[1] and the rest of the English jesuits

---

[1] This is a mistake. Fr. Parsons was then rector at Rome for the second time. But he was made by Aquaviva, prefect of the English mission, and had full power over the seminary at Valladolid, and could admit or dismiss students (More, p. 243).

would receive him back again into their college, if he would go back thither notwithstanding all their former exclamations against him.

"The abbat replied that he would never believe that Father *Parsons* would admit him again into the college, for (said he): 'It stands not with his reputation to entertain such a lewd fellow as he reports you to be; and if he will, then you shall stay there some few days, and then come hither again to me, and I will entertain you and as many students as shall come away with you.'

"Master *Roberts* gave the abbat many thanks, being very glad that he had promised to receive him again upon that condition; and so, taking his leave of his lordship and the monks, repaired to the English college; where, upon his feigning repentance and humble submission to Father *Parsons*, he was admitted once again (*statu quo prius*) into the college, and made as much of as in former times.

"The lord abbat understanding by some of his young monks that frequented the university schools that Master *Roberts* was received again into the English college, and was in as great favour and grace with the jesuits as formerly he had been, was very glad, demurring not a little at the unnatural and unchristian-like dealing of the English jesuits towards their own countryman; and withal conceiving a singular good opinion and liking of *Roberts* far better than ever before, he sent him word in writing by one of his monks that was very intimate with *Roberts*, that if he would come to the abbey he should be entertained with as many English students as would come with him.

" Master *Roberts* receiving this message from the abbat runs away once again (with two or three other students) from the English college unto the abbat, where they were courteously entertained, and within a few days received into the order and habit of St. Benet." [1]

So far at present with Lewis Owen and his *Running Register*. Four other students left the seminary with Roberts, viz., Robert Knaresborough (who died in Spain before ordination), John Hutton, William Johnson, and John Jones. From some manuscript notes by the latter, now preserved at Monte Cassino, we are able fairly well to fix the date of the exodus. John Jones, afterwards so well known as D. Leander of St. Martin, tells us he was clothed at the abbey of San Martino, Compostella, October 20, 1599. As Bradshaw left Valladolid for Compostella in the previous May, Roberts' adventure must have taken place very soon afterwards, at any rate before the summer vacation.

Already we have seen that in 1594 the Cassinese congregation petitioned the holy see to allow its English members to work in the English mission-field. In that same year the bishop of Cassano,

[1] *Running Register*, pp. 85-87.

Owen Lewis, had petitioned the Cassinese Fathers to send monks to England. About the same time some of the English secular clergy[1] also wrote to them to send men to their assistance. In 1601 a petition signed by some of the English lay nobility, who saw the terrible desolation resulting from the conflicts between the jesuits and seculars, was presented by cardinal Frederic Borromeo,[2] archbishop of Milan, to the same effect. All these attempts had been strenuously opposed by the superiors of the English college and their friends, and so far with success. But now petitions began to come in from Spain also, and were being backed by that very power which had been used to frustrate the former negotiations, namely, the Spanish ambassadors. In 1601 a petition from the six English monks at San Martino in Compostella was presented to the Spanish general chapter praying for leave to be sent on the mission; and the general of the Spanish congregation began to stir in the matter.

As soon as there appeared a probability of the Spanish congregation taking up the English mission, the exodus began again from the seminary at Valla-

---

[1] They wrote: "Quid potest impedire vos, quominus qui Christianam reddidistis Angliam eamdem reddatis catholicam?" See *Downside Review*, vol. ii. pp. 175, 176, "Among our Archives."

[2] The interest the cardinal took in the matter was, on the one hand, through his relation and predecessor, St. Charles; and, on the other, through Dr. William Gifford, who had been a trusty member of his household.

dolid. First six went, then six more. The superior of San Benito appealed to the superiors of the other houses in Castile to receive the students, who thus finding the door opened to follow the vocation they had received (to use the quaint words of Lewis Owen), "ran away (like so many sheep to the water) to be monks, yea, many scholars and gentlemen; nay, roaring boys and . . . rid post from England thither to wear St. Benet's cowle."[1]

The superiors of the seminary tried in vain to avert the movement and to hinder an English mission, which would be independent of them and break through the monopoly they projected or indeed had already secured. At length they appealed to the civil power, to the nuncio in Spain, to the archbishop of Valladolid, and even went so far as to denounce the monks to the Inquisition. They said:—

"The benedictines were decoying the students from the seminaries; that the employment of missioners trained under different institutes and formed to different views would be productive only of animosities and discord; and that in point of fact the duties of the mission to which the parties in question proposed to dedicate themselves were incompatible with the obligations of a religious life, and a direct violation of the monastic vow."[2]

It is difficult to believe that Englishmen could

[1] *Ibid.* p. 88.
[2] Tierney, vol. iv. p. 88, *note.*

have made such a statement, when a knowledge of their own history told them that monks had converted England.

The opponents called on the Council of State to interfere; they harangued the people, and demanded both the archbishop and the nuncio to prevent the reception of the postulants. They appealed moreover to the oath lately introduced, at their suggestion, into all the colleges, which bound the students to go out on the mission after ordination. How could the students keep this oath, they argued, when Rome would not grant the mission to benedictines? The nuncio took the matter up. D. Leander tells us in his notes that one winter's night (1602-3) the nuncio sent for the abbat of San Benito or his procurator to come to him at once, and to bring with him the six youths who were the last admitted. The procurator came, and along with him the six postulants. They found the nuncio, together with Fr. Cresswell, S.J., the superior of the seminary,[1] awaiting them. The interview was warm on either side, and the youths refused to abandon their vocation. A last demand was made by the jesuit, that at least they should return to the college and make the

---

[1] Fr. Cresswell had been rector at Rome (1589), but his indiscreet and tyrannical behaviour brought about his removal, February 22, 1592. He was sent to Spain, and became prefect of the English jesuits on Fr. Parsons' departure. After these troubles he was recalled to Rome, and finally died, as rector at Ghent, in 1623 or 1622. He is described as having much "peevishness of temper and tenacity of opinion."

spiritual exercises there, under their late superiors, before taking the habit. But the invitation was absolutely declined; the retreat, they said, could be made with equal facility and perhaps more convenience in their own monastery. The nuncio, seeing they were determined in their refusal to return to the seminary, compromised matters with the jesuit and kept them in his own house to make the retreat, after which he encouraged them to persevere in their holy vocation, for which they had struggled so bravely. The superior of the seminary, moreover, received an order to send to the monastery without any delay any student who wished to become a monk. Two more at once left, and ten followed during the next year; and several from the other Spanish colleges also joined the benedictines.

Fr. Parsons, from Rome, seeing that further opposition was useless, wrote to Fr. Cresswell (September 12, 1604),[1] not to set himself against the current. He says a long experience has taught him that the best way to keep the seminarists in peace is to leave them to themselves, and to be moderate in all dealings with them: "for the more we seem careful and vigilant towards them (what they call jealousy) the worse they are." But Fr. Cresswell was not a man to be talked down. He had his own views. So Parsons wrote again, this time vehemently reproaching Cresswell for hindering the vocations;

[1] *Stonyhurst Collectanea*, p. 458, quoted in the *Revue bénédictine*, 1895, p. 402.

for, on the mere ground of human policy, it was a mistake, he said, to oppose these spontaneous vocations; and he seems to have gathered from the number that something must be wrong in the administration. The troubles went on, until in 1607 the general of the jesuits was obliged to send over a visitor. That Fr. Cresswell was unwise in his dealings with the seminarists seems beyond dispute, and that he could keep ill feelings rankling in his heart is unfortunately too true. Even as late as January 30, 1608, the rancour had not died out; for he could bring himself to write of them to Dr. Worthington at Douai that he thought "it is the devil who attempts by the way of lewd persons under pretence of a monk's cowl, what he could not before effect by appellants' cloaks. For neither are such truly and religiously resolved for the love of Almighty God to become good monks; nor do they any whit savour of holy St. Benedict's spirit, nor even are like well to keep his rule."[1]

So many English had joined the Spanish congregation, both from the seminaries and directly from England, that it became a question with the general what to do with them, especially, as Lewis Owen says, some were dying off—

"Like so many rotten sheep, and those that scaped had not their health, by reason of the unwholesomeness of the air, and that they did not like so well of the fashion and condition of the Spaniards

[1] Tierney, vol. iv. p. ccxviii.

or of their diet; and therefore in the beginning of King James' reign it was agreed between all the Spanish abbats that all, or the most part of the English monks of their order that were in Spain, should be put into one or two abbeys in some temperate part of the country which was best agreeing to their nature and complexion, whereof Onia was one, which is an abbey situated in the kingdom (or province) of Castilla la Vieia, near adjoining to the mountains of Asturia and Biscaia, where they continued many years, sending such monks into England (when they were made priests) as they thought fittest, and receiving other students into their places."[1]

We have said above that Fr. Parsons, writing from Rome to Fr. Cresswell, had counselled a withdrawal of opposition. What was the reason? The following events will show.

The Spanish general, D. Alphonsus de Coral, in answer to the petition of his English monks, in the spring of 1601 petitioned the pope for leave to send his subjects on the English mission, for which the congregation, at a great expense, had educated them at the university of Salamanca. The Cassinese joined in the renewed effort, and added their petition to that of the Spaniards. The old opposition at once broke out again. But the repeated applications, and the continual objections coming always from the same interested quarter (which had

[1] *Running Register*, p. 88.

lately met with a certain amount of discredit owing to the arch-priest controversy) revealed to the pope the true nature of the opposition. A decree of the Inquisition granting the mission to the English monks of both congregations was passed on March 20, 1602, and, after a last attempt to get its withdrawal, was confirmed by Clement VIII. on December 5 of that same year. England was now opened to benedictine missionaries, and at last St. Benedict was going to re-enter his old patrimony, and his sons were again to toil and labour in their own vineyard, but now at risk and peril of the pain of death.

As soon as the decree was confirmed, no time was lost. The news reached the Spanish monks about Christmas-day, and on the 26th, the feast of the proto-martyr, the first missioners set out. They were also the first who had joined the order, D. Augustine Bradshaw, who was appointed as superior, and D. John Roberts. D. Roberts tells us, in his examination before the bishop of London (21st December 1607), "that returning out of Gallicia he stayed in Paris and in St. Omers about half a year, and then came into England."[1] That there was a third in the little party seems to be the case, for from a paper in the State Paper Office, containing information given by an Irish priest lately

---

[1] A copy of this document, preserved in the archives of the *Old English Chapter*, has been kindly placed at my disposal by D. Bede Camm of the German benedictines at Erdington.

at Valladolid and then at Bordeaux, we learn "that three benedictine friars have lately gone to England with plenty of money." The date of this paper is given as March 10. Bordeaux was the port of embarkment; though where they landed and the date are points not known; but only that it was at some quiet port and at nightfall that they were put ashore. Shoreham was a favourite place of secret landing, and was within easy reach of London. Wherever the spot, it was not long before the monks made their way to the capital, where we find Roberts was in the early days of that April (1603) frequenting the chambers of Bluet, the secular priest, then in the Clink.

The Italian fathers were just as eager as the Spanish; and knowing the news sooner, were able to start earlier than the others. These first missioners were D. Thomas Preston and D. Anselm Beech. They landed some time in the early spring at Great Yarmouth. Hard by, at Great Breecles near Wymondham, they first settled; and there, in the house of a Mr. Francis Woodhouse at Cisson, they stood face to face with one of the old Westminster monks, D. Sigebert Buckley, an old feeble man, well over eighty years of age, who had spent half of his life in prison for conscience' sake.

How happy must have been the meeting between the patriarch and the younger brethren. How the old man's heart must have leapt for joy when he saw in them the men he had so often prayed for, those who were to keep alive that order of which, to his knowledge, he was the last survivor. His long imprisonments, his many toils, his tears and prayers, were not to go without reward. And the old monk of St. Peter's abbey rejoiced the more that it was from Rome, from Peter's own chair, that, like Augustine of old, these benedictines came.

Tenderly and lovingly, as their special care, did the two monks take charge of the old man, who was to them the representative of the ancient glories of the benedictine name in England. They lavished upon him every reverence and attention while he lived, and watched over him as sons do an aged father. But as yet they did not realise the full importance of the meeting.

Here, then, calmly as though they were in their cloister, the monks of either congregation, joined by new comers, pursued their mission of life and death.

Their history was like that of the early missioners: *There was no crying out in the street.* The spirit of John Fecknam had fallen upon them. They, too, "went on planting:" and not in vain.

CHAPTER XII

DOUAI AND DIEULEWARD

THE missioners of the Spanish congregation[1] were from the beginning very successful. Welcomed by many of the clergy and laity, their true worth was soon found out. The benedictine spirit made itself felt, and won for them friends high and low. Many who had before favoured the other comers were struck by the peaceful and unostentatious way in which the monks set about their work. D. John Roberts especially seems to have made a mark—Lewis Owen tells us:—

"He became very famous among the English papists, and many resorted to him; some of them (especially such as were of the jesuit faction) out of curiosity to see a benedictine monk once again in England, and others came out of a blind zeal for his fatherhood; but, however, they all did administer and contribute very largely to his relief and the rest of the English monklings."[2]

This influence was used wisely, and through it D. Roberts made many converts:—

---

[1] We shall use in future the terms "Spanish" or "Italian" fathers to mean the English members of these two congregations.
[2] *Running Register*, p. 89.

"Nor did he neglect his lord and master's[1] business, but bestirred himself day and night in negotiating his affairs, and within a short time (with the help of the secular priests and their benefactors, and favourites who then were, and still are, altogether tooth and nail against the jesuits) he got here many proselytes and popelings, and having done so, transplanted them into Spain to be trained upon the monastical discipline."[2]

The necessity of having some special house for the English monks had been already engaging the attention of the Spanish congregation. Many young men going over into Spain cost both money and time; and the advantage of securing some place nearer at hand was apparent to all. One place in Spanish territory, but near to England, would at once suggest itself as suitable for the proposed foundation. Douai, already so well known to English catholics, was within easy reach, and its climate was less trying to Englishmen than Spain. It was also the seat of a famous university, whose degrees were highly esteemed. Moreover, it was in the midst of many ancient and wealthy benedictine monasteries, some of which, such as Arras, Marchienne, and Anchin, had years ago contributed largely to the establishment of the English college, and were still befriending it. This other point, the presence of the college for the secular clergy, among whom the bene-

---

[1] Owen here means, of course, the pope.
[2] *Ibid.* p. 89.

dictines had so many friends, made Douai one of the centres of English ecclesiastical life, and therefore marked the town out as a suitable place for a foundation of English benedictine monks. It was, we think, most probable Dr. William Gifford, the dean of Lille hard by, and well known to be anxious that benedictines should labour on the English mission,[1] who

---

[1] William Gifford, one of the earliest to join the Spanish benedictines after 1605, was of the noble family of Giffords or Giffards of Normandy, and by his mother connected with the Throckmortons. He was born 1555. After four years at Oxford he went to Louvain, where, for four years, he studied theology under Bellarmine. He went on to Paris, whence Allen called him to Rheims, and sent him on to Rome in 1579 to continue his studies. He then, in 1582, returned to Rheims to teach theology. He took the degree of Doctor of Divinity in 1584 at Pont-à-Mousson, and continued his work at Rheims. He lost his inheritance in England on account of his religion, but found great benefactors in the duke of Guise and his brother, the cardinal archbishop of Rheims. They gave him a yearly pension of two hundred golden pieces. He went to Rome in 1591 as one of the household of cardinal Allen, and acted as his head chaplain and almoner; and in 1594, upon Allen's death, filled a similar post in the household of the great St. Charles of Milan. The pope conferred upon him about 1596 the deanery of St. Peter's at Lille. He was no favourer of the Spanish and other policy advocated at that time by Parsons, who took care to represent the dean as unfriendly to the state. The duke of Feria writes to the king of Spain (January 3, 1597): "In Lille there is a Doctor Gifford, the dean of that place, a man of good abilities but of ambitious views, possessing, I am told, but little discretion, and yet the confidential adviser of the nuncio, Malvasia. At Rome he is not in bad estimation. His character, in fact, stands higher than that of any individual belonging to his party; and to increase his importance, by accomplishing his purpose, he will never hesitate to effect any mischief." He held this post for nearly ten years, and during that time kept open house, especially to exiles for the faith. On August 1, 1603, he received instructions from the nuncio to go to England and, on the occasion of James's accession, offer in the pope's name (Clement VIII.) to "recall all those whom his majesty should reasonably judge to be harmful to the king-

drew attention to the advantages Douai offered for a foundation. Already D. John Roberts, as we learn from his examination before the bishop of London, on leaving Spain had spent some time at Paris and then at St. Omers, in the immediate neighbourhood of Douai; and it is only some important business of this kind, from what we know of the man's ardent character and zeal, that could have kept him from

dom and state." Had James accepted the offer, how different would have been the religious history of England? When turned out of his deanery on account of his defending the benedictines in the attempt to drive them out of Douai, he retired to Rheims, where, as will be seen, he was able to continue his good offices. He was made rector of the university, and there perhaps found his vocation. He helped largely in founding the monastery at Dieuleward, and giving up all his honours in his fifty-third year, he took the habit of St. Benedict in the abbey of Rheims on July 11, 1608. In the following spring Dr. Gifford (now known as D. Gabriel of St. Mary) was sent to that house, where he had for his novice Master D. Nicholas Fitzjames, the first received at Douai. Here he was professed, July 11, 1609, and gave furniture and many books to the monastery. Under circumstances to be mentioned in the text, in 1611 he stayed at St. Malo on his way to Spain, and there founded another monastery for the Spanish monks at the request of the bishop, who was much struck by his religious behaviour. He was frequently called to Paris, and was famous as an eloquent preacher. The part he took in the affairs of the Union, and the high mark of esteem his brethren paid him, by electing him the first president, will be told in the text. He became bishop of Archidalia, and coadjutor to the cardinal, and in 1622 succeeded as archbishop of Rheims, and thus became duke and first peer of France and legate of the holy see. In the midst of his splendour as archbishop he retained all his customs as a simple monk. He wore the habit, kept the fasts, and rose at the usual hour. He was a model pastor, and of unbounded charity; he was instant in visiting his diocese and preaching and catechising in the villages, sometimes seven or eight times a day. He had seen St. Charles at work in Milan, and that was enough to give him an excellent idea of the pastoral office. The archbishop died in 1629, leaving a memory rich in virtue.

entering at once upon the mission field. Very soon after his arrival in England, early in 1603, he was apprehended as a priest and confined in prison; but with many other priests he was, on the accession of James I., released and banished the kingdom. He then left London, May 13, 1603, in company with Fr. Weston, S.J., of Wisbeach fame. While the latter went to St. Omers, the benedictine[1] on May 24 paid a passing visit to the secular college at Douai, and thence went to the abbey of Marchienne, with the intention of proceeding on to Antwerp and Brussels before returning to England. But evidently his visit to Douai and to Marchienne changed his plans, for, instead of returning at once to mission work, we find him posting off to Spain. Douai, he saw, was the spot for the foundation; and most likely the good monks of Marchienne had given him encouragement. And being a man of action, he lost no time in consulting the general of the Spanish congregation. This was in the early summer of 1603.

As far as we can trace his movements, he seems to have returned from Spain directly to England; at least in the autumn he was devotedly attending the sick during the plague which raged in London until late that year. The winter (1603-4) was spent in mission work; and he was probably making the

---

[1] "Eodem die (Mai 24) transit per nos D. Joannes Roberts, ordinis Sancti Benedicti, ex Anglia relegatus. Hinc vero ad monasterium Marchianense, inde Antwerpian et Bruxellas perrecturus postea in Angliam reversurus" (*Third Douai Diary MS.*).

converts, and, in view of the new foundation, sending over to Spain the postulants Owen refers to in the passage above. Now also would he be maturing the plans for Douai. There is no record, at present, of any other visit of his to the continent during the winter.

But an occasion did arise a few months later of which he availed himself. In the spring of 1604 he set out for Spain, to attend the general chapter.[1] This was very likely the result of his recent visit to the general. As he was embarking, he was arrested under suspicion and put into prison. But not for long. D. Roberts had powerful friends who frequently interested themselves on his behalf, and on more than one occasion obtained his liberty. So it was on this occasion; for by the first week in April he was journeying to Spain. He would certainly pass by Douai, for he stopped on his way at Paris, where he had an interview with the nuncio Bufalo. But what was decided at chapter we do not know, neither what his immediate movements were. But to this period may be attributed this portion of Owen's narrative :—

"Being thus applauded and extolled by the Spaniards and his own countrymen, he procured divers letters from the general, provincials, and

---

[1] This seems to imply that D. Roberts held some position of authority among the English monk-missioners. Owen speaks of him (p. 89) as having the title of "Provincial"; a title, however, as far as the name is concerned, of later date.

others the chiefest of the Spanish abbats of the Low Countries, for the maintenance of a congregation of English monks in the university of Douai; signifying unto them what they had done and still did for them in Spain, and what a meritorious deed it was to help their own spiritual brethren in so good a work as was the conversion of a whole kingdom from heresy to their holy mother, the church of Rome, and that the English monks (yea, all English catholics) would not be unthankful unto them or their successor for their charity.

"Father Roberts (having received these and many other letters to that purpose, together with a good *viaticum* to defray his charges) took his leave of Spain; and with all speed came (together with another English monk whose name was Father White, *alias* Augustine,[1]) into Flanders; where he solicited his business so well, that all the abbats in the Low Countries were content to contribute to such a good work. For some of them promised to give him corn and others money—whereupon he immediately hired a convenient house near St. James' Church in Douai, and accommodated a lower room for a chapel to say mass, and gathered ten or twelve other English monks unto him, whereof he was the prior."[2]

But Lewis Owen goes on too fast. The foundation at Douai meant men; and the mission could not at

---

[1] "White" was the *alias* of D. Augustine Bradshaw.
[2] *Ibid.* p. 90.

once spare them. Therefore D. Roberts returned to England and continued his work in London, and lived " in one master Knight's house in Holborn over against Chancery Lane."[1] He may, of course, have returned by Douai and presented his letters to the abbats and have secured the " convenient house " at the same time. But it is certain that the foundation was not then made.

D. Augustine Bradshaw had come back from the chapter of 1604 as the general's vicar over the Spanish fathers on the English mission. He therefore had to have a word in the matter and to fix a date. Now there were other cares occupying him just then, and he was full of work which had fallen to him. Besides the ordinary mission work there was the duty of looking after an increasing number of subjects. Perhaps, also, he did not enter very heartily into the plan of the Douai house, which seems all along to have been due to the initiative of D. Roberts. Whatever the cause, the vicar took no immediate steps; and when soon after he relinquished active missionary work in England, it was for quite another purpose than that which D. Roberts had conceived. In the September of 1605 Lord Arundel of Wardour, who had been appointed colonel of the English regiment in the service of the archduke Albert, " brought Father Augustine Bradshaw out of England with him to be chaplain major of that regiment," a position which one of the

[1] *Ibid.* p. 89.

other chaplains, Father Coniers, S.J., seems to have resented.¹ So, soon troubles began to brew, and D. Bradshaw had his hands full.

To go back to D. Roberts. Very soon after his return to England in the autumn of 1604 he was again arrested. Owen carries on the story thus: "In the end this our provincial was arrested (by a pursuivant who had for a long time sought for him) in one Master Knight's house, a scrivener, that dwelt in Holborn over against Chancery Lane, where this English provincial had his cell or chamber, and afterwards was committed to prison upon the lord archbishop of Canterbury's command." ²

In the following spring of 1605, "by the means and intercession of some great personages in this land," he was released and banished. Now was the time, we conjecture, when he went over to Douai and took possession of "the convenient house near to St. Jaques" "whereof he was prior." It was, perhaps, during this time that the English monks came under the notice of Philip Caverel, abbat of St. Vedast's at Arras, who was afterwards to be their munificent founder. At that time he was building a college at Arras (begun some time before) for the jesuits. One day as he was watching the

¹ Father Coniers had been confessor at the English college of Douai and most certainly knew of the proposed benedictine foundation. He left Douai to be one of the chaplains, September 17, 1605. See *Downside Review*, vol. xvi. p. 30.

² *Running Register*, p. 89.

progress of the buildings he met an old Welsh priest, John Ishel,[1] a chaplain at Notre Dame, who was gazing very seriously at the work.

"The abbat asked him what he thought of it; the chaplain replied that it was a stately fabric and not misapplied, yet it was his opinion that his lordship would do better to begin his charity towards his own order; and that there were at Douai a considerable number of benedictines that had not a home to put their heads in, or wherewithal to subsist. This news made some impression on the abbat's mind, who, besides a natural tendency to do good to all, had a singular tenderness for the order of which he was so considerable a member and ornament."[2] Thus Weldon in his characteristic style.

While we are leaving D. Roberts at Douai founding the house of St. Gregory's, we must for a while go back to England, where political events were rapidly coming to a crisis. Driven to desperation by the renewal of persecution, and disappointed by the policy forced on the king, some few catholics, none of whom were in any way mixed up with the benedictines, determined to strike a decisive blow

[1] Weldon places the account of Ishel at another date, an altogether impossible one. That John Ishel, a Welshman, may have been really interested in his fellow-countryman's (John Roberts) work is likely enough. But that he did the part ascribed to him by Weldon is out of the question. *En passant* it is worthy of notice how many Welshmen were associates in the work of the revival of English benedictinism.

[2] *Chronological Notes of the English Benedictine Congregation*, pp. 63, 64.

for liberty. Rumours of a movement of some kind had reached the pope, and he had written to the persecuted catholics of England imploring them to be patient, and not to attempt any forcible measures. The conspirators, unhappily, succeeded in deceiving their friends, and by putting a supposititious case, got from them a declaration, which they twisted into an approval of their policy. The Gunpowder Plot was unfortunately the result. It gave the government the desired opportunity of enforcing more severely, and of increasing the laws against catholics.

D. Benet Weldon, whose work has for so long been accepted as history, tells us after his peculiar fashion how the discovery of the Plot affected the Spanish fathers. It will serve as a specimen of his accuracy :—

"Wherefore Fr. Austin Bradshaw, vicar-general of the English Spanish benedictine missioners, seeing such a dismal storm, found himself in a necessity of withdrawing out of the land; and fearing the violent cruelties in force would soon bereave his mission of a continued succession unless they could procure some refuge both to shelter themselves in when such violent storms broke out, and a nursery for the education of such as the Spirit of God should dispose to such a vocation, for both which purposes Spain was too remote, he went to Douay, where he obtained a dormitory in Anchin college. Thither he called some of that congregation who were intended and designed immediately for England; he gave orders likewise to such of his obedience that were there already to send over some youths to be educated in this new obtained place."[1]

The truth of D. Weldon's narrative being that the Gunpowder Plot concerned the foundation at Douai in no other way than by justifying D. Roberts' forethought. The whole account Weldon gives of the history of the benedictines in the seventeenth century is so confused and impossible, when confronted with ascertained facts, that he may once for all be dismissed from serious notice as an altogether unreliable authority. And to quote a recent writer: "It is every way regrettable that (he) has been so long allowed to run an honoured career in that guise."[2] As a matter of fact D. Bradshaw, as chief chaplain of the English regiment, was engaged in quite other matters of which Weldon knew nothing, and his business engrossed him far away from Douai. Besides his duties in this respect, he found his hands full also with other matters resulting from his position as chaplain-general. In fact early in the year 1606 he is found defending himself at Brussels as best he could against the attacks of his jesuit colleague, Fr. Coniers, backed by Fr. Baldwin; and their powerful friends at the courts of Brussels and Madrid at last succeeded (May 1606) in getting

---

[1] *Chronological Notes*, pp. 62, 63.
[2] *Downside Review*, vol. xvi. p. 30.

"all the principal officers and almost one-half of the captains" cashiered.[1] D. Bradshaw does not appear at Douai for the first time as prior until the autumn of 1606. The value of the rest of Weldon's account can be gathered from the preceding pages.

D. Roberts returned from Douai on the eve of the Gunpowder Plot, and on the 5th of November, the very day of the discovery, was "taken in the upper end of Holborn, in the house of Thomas Pircie, his first wife, and was then committed to the gatehouse by the lords from the council table."[2]

But he was not kept in prison; for, as he himself says, after examination by the council he was declared by them a man of good repute, "and in liberating me testified that no imputation whatever rested upon me."[3] He seems to have been a

---

[1] "In April 1606 disaffection showed itself in the regiment, fomented by Sir Thomas Studder (see Foley, i. p. 486), the sergeant-major, 'wherein his lordship will find it difficult to procure satisfaction, because he is suspected by the faction of the jesuits.' It is a miserable story. Meanwhile, Captain James Blount, one of his officers, had gone with recommendation to Spain, and managed 'to blast his late colonel, the Lord Arundell, at the Spanish court.' On 28th or 29th May the blow fell suddenly, to Arundell's amazement, in the 'cashiering of all the principal officers and almost one-half of the captains.' And thus the 'valiant' Arundell fell; and Father Augustine's functions as chaplain came to an end too. The cashiering of the nuncio Frangipani and the exile of Dr. Gifford are items of the same politics."
—*Ibid.* p. 31.

[2] MS. Examination of John Roberts, from the archives of the old English chapter.

[3] *Downside Review*, vol. xiv. p. 126. Of this we are assured by the certificate of the justice by whom he was arrested (*S.P.*, Dom Jas. I., November 5, 1605).

prisoner on parole; for in his examination he says he continued such "for the space of nine months, and was then banished with the rest about August last (1607) was twelve months." But if D. Roberts remained all this time in England (and we doubt it), his care for the new house at Douai was meanwhile active. The letters from the Spanish general to the abbats of the Low Countries had been presented and had borne fruit; and, moreover, abbat Caverel had begun to take a special interest in them, out of the admiration he had conceived for D. Roberts.

"The abbat of Arras (who is a man of great revenues and a great favourite with our English fugitives, and one, as they say, that is a good man to all poor men admiring at the forwardness and zeal of this English prior) promised to build a cloister at his own proper cost and charges for the English monks in Douay, and to give them some yearly pension besides, if that they could procure leave from the king of Spain and the archduke and the archduchess." [1]

Here was an opportunity for D. Roberts to avail himself of "the means and intercession of some great personages in this land" in obtaining the requisite civil authorisation for his house at Douai. Early in 1606 the king of Spain wrote to the archduke in favour of the new foundation; and the Spanish general, Perez, did the same. On the

[1] *Running Register*, p. 91.

strength of these letters the archduke wrote to abbat Cavarel, and recommended the English monks at Douai.[1] The nuncio, Carafa, sometime in the latter half of 1606, wrote also to commend them to his good offices. The conditions the abbat had made were fulfilled, and moreover D. Roberts was again on the spot to forward the work both in Flanders and in Spain, to which place he went when released in August 1606.[2] What was the cause of his journey to Spain we must now narrate. To use the words of the *Running Register:* "But alas! the English jesuits (perceiving the way the cry went) made all the friends they could to prevent the monks in their proceedings."[3]

The benedictine mission, even in its earliest days, had been attended, as we have seen, with no small opposition, and those who had tried to prevent it were still living. Now that the Spanish fathers were attempting to secure a footing at Douai, a university town where the monks would have all

[1] A certificate on behalf of the English benedictines given by the echevins of Douai, and dated October 12, 1607, is assurance that 1606 is the date of the archduke's letter: "depuis un an ou environ seraient venus resider (they say) en cette ville certains religieux bénédictins anglais recommandés de leurs altesses sérénissimes."—*Downside Review,* vol. xvi. p. 25.

[2] In the examination before the bishop of London in 1607, D. Roberts says "that during this his second being beyond the seas, he was at Douay, Paris, Valladolid, Salamanca, St. James in Gallicia, and returned through France and stayed in Paris and Douay, when he came into England about the beginning of October last" (1607). An absence from England of some fourteen months.

[3] P. 91.

the advantages of learning, and be thus better qualified than others for the work in England, a deadly opposition once more broke out against the proposed foundation, and heaven and earth were moved to hinder it. The attempt to prevent the benedictines from establishing themselves at Douai was but natural if we take the point of view adopted by the English superiors of the society, whose policy however was fraught with misfortune and failure both to the cause they desired to serve and also to themselves. They saw that the influence and success of monks, whose very name called up hallowed associations with much that Englishmen held dear, would be fatal to that monopoly they had so carefully planned and cultivated, and which was of such vital importance if the control of the clergy was to remain in the hands of arch-priests "who walked in amity and fidelity to the society."

It is not a historian's province to palliate or to make out a case. It is enough for him to present ascertained facts which tell their own tale.

The position of D. Bradshaw as chaplain-general at the camp was felt to be a danger to the influence of the English jesuits. He was therefore removed. And now all attempts at founding a monastery at Douai must be firmly and steadily resisted, for there was another danger ahead, and one perhaps more immediately to be feared than the presence of a few monks. There were plans in process of development regarding the secular college at Douai, which were then occupying the attention of the jesuits; and an English benedictine monastery in the same town would be a serious obstacle to their success. Learning, the jesuits felt, was altogether an inconvenience in the hands of the clergy, for it meant power, and this latter was just what they were determined to keep in their own hands. In accordance with this policy, since the clergy strenuously opposed the giving up of the control of the college (the one ewe lamb left to them), a president subservient to the interests of the society had been appointed by the authorities in Rome, who, in this as in almost every other matter, acted on the advice of Fr. Parsons. Dr. Worthington, third president of the secular college at Douai, was a useful choice; he had made a secret vow of obedience to Parsons, and had promised to be directed by him in all things.[1] By this means, through the president, a mere handful of English jesuits (whom, once again we repeat, were but a few, and by no means representative of that generous body of missioners who stood shoulder to shoulder with the clergy and monks, and with them met a felon's death) came to have almost the same control over the college of Douai as they had over all the other houses in which the clergy were trained.

It was a cleverly planned piece of work, and it was being consistently carried out. The intellectual status of the clergy was to be lowered; that was

[1] See his letter to Parsons, Tierney, vol. v., appendix, p. iv.

the first step. Already (in 1597) had measures been taken to put obstacles in the way of the higher studies, and now, through the new president, the project proceeded further. On the plea of expense the staff of professors was reduced. Theology and philosophy were no longer taught in the college, and even for humanities the students had to attend the free classes held by the fathers of the society in Douai. Here was indeed a falling off from the intellectual activity of the college in former days, and the result brought discredit upon the clergy. Priests unprepared[1] and untried, often converts of recent date, kept pouring into England,[2] and it is no wonder that many and grievous were the complaints made by the laity, and that great scandals were not unknown. This came to such a pass that in many cases the doors of catholic houses were shut against them, and the laity refused to support men so unfit to be pastors in such troublesome times. The clergy in England

[1] From the *Douai Diary* MS. quoted by Tierney (vol. v. p. 6, *note*) we take a case: John Farmer, confirmed on March 22, 1605, three days later received the minor orders, next day subdeacon; on the 9th April, deacon; on the 24th, priest; sent to England May 16. A layman on March 22, a priest on April 24.

[2] From 1604 to 1608 more than forty-one priests were sent off from Douai alone. Writing to Richard Smith, the agent in Rome, the archpriest Birkhead says (October 9, 1609): "More workmen do daily come over, and think much they have no relief from me, which I assure (them) they should have if I had it. But exceeding little cometh to my hands. The great gobetts go where the distributors please, who are all for our opposites. . . . I believe it is done to weary me" (Tierney, vol. v. p. 7, *note*).

were up in arms, and were clamouring for the removal of Dr. Worthington. But his friends in Rome were by no means willing to part with so valuable a servant.

With these threads of the story in the reader's hands, the state of affairs at the secular college at Douai at the moment of the arrival of the monks can be understood, and the all-importance to the jesuits of hindering the foundation. For such a project upset the plans so long and so carefully matured, and which were now on the eve of a sure realisation. The removal of D. Bradshaw from his post at the camp had been only a preliminary skirmish; but now, when, in the autumn of 1606, he took up his residence as head of the little community at Douai, Dr. Worthington was called upon to open fire. Elated with the success which had attended their plans, both as to D. Bradshaw and to his strenuous friend, Dr. Gifford,[1] whose banishment from Lille they had secured, the fate of the benedictine establishment

[1] "On the other side Dr. Gifford, who was then dean of the collegiate church of St. Peter in Rissell (alias *Insula*), a city in the confines of Flanders, and the other doctors and secular priests before mentioned took the monks' part, and much ado there was about the matter in the court of Brussels; but in the end the jesuits prevailed, and Dr. Gifford was banished out of the archduke and archduchess's dominion; howbeit he was permitted to make the best of all his spiritual livings in the Low Countries, and to depart within a very short time." So Lewis Owen, p. 91. Already in the spring of 1606 Dr. Gifford seems to have expected such a termination. Writing to Thos. Phelippes, he says: "He wished to serve the king by his correspondence or *to retire*" (*Cal. S. P.*, Dom Jas. I., vol. i. p. 314).

at Douai seemed settled. No sooner had D. Bradshaw taken up his residence in the town than the president set off to Brussels to secure his ejectment. This was in the September of 1606. At the archducal court he found a friend and supporter in Fr. Baldwin, S.J., who was established in the place of Fr. Holt as a kind of overseer-general of the English catholics residing in the Low Countries, and was, moreover, the distributor of the royal alms set aside for their support. Dr. Worthington drew up a petition to the nuncio, Carafa, against the foundation at Douai, and took advantage of the recent departure of some students who had been dissatisfied with the way things were going on at the college, and had joined the benedictines. Not only at Brussels but at Spain also was the opposition carried on. To the king the jesuits appealed to forbid the foundation; and, in spite of the papal leave, it was loudly asserted that for monks to go on the mission was against the very essence of the monastic state.

D. Bradshaw as vicar undertook the defence and certified the Spanish general of the whole affair,[1]

[1] Owen says D. Bradshaw went to Spain on this business. From his known movements, such a visit could only have taken place between August 7, 1607, and February 1608; or October 1608 and April 1609. It is however not improbable that he did not go to Spain at all, but conducted his defence by letter. The *Running Register* is, as we should suspect, accurate as regards D. Roberts, the author's brother-in-law; but not always so as to the doings of others. If there was a journey to Spain, as Owen says, we are inclined to think it took place at the former of these two periods.

"which made the monks to swear many a *Boto a dios* that the jesuits (who were *upstarts*, and *los mas novicios de todos los religiosos;* the inferior order of all religious orders) should not domineer over them who were of the first order of monks that ever was; and so, with great indignation, they went unto the king and with opened mouths exclaimed against the English jesuits for hindering so good a work.

"Father Creswell and the rest of the Jesuits that lived in the court of Spain, together with their brethren the Spanish jesuits, stood stoutly to their tacklings; alledging that the monks would do more hurt than good, in the conversion of England; because that they were (for the most part) unlearned, idle, lazie fellowes, and withall men of no account in England, and a thousand such accusations; that all the principallest men in the court were *pro et contra*, some with the benedictines and others with the jesuits. And therefore to pacify this uproar the king wrote to the pope to know his pleasure. But his holiness kept them in law in Rome and in Spain for some two years."[1]

But while enemies were thus at work for their destruction, their friend Dr. Gifford, who, upon his banishment from Lille, had returned to Rheims and had become rector of the university of that town, was not going to sit idle and see the monks thus treated. He, too, had powerful friends; and if the foundation at Douai could not be made, some other

[1] *Running Register*, p. 92.

locality must be found for them where they could be safe at least from intrigues at the Spanish court. Dr. Gifford was on intimate terms with the princes of the house of Guise-Lorraine, through whom he was afterwards to be raised to the see of Rheims and become first peer of France. Cardinal Charles of Lorraine was archbishop of the newly erected metropolitan see of Nancy, and for the foundation of his chapter was appropriating the revenues of several old collegiate churches in the neighbourhood. Among them was the old church of St. Lawrence at Dieuleward or Dolwart in Lorraine. Before the pope would sanction the proposed transfer of the revenues, a stipulation was made that due provision should be made at Dieuleward for the continuance of divine worship. Dr. Gifford heard of it, and, through his influence with the cardinal and prince Erric, the bishop of Verdun, the church, a cloister, a small cottage and garden were offered to the benedictines. D. Bradshaw went into Lorraine to inspect the place, and accepted it. And on December 2, 1606, the dean and chapter of Nancy made a deed of gift of the property to him. But he did not stay to take possession; but left Mr. Arthur Pitts, the dean of a small collegiate church at Liverdun and confessor to the nuns of Remiremont, to act as his procurator. By the 24th of that same month all the legal formalities were completed, and St. Lawrence's passed into the hands of the Spanish monks at Douai, who now had a place of refuge in case they were turned out of Douai. But no further steps were taken at Dieuleward; for the monks had no intention of yielding up their house at Douai. They met every attack with that steady calmness which came from a consciousness of the justice of their cause.

Here at Douai, in the midst of all the uncertainty, they were going on quietly in their home-life, and were ever increasing their numbers. On May 12, 1607, they moved into more convenient quarters hired from the Trinitarians; and on this day their first novice, Nicholas Fitzjames, was clothed.[1] This new departure may be perhaps due to the initiative of D. Roberts, who was banished in the spring of 1607 (most likely in the April), and for six months was a conventual of St. Gregory's.[2]

Just before the arrival of D. Roberts (and it is by no means unlikely that he had obtained his banishment so as to be on the spot to help in the conflict) the jesuits, acting through the president, had approached the holy see. " It is currently reported here," writes D. Bradshaw in March, " that the president, by our jesuits' instigation, hath sent a petition to his holiness for the removing us out of Douay."[3] The case seemed so

---

[1] *Liber Graduum.* Nicholas Fitzjames, of a Somersetshire family, was a student of the old benedictine college at Oxford. He entered Gloucester Hall with his four brothers, 17th March 1582, being then but a mere child. At the time of his clothing he was about twenty-two.

[2] *Apostolatus*, i. 248.

[3] *Downside Review*, vol. xvi. p. 32.

hopeless, that a few months after (June), when he had an interview with the nuncio Caraffa, the vicar writes that the nuncio "told him that he sent for him to leave Douai; for that the jesuits and the president (said the nuncio) will never let you be quiet."[1]

In Rome Fr. Parsons[2] took charge of the case against the monks. "Regarding the benedictines as the 'adversaries' of his order (*Stonyhurst MSS. Ang. A.* iii. 94), Father Parsons hesitated not to assail them with the most unmeasured language—on the one hand he maintained that their object was to allure the students of the seminary to their own

---

[1] *Ibid.* 32. There had been many great disturbances at the college. On one occasion seven students were expelled because they wished to become benedictines.

[2] Parsons seems to have had a desperate dislike to and fear of the benedictines; though why we cannot imagine, save that they were obstacles in the way of his policy. In the *Memorial for a Reformation* drawn up in 1596, when he was still clinging to the hope of making England catholic by force of arms, he recommends the formation of a council which must "presently at the beginning publish an edict or proclamation with all severity, commanding under pain of great punishment that no religious or ecclesiastical person whatsoever do enter the realm without presenting himself before the council within so many days after his entrance to show the cause why he cometh, and the licence and authority by which he cometh, and to stand by the determination of the council for his abode or departure again" (pp. 74, 75). In this same work he insists upon the restitution of the abbey lands as a conscientious obligation; but proceeds to maintain it "would not be convenient to return them again to the same orders of religion that had them before." He suggests they should be given, among other purposes, all of which lay in the direction of the society, for "*divers houses of other orders that do deal more in preaching or helping souls.*" Of course, in other words the property of the monks should be given to the society.

order, on the other, he declared that the only persons whom they had hitherto induced to join them were men distinguished during their residence in the colleges for their undutiful and turbulent behaviour. The parties, he said, had quitted the seminaries in sedition, and embraced the religious institute without the knowledge of their superiors. They hated the jesuits, they had slandered the society; and they had sought by their letters to create divisions and excite disaffection among the students from whom they had deserted. Nor was this all. The benedictine mission had been expressly established that its members might support the jesuits against the appellant priests, but instead of this, they leagued with the appellants against the jesuits; they even countenanced them in their criminal intrigues with the heretical government of the country; and they still continued to number one member among them who, though he had originally condemned the oath of allegiance, had subsequently maintained that it might be lawfully taken."[1]

It was pitiful to see Fr. Parsons, powerful mind as he was, yet unhappily ever consistent with himself, thus advocating a bad cause.

D. Anselm Beech, the Cassinese, was in Rome, and was acting as procurator for the English of both congregations. He drew up a paper and

[1] Tierney, vol. iv. p. 88, *note;* and *Add. MSS.*, 21, 203, Plut ciii. F., f. 14.

presented it to the pope in 1608. It was followed soon by another from the same person, and was written at the request of cardinal Bianchetti. D. Beech had but little trouble in showing that Fr. Parsons' memorial was both false in its statements and frivolous in its accusations. He said:—

"It was not true that the benedictines had sought to aggrandize their own body at the expense of the seminaries. It was not true they had received the disaffected members of the colleges, or committed any of the acts imputed to them by their opponents. But they had established houses for the supply of the English mission, and had been assisted in the work by the abbats and prelates of the country. In Flanders they had even been employed as the instructors of the other monasteries; and hence, unfortunately, had arisen the jealousy of the society, hence the hostility with which its members had pursued them, and the accusations they had constantly poured out against them."[1]

He ends up his paper with these noble words:—

"Yet after all the benedictines have no private wishes to gratify, no personal objects to accomplish by the maintenance of the present quarrel. Our opponents seek to drive us from the establishment at Douai; they covet a monopoly of that mission, in which our substance and our blood have been expended; and they appeal, for the justification of their ambition, to the superior qualifications of

[1] Tierney, vol. iv. p. 89.

themselves and their disciples. Be it so. Our colleges are established only to propagate the Gospel; our desire is to promote the glory of God, not to engage in controversy with the society: and if, to avoid the latter, we shall be required to abandon the work in which we are engaged, we will cheerfully withdraw our fathers from the missions and show the world that we seek no interests but that of the church, no honour but that of being obedient to the holy see."

Rome was a long time in coming to a decision. And wisely too. In the heat of controversy it is sometimes difficult to arrive at a clear understanding before passing sentence. Nor are men's minds sufficiently calm to accept a decision. Besides, there were arrayed against the benedictines all Father Parsons' powers of diplomacy; and he was a master in the art and well acquainted with all the ins and outs of the Roman *Curia*. As the recognised and credited adviser on all English subjects, Parsons was for a long time more than a match for D. Anselm Beech.

Meanwhile at Douai the monks got a testimony in their favour from the town authorities who, in October 1607, bore witness that "during the time they have conducted themselves virtuously, to the contentment and edification of the inhabitants." The *rector magnificus* of the university made a like attestation. Having done on the spot what he could for the defence of his house, D. Roberts returned in the October to England, and on December 17, 1607, was again arrested and, after examination before the bishop of London, was confined at the Gatehouse prison, "where he continued for a month or more, spending like a little prince; for he wanted no money: he had the liberty of the house all day long, and his friends had accession to him; but at night he was locked up in his chamber where nobody lay but himself; for he was a good guest, and spared no cost; and withall liberal to his keeper, wherein he knew full well to be the only way to purchase favour in a prison-house.

"Moreover his friends that came to visit him bestowed money upon him that let them in, and afterwards he conversed privately with them in his chambers; but in the end they brought him a cord and a file and (as some say) mercury water, and by that means he did with the water eat, or else with his tool, file the iron bars of his chamber window, which was in the upper part of the house, and afterwards came down with the cord, and so escaped away and got over to Douai."[1]

Louis Owen, writing in 1626, seems to have been unaware that D. Roberts, upon his escape, lived quietly in London for about a twelvemonth, if the statement of Fr. Miles, S.J., is to be relied upon as to dates. Fr. Miles tells us in 1613, that about his sixteenth or seventeenth year (he had become a catholic when fourteen, but had lapsed) a catholic

[1] *Running Register*, p. 93.

friend "took me to a prison to Fr. Roberts, a monk and now a glorious martyr, by whom I was reconciled in 1607 as I think, and in the time of Lent. . . . But after a year I went to the prison called Newgate on the feast of SS. Peter and Paul, and after hearing two or three masses, the officers entered and seized and detained me with many others." A week or so afterwards he was released. "After the lapse of half a year Fr. Roberts returned to England, for he had been banished immediately after my conversion, and being a second time seized upon, was thrust into the prison called the Gatehouse, together with the glorious martyr, Father Thomas Garnett. . . . I then spent a year with them privately in London, after which I left England with Fr. Roberts, Fr. Broughton of the same order, and another priest, all of whom were at that time sent into exile. When we landed, Fr. Roberts proceeded into Spain."[1]

But while D. Roberts was living quietly in London after his escape, the dispute at Douai was still unsettled; and from the delay, the benedictines

---

[1] Foley, vol. i. pp. 469, 470. Fr. Miles' statement is so loose, and is also a translation from the Latin, that one is uncertain sometimes of the exact meaning of a phrase; and his dates are not to be taken exactly. As D. Roberts returned to England October 1607, "the lapse of half a year" from June 29 is a very general way of speaking. But the martyrdom of Fr. Garnett, S.J., helps to fix the date. He was executed June 23, 1608. The introduction of Fr. Broughton's name, too, is valuable. He was professed at Douai, September 14, 1609 (*Liber Graduum*). It would seem, therefore, that he passed his novitiate on the mission; and the year, passed privately in London, was from the summer of 1608 to that of 1609.

seemed to think it not improbable that they might have to leave that town. So steps were at once taken to begin at Dieuleward, which had hitherto been left untenanted. On July 11, 1608, Dr. William Gifford, at that time rector of the university of Rheims, received the habit for the house of St. Lawrence at Dieuleward, at the abbey of St. Remigius, and took the name of Father Gabriel de S. Maria. On the thirtieth of the same month at the same monastery Clement Reyner, a secular priest, was clothed for the same house by D. Leander Jones, and on August 4th, four others, Joseph Haworth, a cleric, Anthony Walsgrave, priest, Peter Wilford, priest, and Robert Babthorpe, layman, were also clothed by D. Leander. The following day, D. Leander with his little company, leaving however D. Gifford behind, set out towards their new home. On their way they were joined at Verdun, where they rested a few days, by Fr. Nicholas Fitzjames, lately professed at Douai, and Fr. Francis Walsgrave, who probably had instructions for them from the vicar. Here after consultation they separated. D. Leander, with three (Haworth, Wilford, and Babthorpe), went to take up their abode in houses of the Lorraine congregation (St. Michel and Moyenmoutier), where the novices might continue their studies. The others, Fitzjames, Walsgrave, Reyner, and a layman Robert Warden, set out for Dieuleward, at which place they arrived on the eve of St. Lawrence, August 10th.

What they found on arrival was not encouraging. An empty church wanting in all ornaments, a bare cloister, a small little cottage without any furniture, not even a stool. At first they were obliged to accept the hospitality of a neighbour, one Didacus Pierson; and stayed with him for eight days. With their own money (they only had 300 francs of Lorraine) and some gifts of Mr. Arthur Pitts they were then able to provide what was absolutely necessary to furnish the little cottage. They had to set about building a portion of the monastery. This work began in the September; and towards the expense their friend, Arthur Pitts, contributed the sum of twenty-four pounds. The walls were as high as the future dormitory, and were ready for the beams, when, on the evening of December 5th, a great storm arose and destroyed the work. But the disaster was soon repaired. Sometime in the following April, 1609 (about the 23rd), D. Gifford came from Rheims with a layman, Thomas Merriman. Immediately upon their arrival the works were pushed on. A new refectory, kitchen, and extra cells were begun, and arrangements made to accommodate eleven religious. The vicar, D. Bradshaw, after a visitation at the end of May, appointed D. Nicholas Fitzjames superior, with the title of "sub-prior"; and gave him certain rules for the government of the house. D. Fitzjames it was who, on July 11, 1609, received the vows of D. Gifford, the first professed monk of St. Lawrence's monastery.

The others, who were clothed about the same time, were duly professed; while those staying at St. Michel and Moyenmoutier were likewise, by agreement, considered to have taken their vows.

Things were so settled at Dieuleward (and maybe the horizon, hitherto so black, showed signs of breaking at Douai), that on the 18th of August D. Fitzjames, together with D. Gifford, went to Moyenmoutier (where the chapter of the Lorraine congregation was then holding its sessions) to take back their subjects who had been studying there; a proposal which gave offence to the chapter, as D. Bradshaw had undertaken to leave them there for three years. About September 14th, the studies of philosophy and theology formally began at Dieuleward. On the 25th, D. George Browne, a professed monk of St. Sinbert in Spain, was appointed prior by the vicar, and he was the first to hold that office. But a short while after, that is to say in the October, letters came from Spain authorising D. Browne and D. Mark Crowder (the "Broughton" of Fr. Miles' statement) to go on the English mission.

What was the meaning of this sudden alteration of plans? There had been a change in the numbers at St. Lawrence s going on lately; and many, together with D. Leander, had been recalled to Douai. What did it all portend?

Now comes in the value of Fr. Miles' statement. D. Roberts, together with Miles, Broughton, and another left England, most likely sometime early in the July of 1609; and while Miles went to St. Omers and Broughton to Douai to be professed, D. Roberts, as soon as he landed at Calais, set out for Spain. As we have seen, he was a man of action. He saw it was no use working for the defence of his house from a distance. He must be on the spot; for in Madrid was now all the difficulty. Rome had decided in favour of the monks. Decrees dated December 10, 1608, and April 23, 1609, had, on part of the pope, confirmed the establishment at Douai. But the papal decision had not quieted the parties at Douai adverse to the monks. They put their trust in princes; and prosecuted more keenly than ever their suit at the Spanish court.[1]

[1] They represented the decrees as a triumph for the jesuits. Dr. Singleton, a man devoted to the society and who had been made one of Dr. Worthington's assistants, with the object of keeping him up to the mark, writes (April 9, 1609) to Father Floyd, S.J.: "This summer our nuncio of Flanders goeth in progress and intendeth to visit Douay seminary and the benedictines' monastery; upon which visitation and information afterwards dependeth the benedictines' removal or stay at Douay, as Mr. Fitzherbert writeth to me. *But this is a secret till it be done.* You must understand that the benedictines in England receive, as they call them, many *donates* in England, and omit nothing to make themselves populous and a great multitude, imagining to do by numbers what they cannot by virtue" (Tierney, vol. iv. p. ccxix). But how Fitzherbert, the secular agent in Rome and a sworn ally of Parsons (he became a jesuit a few years after), could write this in face of the decree of December 10, 1608, we venture not to explain. But it shows that an attempt was being made to get the decree set aside. The president did not consider that the decree which forbade any influence on one side or on the other with the vocation of the students bound him; and he was delated to Rome for having made an ordinance

In Spain, therefore, the business must be carried on, and there D. Roberts speeded.

"All this while Father Augustine, the other monk, was very diligent in negotiating his suit in the court of Spain, but could not bring it to any perfection; for the jesuits were too strong for him. Whereupon Master Roberts with tooth and nail began to second his brother friar Augustine; and within a very short time obtained leave from pope Paulus Quintus and the king of Spain, to build a cloister for the monks in Douay or in any other city or towne, in any of the king of Spain's dominions in the Low Countries."[1]

Evidently, then, very soon after D. Roberts' arrival in Spain, matters began to move, and the prospect to appear more hopeful. On the 27th of July 1609, the theological faculty of Salamanca (where D. Roberts went in 1606 or 1607) gave their opinion that the monks could undertake the mission, as there was nothing in their state to hinder such a work.[2] By the September, it must have become known that D. Roberts was successful; for, bearing in mind the scandalous state to which the secular college at Douai had of set purpose been reduced by Dr. Worthington, it is noteworthy that theological lectures were suddenly resumed in that month, and there seems to have been an unwonted ferment at

to the effect "that whosoever would be priest in his college must first take an oath or promise at least not to enter into any religion except he enter into the society." See also Tierney, vol. v. p. lxxxix, *note.*

[1] *Running Register*, p. 93.   [2] *Apostolatus*, i. 244-245.

the college. This and other events, which it is not our purpose to enter into now, show that the president knew his attempt had failed; and that in Douai another place for study for Englishmen, and for benedictines too, was about to be fairly established.

D. Roberts returned to Douai about the beginning of October; and it was he who brought from the Spanish general the leave for prior Browne and D. Mark Crowder to go on the English mission.

Here, at Douai, for some little while, probably until the beginning of 1610, D. Roberts remained preparing himself for what he doubtlessly knew awaited him in England. His work was nearly over. By his energy and wise forethought he had secured the safety of his house: and now, after a short rest, the brave monk set his face steadfastly towards England. As far as we know he never set eyes again on the house which is proud to call him founder. Arrested for the last time on Advent Sunday, 1610, whilst standing at the altar saying mass, he was dragged off to prison in his sacred vestments, was tried and condemned on December 8, and two days after suffered, in company with a secular priest—Thomas Somers, or Wilson—a felon's death for conscience' sake.[1]

[1] See Challoner's *Memoirs of the Missionary Priests* (ed. Edinburgh, 1878), vol. ii. On the scaffold, addressing the people, he said "that he was sent into England by the same authority by which St. Augustine, the apostle of England, was sent, whose disciple he was; being of the same order and living under the same rule in which he lived; and that for the profession and teaching of that same religion which St. Augustine planted in England he was now condemned to die" (pp. 43, 44).

When the royal decision came which authorised the establishment at Douai, the archduke Albert gave a formal permission to the monks, and annexed to it a condition of two yearly masses in perpetuity for himself and the archduchess. "The which was no sooner granted but the abbat of St. Vedastus in Arras (according to his promise) began to set to work to build a priory for the English monks in Douai, and came himself in person to lay the first stone of the foundation, which within the space of one year was thoroughly finished.[1]

[1] Weldon tells a story which is so circumstantial that there must be some truth in it; but as it is difficult to test it, and as there are manifest anachronisms, we give it (shortened) as a note, leaving the reader to attach such value to it as he thinks proper:—

"Now these enemies ... spared neither time nor themselves, neither their credit nor their own consciences, painting them out for vagabonds, dangerous men and counterfeit monks; and seeing all this artifice did not succeed, they got a surreptitious bull from Rome directed to the archduke and the nuncio Bentivoglio, to break up their conventicle and expel them the university under pain of excommunication if they obeyed not within twenty-four hours after the intimation, and then to employ the assistance of the secular arm and compulsion." The nuncio (1610) cited Fr. Bradshaw, the superior, to Brussels; he, upon advice of abbat Caverel, did not appear.

"Second orders came, which were not regarded; at last came a formal precept full of threats. D. Austin made a report thereof to the abbat of Arras, and demanded again his advice. The abbat answered that he saw their enemies were too strong for them, and it was impossible for them to fix at Douai; told them it was indifferent to him where he placed them, and called for his book of maps to seek for a convenient place in some other town. While he was turning the book, Father Leander arrived from Douai, entered with a letter from Rome directed to the superior, or, in his absence, to the most ancient of the English fathers in Douai. It was from a benedictine cardinal, the only one that then was (Annas d'Escars, cardinal of Metz), to inform them a bull much to their prejudice had been surreptitiously

"Moreover he built a fine church for them joining the cloister, and gave them a certain yearly stipend or revenue towards their maintenance for ever; and also procured all the other abbats of the obtained. Out of love to his order and justice, he gave them notice of it; and upon any question about it they should, if need were, produce his letter. The abbat much rejoiced at this, and looking at it as a singular providence, commanded Fr. Bradshaw and Fr. Leander to make presently for Brussels, and without permitting them to return (to Douai), himself furnished their expenses." We may imagine the good fathers on their way to the nuncio, full of thankfulness to divine providence, and yet not without a sense of the humorous side of the fact that they were now masters of the situation, and were about to turn the tables upon their opponents. The nuncio received them with great coldness, and was pleased to express himself in very high terms at their neglect in obeying his orders. He scolded them right well; and ended up by saying: "To be short, you must disperse and quit Douai. Such is his holiness' pleasure." The two monks begged to see the date of the bull; and this request only served to increase the anger of the good nuncio: "Do you take me for an impostor?" said he in great indignation; "this shall not serve you." But upon being shown the bull, Fr. Leander humbly produced the cardinal's letter, and asked the nuncio whether he knew the hand: "Yes," said he, "and the person, too." He then read the letter, and was disgusted to find that he had been made a tool of by their unscrupulous opponents: "He told them he saw they had been injured, and himself abused; bade them return home, and be secure that he would never trouble them with any summons till he had better warrant for them, and had first heard what the fathers at Douai could say for themselves. They came home in triumph, without any opposition from the town or university. But this storm was scarce to blow over before another, no less furious, began to arise against them. Their adversaries seeing their malicious designs frustrated on this side, applied themselves to the archduke, produced their pretended bull, begged his assistance towards the ejection of a company of vagabonds who under the mask of a religious habit machinated disturbance in the state and academy. The duke, tired with their importunities, and not suspecting so much as that they were the same persons he had formerly recommended to the abbat of Arras (Philip of Caverel), gave an order to a huissier of Mechlin to expel them the town without possibility of returning.

Low Countries of their order, to give them likewise some yearly pension to help them to live."[1]

Philip Caverel, a name ever to be held in benediction, began to redeem his promise. For a long time he had contemplated building in the university town a college, like those belonging to the abbeys of Marchienne and Anchin, so that the young monks of his own abbey might assist at the lectures. His benevolence towards the persecuted English monks made him defer his project. He laid the foundations of a large conventual church and a monastery for the English monks.[2] The building was so far advanced that in the October of 1611 the monks were able to move into what was to be their home until the great Revolution. On the 15th of October

---

The officer presently prepared for his journey and was ready to take horse, but knowing that the abbat of Arras, his benefactor, was at Brussels, went first to receive his commands for these parts. The abbat asked him the cause of his journey, and having heard it, desired him to stay an hour or two till he writ some letters. He went to court, had audience of his highness, asked the reason why his highness had issued out such a commission against men of an unblamable life whom he had formerly commended, and for whose behaviour himself (the abbat) was ready to answer. The duke replied that they were not the same persons whom he had commended to the abbat's charity. 'Those were members of the Spanish congregation, these wanderers are no benedictines.' But being disabused and better informed by the abbat, he promised they should live unmolested for the future, and encouraged the abbat to build for them, gave his consent to their establishment with an obligation of an anniversary mass for himself and the archduchess for ever."

[1] *Running Register*, pp. 93, 94.

[2] The community were already under the patronage of St. Gregory the Great, the monk-pope, who sent the prior of his own monastery to convert England.

the chapter of Arras, in which diocese Douai then was, upon the petition of D. Bradshaw, the prior, granted a licence for the transfer of the convent to the new buildings, with the right to celebrate the divine offices publicly.

Once established, the monks began to get congenial occupation. From a document written by the abbat of Marchienne, dated October 4, 1614, we can gather some of their employments:—

"I certainly knew that out of the said number of monks there are several of them doctors in divinity and arts and licentiates. Some of them have much vexed the heretics by most useful and learned writings, whose books I have read with joy; and for the experience I have had of their extraordinary religious comportment I have received eight of them into my college of Marchin, who either by their continual studies prepare themselves to teach philosophy or actually do teach it, to the very great satisfaction of all and their own commendation. Likewise in the college of St. Gregory's there are many of the monks who are egregious professors of divinity, the others learn it or philosophy . . . and the better to maintain themselves and prepare themselves for the English mission, exercise themselves continually in hearing confessions, preaching, and pious examples in the places in which they live, and are wonderfully profitable to those who are under their care."[1]

Some of the monks held chairs in the university

[1] Weldon's translation, pp. 88, 89.

itself. D. Leander Jones (who became prior of St. Gregory's in 1612) for twenty-four years was the professor of theology and Hebrew; and another, D. Rudesind Barlow, was a noted canonist. From the very first St. Gregory's established a tradition of study and learning. The fees they got by teaching, together with a small pension from abbat Caverel, was about all they had to live upon.

Of the good abbat's "subsequent benefactions" we shall speak in another chapter. Suffice it here to say he seemed never to weary of his kindness to the monks of this monastery of his predilection. Among other gifts he gave them a country house at Escquerchin, two miles out of Douai, where they could resort for recreation and change of air. And when he died (December 1, 1636) he left his heart to the monks of St. Gregory's, to be buried before the high altar of the conventual church, with the touching inscription—"*Cor meum jungatur vobis.*"

Of this worthy abbat a few words will not be amiss, for he imprinted his own characteristics on the monastery he founded.

He succeeded Jean Sarrasin in 1600, and was the third of the three great abbats who in succession had ruled at Arras. M. Henri Louquet, the present archivist of Arras, says of him: ". . . La discipline monastique trouva en Philippe de Caverel son restaurateur le plus energetique."[1] He was the president of the congregation of exempt abbeys in

---

[1] *Journal des traveaux d'art* de l'abbé J. du Clergy, pp. 1, 2.

the Low Countries, beginning, as Weldon says, "the execution of the statutes he framed from the forming of his own household and domestics."[1] He enjoyed the confidence of his prince, and was appointed president of the states of Artois. Like his predecessor, Jean Sarrasin, though a thorough monk he was also a statesman in the true sense of the word. As plenipotentiary he sought to bring about a peace between Spain and Holland; and won the admiration even of those who were at first inclined to look upon his religious dress as an insult to their own religious opinions. He was truly the father of his monks; and rebuilt the greater part of his abbey. The poor and the destitute flocked to him in their distress and ever found him a loving and compassionate protector. How he befriended the English monks we have told. But it was not to his own brethren that he showed kindness. His spirit was too large to be cramped within his own order. For instance, at the very time his protégés were being persecuted at Douai he was building (for the jesuits) a noble college at Arras, which he also endowed. The English franciscans also received abundant help from him when they settled at Douai. Such then was Philip Caverel. He had the same large, noble spirit as his brother of Westminster, John Fecknam; the same love of the poor, the same munificence, the same spirit of "planting." If Philip Caverel had the brilliant

[1] P. 176.

success which the world alone acknowledges as a mark of merit, he was not behindhand with John Fecknam in those more solid qualities which result from a monastic training. If Fecknam was a confessor for conscience' sake, Caverel knew the all-importance of following it in forming men's lives. He right willingly, therefore, helped on men whose conscience was their only wealth. The work Caverel did for England has lasted; although his own abbey of St. Vedast and the college he later on founded at Douai have passed away, St. Gregory's lives to-day and keeps green the memory of her great benefactor.[1]

Before closing this chapter, we must direct the reader's attention to the remarkable fact that these poor hunted-down and calumniated monks, in the midst of their own trials and the difficulties of the new foundation, went on "planting" for others. And notably for the clergy whose cause they were advocating. It is clear, also, that in the struggle for life and death through which they were passing, they never lost their own peace, but calmly went on doing whatever good presented itself, and during these trials laid the foundations of a spirit that was never quelled by opposition, and never turned aside from the clear path of duty.[2]

---

[1] In the minster now rising at Downside is a chapel dedicated to St. Vedast. Each year, in November, a solemn mass of Requiem is sung for the repose of Philip Caverel's soul and for all benefactors.

[2] In all this storm the benedictines of Douai had kept their souls in patience. A principle was at stake here at Douai as there had been at Wisbeach. That experience was in their favour. They

It is not our purpose to tell here the story of the secular college at Douai. The establishment of St. Gregory's once for all broke down the monopoly hitherto existing; and by degrees the clergy emancipated themselves.[1]

fought aboveboard, and, by the strength which the monastic character gives, they met and brought to nought the secret attacks of misguided opponents. The contest the benedictines engaged in was a double battle; they were fighting a battle both for themselves and for the English clergy who were seeking to free themselves from the same thraldom. In a letter to his agent in Rome, Birkhead, the arch-priest (May 30, 1611), writes: "I took great unkindness of the Italian benedictines for denying to send our letters, and much more at Mr. Beach, for yielding to the humours of others against our proceedings, having received so much kindness of me, as he cannot be forgetful thereof. . . . Those benedictines of Spain deal far more sincerely with us. Father White (D. Bradshaw) hath assured me and Mr. Farrington at his being here, to join most unfeignedly with us and to help us by all means possible" (Tierney, vol. iv., appendix, xxxiii, *note*).

[1] Fr. Parsons ceased his troubled career, April 15, 1610; and immediately Dr. Worthington was released from his vow he seems to have been anxious to be reconciled with the benedictines: and it was his first care with D. Bradshaw to adjust "the terms of a lasting and friendly agreement." "I understand the president and Fr. White (Bradshaw) are reconciled together, which was a harder thing in my opinion than to reconcile us to him" (Birkhead to More, October 14, 1611). And then again: "Father White telleth me plainly that the president and he are good friends, and that he is much changed from what he was, and that I may deal with him confidently" (Birkhead to More, November 4, 1611). It is pleasant thus to see the benedictines aiding in reconciling the president to the brethren he had so greatly wronged. Of the death of Parsons, Birkhead writes to Smith (August 25, 1610): "You write that Paul (the pope) thinketh we shall be more quiet now that Father Parsons is dead; but, when you come, I can tell you of some that, I fear, will prosecute matters as hotly as he; and so God knoweth when peace will have place amongst us." Dr. Worthington, after attempting to give up the control of the seminary to the society, then turned against them and

D. Bradshaw in 1611 used his influence with abbat Caverel to grant to the English clergy the buildings of Arras college in Paris, for the purposes of a place of higher studies, and for a residence for writers of controversial works. The new college was to be conducted after the plan of the college at Chelsea, lately founded (1609) by king James I. It was first proposed to erect a "house for writers" at Douai, "but the opposition raised by the jesuits rendered it imprudent to persist in that part of the scheme."[1] This kindness endeared the benedictines much more to the clergy. We find one of the original members of the college, many years after (October 9, 1636), leaving by will a considerable sum of money to St. Gregory's in acknowledgment of the kindness of the monks. And, in view of further services, rendered later on by D. Leander, which healed a breach, he also left a sum of money to institute yearly a "reconciling feast," to which the benedictine superiors and the heads of the seminary should assist, and, over a good dinner—*more anglico*—forget the past. The name of this worthy deserves to be recorded. It was Richard Ireland, sometime master of Westminster school.

made friends with the secular brethren. But he was deposed; and studies began to flourish again. When Dr. Kellison was appointed as fourth president, he wrote to Harly, provost of Cambray, telling him of the speech he made on the occasion: "Marry, said I, if any desire to be jesuits or benedictines, let them well examine their vocation; and then if they come to me they shall have all assistance I can give them." For the whole story see Tierney, vol. v., additional article, ii.

[1] Tierney, vol. iv. pp. 135, 136.

Dodd speaks of him as "a man of a very pacific disposition;" and adds that in his own day the ceremony was still observed.[1]

We have now traced the history of the foundations of St. Gregory's and St. Lawrence's, the two houses which were destined to play the most important parts in the revival of English benedictinism. Other houses were soon established, one at St. Malo in Brittany, in 1611, one at Chelles near Paris in the same year, and another in Paris, itself, in 1615. All of these will, with other houses of later date, be treated of in subsequent chapters. But at the period in our narrative to which we have now arrived, it will be seen that the Spanish fathers, before the great constitutional change which was before them, had already firmly established themselves on the continent; while in England their missions and numbers were increasing. From the abbat of Marchienne's testimony, quoted above, we know at that date (1614) there were then "about fourscore monks" under the obedience of D. Leander, the new vicar.

Thus had God blessed and prospered the house which D. Roberts, the martyr, had founded, and to which Philip Caverel had been so great a benefactor. If the martyr planted and the abbat had tended, it was surely God who gave the increase.

---

[1] Dodd, vol. iii. p. 88.

CHAPTER XIII

THE RENEWAL OF THE ENGLISH CONGREGATION

WE must now return to England, where we left the Italian and the Spanish fathers at work in the mission field. The Spanish were successful and soon grew into a large, important body. They had men; and as Lewis Owen tells us: "They got great alms from England, and received every year ten or twelve students into their order." They moreover now had many friends and a footing at Douai, and another house at Dieuleward. Altogether they were doing well, and were every day growing more and more into estimation with the catholic body. But not so the Italians. They were at no time so many as twelve in number; their distance from Italy was itself a hindrance to getting new members. But they had received into their congregation one or two secular priests; to whom, however, they were unable to give anything of the training necessary to make monks. Altogether they had a hard struggle for existence, and in the immediately succeeding years repeatedly complained that they could not find benefactors, and put forward this as one of the grounds for the necessity of a union. The two congregations, be it remembered, were distinct; each with its own superiors, special practices, government, observances, and traditions.

The story to be told is now for the first time placed before the English reader; it is based on the calm and guarded narrative of men themselves concerned, and on the original documents they record. It moreover comes with all the authority derived from the countenance of a man of so high a character as the historian and statesman, cardinal Guido Bentivoglio, through whose hands, first as nuncio in Brussels and then at Paris, the whole business passed.[1]

The reader will remember how the two first Italian fathers soon after their arrival in England fell in with old Father Sigebert Buckley,[2] a monk of West-

[1] In the dedication the authors describe the restoration of the English congregation as "*opus manuum tuarum*"; and speaking of their book they add: "Cujus disceptationis totius et controversiæ te judicem facimus, sed maxime quoad illam partem quæ comprehendit narrationem eorum quæ facta sunt in congregatione nostra nupera restauratione, aut erectione, quæ omnia aut pleraque tuis oculis inspexisti . . . Accipe igitur opellam tibi in gratitudinis obsequium a tota congregatione nostra oblatam quæ certe non debuit alium quærere patronum aut judicem postulare quam te, *Cardinale Illustrissime*, quem ut altorem et nutritorem tenellae adhuc congregationis habuimus indulgentissimum."

[2] D. Sigebert Buckley was born in 1517. Nothing is known of his early life, but it is by no means unlikely he had been a novice, or at least brought up in a claustral school. His coming to D. Fecknam would seem to suggest an early connection with either Evesham or Westminster. He must have been about forty when he joined that abbat after the restoration of Westminster in 1557. The exact date when he joined the Westminster community is not known, nor what became of him immediately after the closing of the abbey. But it seems that he was either a native of Staffordshire or worked there as a priest, for in a

minster, whose one great wish was to see the restoration of his order. This was in the winter of 1603-4. But the man who was to see the true value of D. Sigebert was a clever lawyer of the name of David Baker[1] of Abergavenny (afterwards

list of names of priests then confined at Wisbeach is that of "Father Buckley," with the county of Stafford affixed (Harleian MSS., 6998). He was at Wisbeach during the disturbances under Weston's encroachments, and sided with the secular clergy. His imprisonment lasted nearly forty years, and would, therefore, have begun about 1570, just after the publication of Pius V.'s bull of deposition. He suffered imprisonment in the Tower, at Wisbeach, and at Framlingham, from which last prison he had been just released when the Italian fathers arrived. The wife of his host was a catholic; but Mr. Francis Woodhouse, at least outwardly, was not.

[1] In Wood's *Athenæ*, ed. Bliss, vol. iii. p. 7, is an interesting account of Father Baker taken from "A Breviate" of an autobiography. He was born December 9, 1575. His father was well off, and held the position of steward to Lord Abergavenny. He was first sent to Christ Church Hospital in London, then to Oxford (Broadgates Hall College), 1590. Naturally of a good disposition, though passionate, he here fell into "many vicious habits," and gave up all such practices of religion as he had been accustomed to. He had been intended for a parson, but gave that up on leaving Oxford. He went to London, to Clifford's Inn, then to the Inner Temple (1597), to study law. Here in London he lost all his faith and most of his morals. He returned home, and held the appointment of recorder in his native place. Once when returning from his rounds, being absorbed in some legal difficulty, he let his horse, instead of following the road to the ford over which he wanted to pass, take a narrow path which led to a narrow wooden bridge, which, "wide enough at first entrance, grew still more and more narrow and of an extraordinary height from the water." He did not see his danger, "till the horse, by stopping suddenly and trembling with neighing and loud snorting, gave his rider notice of the danger which he soon perceived to be no less than present death." He could neither go forward nor backwards, and being no swimmer, dared not jump into the water, which was very deep and with a strong current. His danger was God's opportunity: "Whereupon he framed in his mind such an internal resolution as this: If I escape this danger I

the famous D. Augustine Baker), a recent convert just then arrived in London. As he had conceived a great desire for the spiritual life, the priest who had received him advised him to go to London, where he would find benedictines who could assist

will believe there is a God who hath more care of my life and safety than I have heed of His love and worship. This he thought, and immediately thereupon he found his horse's head was turned, and both horse and man out of danger." He entered into himself, and some catholic books falling into his hands, doubts arose, and he was finally reconciled to the church by Rev. Richard Lloyd. "On the first general confession made by him in order to his reconciliation, all his habitual and deep-rooted vices were at once most miraculously ever rooted out of his heart, and the serpent's head with one blow was mortally wounded and crushed." After the occurrences mentioned in the text, Baker was allowed to lead a very retired life, and devote himself to prayer. He lived with a young nobleman, most likely lord Burghersh, son of the earl of Westmoreland. But they sorted not well together. He then went to Sir Nicholas Fortescue's, and lived there a very retired life, giving many hours a day to contemplative prayer, to which he had a great attraction. In 1619, being then in his forty-fourth year, he went over to Rheims, and was ordained priest probably by bishop Gifford, then the coadjutor to the archbishop. He was then sent to Devonshire on the mission to the house of Mr. Philip Fursdon of Fursdon, who had a relative at Douai. He remained here for about a year, and now began his work of historical collections, for which he had a particular talent. He was on intimate terms with all the learned men of the day, with Sir R. Cotton, Sir Henry Spelman, John Selden, and Godwin the bishop of Hereford; and to his labours both Dugdale and Dodsworth are indebted later. His principal work of this kind was the collection of material to prove the existence of the old English congregation, and the result is seen in the *Apostolatus Benedictinorum in Anglia*, which is, in its pre-reformation parts, really his work. D. Leander turned the English notes into Latin, and added an account of the history of his own times and the canonical aspects of the questions discussed; and D. Clement Reyner arranged the whole and published it. The real credit for this book, which is still remarkable among those of the kind for its correct apprehension of monastic England in later mediæval times, is due to Baker. Of his work as a him in his vocation. Here, by some chance, he fell in with the Italian fathers, who invited him to go with them to Italy, whither they were bound for a general chapter. It was about this time that he heard of D. Sigebert, and a coincidence which occurred just then opened his eyes to the importance of the old man's existence. He tells us the occurrence in his "Treatise of the Mission," hiding, as was his wont, the part he took in the business.

"The great light and knowledge that these fathers had on that point (the existence of an English congregation of which D. Buckley professed to be the sole survivor) was by occasion and means of an old printed *Turrecremata* upon our Rule, which one whom I well knew (*D. Baker himself*) happened to buy among the booksellers of Duck Lane; the which book he showing to the chief of the Italian Fathers (*D. Preston*), he looking into the book and turning to some place of it, found in the latter end of it, in an old written hand, an abstract or summary of the decrees of a certain

great ascetic we shall speak in the account of the convent of Cambrai. Suffice it here to say that after training the nuns for nine years in the spiritual life, he did the same work at Douai, which was the monastery of his choice. He then was sent on the mission again in his sixty-third year, and lived in Gray's Inn Lane, where he died of the plague, August 9, 1641. He was buried in the church of St. Andrew's, Holborn. "He was esteemed the most devout, austere, and religious person of his order, and one that did abound and was more happy in mental prayer (though it was a long time before he could obtain it) than any religious man (not excepted the carthusians) whatsoever." Four out of six of his volumes of Collections of Ecclesiastical History are now at Jesus College library, Oxford.

general chapter of the order in England held in the time of Henry VI., king of England (and if my memory deceive me not) in the year of our Lord 1442, and there was expressed there the title of the session, place, day and year, and names of the presidents, specifying that it was of the whole order in England that was not subject to transmarine houses; and indeed it was the greatest general chapter that ever (as I think) was held in England of the order. This, I say, gave the first light, and sometime shortly afterwards a little more was found; but plenty and clearness therein came not to be had till many years after, &c."[1]

His lawyer's instinct told him at once that if there was a congregation it was a corporate body; and D. Sigebert Buckley, survivor thereof (argued Baker), was heir of all the rights and privileges of the historic English congregation; and what he had he could hand on to others. Of survivors of the ancient benedictines of England he alone appeared; to the best of his knowledge and that of others he was the last: though it was true that he had spent the greater part of his life in prison, and had only just been set at liberty. His constancy in long confession to the limits of an extreme old age, also seemed to point him out as a providential instrument.[2]

[1] Quoted in D. Allanson's manuscript, *History of the English Congregation*.
[2] That there were other monks, or rather one other, living at the time is certain, though D. Buckley was most probably ultimately the sole survivor. In a MS., *Benedictine Obits*, in the Bodleian, the

So Baker suggested to his new friends "that a further use might be made of that good old man, by and from whom might be procured a continuation and succession and induction of the old benedictine monks of England (and particularly of Westminster), if the said old man would receive and admit them; which being demonstrated to him (the old man) both by ancient and modern laws and canon, Buckley did accordingly receive them,"[1] as it was the answer to his dearest wish.

And to whom could be more fittingly or properly handed on the succession, than to the man who had himself conceived the design, and who had already,

writer, speaking of Fr. Augustine Bradshaw (White), says: "At his coming to Hinlip in 1603 he was met by chance there by one Lyttleton, who had formerly been a monk of Evesham, and was now best known by the nickname of 'parson tinker.' This man was observed to cast his eyes upon Father Augustine, and being not able to hold, he asked Mr. Thomas Habington what this gentleman was, who confidently told him that he was a brother of his. 'A brother of mine!' said Mr. Lyttleton; 'I have not had any living these forty years!' 'I mean,' replied the gentleman, 'a monk of St. Benedict's order.' At these words he seemed to alter countenance, and he seemed moved, and at length besought Mr. Habington for the passion of Christ, that he might speak to him. All being related to Father Austin, a way was made to bring them together. As soon as Lyttleton came into the room, he fell upon his knees, and with floods of tears told what he was, beseeching Father Austin to reconcile him, which he, remaining there a day or two, did. This old man being thus reclaimed went home, and presently fell blind, and so remained almost two years deprived of his benefice, and had he not been bedridden he had been imprisoned for his conscience, and so died with great repentance, being nearly one hundred years old" (Gasquet, *Henry VIII. and the English Monasteries*, vol. ii. p. 480).

[1] A. Wood's Memoir of Baker, *Athenæ Oxoniensis*, ed. Bliss, vol. iii. p. 11.

without any idea of this work, offered himself as a postulant for the benedictine habit and profession? In so delicate and vital a business, it was however necessary to proceed with care and circumspection. The first step was to put the matter before the coming general chapter of the Cassinese congregation, who, in 1604, approved of the design. Baker, whose great desire was to keep up the succession, was sent to Italy and clothed at St. Justina's at Padua on May 27, 1605. But his health failing from the climate, he was allowed towards the end of his novitiate to return to England, whither he hurried and found his father dying. After his father's death, Baker settled his affairs and returned to London, where he put himself into the hands of the Italian fathers.

But while he was at Padua the Gunpowder Plot had taken place, and poor old D. Buckley, with many others, equally harmless and blameless, was again imprisoned. Buckley was in the Gatehouse prison at his old home at Westminster. This imprisonment of the old man not improbably caused a further delay in the project of the Italian fathers. At length two secular priests working on the mission, Robert Sadler and Edward Maihew[1] were received into the Italian congregation, and clothed as novices

---

[1] Both Sadler and Maihew had been brought up at the seminaries; and the latter, at least, was at Rome with the first seminarists who had joined the order. These two had been for many years on the mission, and had to go through their novitiate without any conventual life. D. Maihew remained for nearly eight years more on the mission before he ever lived in a monastery. D. Sadler, who died in 1621, never was a conventual.

towards the end of 1606. The time of probation expired, they were the two chosen to be aggregated to the old English congregation.

To Sigebert Buckley, then for Christ's sweet sake a prisoner in the Gatehouse, came one day in dreary November (it was the 21st, 1607) D. Preston, the superior of the Italian monks, and the two secular priest-novices, Sadler and Maihew. There, in the presence of the old man, they made their profession in the hands of D. Preston, and old D. Buckley, with his trembling hands, helped to put on their habits.[1] Being thus professed into the Cassinese congregation, they were then aggregated by the old man to the monastery of Westminster, which belonged to the English congregation.[2] The link was forged, as it was afterwards remembered, on the very anniversary of the restoration of Westminster, under Fecknam; and this coincidence gave great hopes of a prosperous future to the restored congregation. The old man's last wish was gratified. His eyes had seen the salvation of his house and congregation. They had now done their work, and he was blessed. Blindness, it is said, fell upon him almost

---

[1] D. Maihew says : ". . . et statim effectus est cœcus. . . . Quæ mihi comperta sunt scribo : nam rei gestæ interfui, imo ipso die ipse adhuc occulorum usu non privatus, professionis meæ monasticæ adstitit, et unus fuit qui habitum mihi in professione imposuit" (*Trophæa*, Tabula Tertia, p. 378).

[2] "Supradictus senex . . . sacerdotes illos qui sub Congregatione Cassinensi professionem jam emiserant, suo cœnobio Westmonasteriensis atque Congregationi Anglicanæ aggregavit et incorporavit" (D. Maihew, in his *Trophæa*, Tabula Prima, pp. 141, 142).

immediately after the ceremony, and no more did he see the light till it burst upon him in heaven.

A few others were in course of time aggregated to the old English congregation, but, with one exception, not by D. Buckley. Not long before his death, apparently but some two months, he himself professed into the monastery of Westminster and the English congregation, under the name of Augustine, David Baker, who had first conceived the idea of the continuation of the ancient English benedictine line. And so, in spite of difficulties and delays, Baker was destined to be the sole direct link, by immediate profession, between the old congregation and the new.

The testimony of D. Maihew, a principal actor in all that passed, is explicit and formal. He says:—

"The aforesaid venerable old man received the profession of one of ours as a member of his own monastery of Westminster, and with his own hands clothed him with the religious and sacred habit as is wont to be done at profession; who, bound by the monastic vows, the old man himself receiving them (*ipso acceptante*), and clothed by him with the holy habit, did confer those same benefits upon several others of ours. Hence we are sons of our first apostles, not only by aggregation, but also by monastic profession and habit.[1]

---

[1] *Trophæa*, Tabula Prima, pp. 43, 44. Of himself Maihew says: "Verum ipsomet die professionis cœnobio Westmonasteriensis et Congregationi Anglicanæ a R. P. Seberto unico ejusdem monasterii relicto monacho

Happy and contented, rejoicing in the answer of his heart's desire, comforted, maybe, with a glimpse of the future in store for the benedictine name in England, the old man on February 22, 1610, slept in the Lord. Ninety-three years had been the days of his mortal pilgrimage, and nearly forty of these had he passed in prison. His Italian friends who had treated him with loving care and honour were able to bury him with catholic rites, but in all secrecy, in an old chapel or country hermitage near Ponsholt, and the seat of the Nortons, in the parish of Westmeon, on the borders of Hampshire, where he had retired when released from prison in 1609. But before he died everything had been done to legalise and ratify his act, so he knew his labour was not in vain. The following is the important instrument of aggregation executed by him on November 8, 1609:—

"At the house of Thomas Loveden at Ponsholt, and witnessed by Dom Maurus, monk of the Italian congregation, notary apostolic, Anthony Norton,

cum licentia suorum superiorum aggregatus est" (Tabula Tertia, p. 388). It is in more recent times commonly stated, and has been generally received, that FF. Sadler and Maihew were *professed* by D. Buckley. But the deed of aggregation to be given presently, besides the other evidence already quoted, shows that this was not the case. That this "one of ours" who was professed directly by D. Sigebert and then clothed and professed others, was D. Baker, does not admit by any possibility of a doubt; for D. Buckley died 22nd February 1610, and on the 27th December 1609 the English congregation consisted of only three members besides D. Buckley himself, viz. DD. Robert (Sadler), Edward (Maihew), and Augustine, about whose identity there can be no question.

Henry Norton. In the name of God, Amen.—I, Dom Sebert, otherwise Sigebert, priest and professed monk of the monastery of St. Peter of Westminster, of the English congregation of the order of St. Benedict, (lest the rights and illustrious privileges formerly granted by the liberality of princes and pontiffs which for some years past, God so permitting, are preserved in me, the sole survivor of all the English monks, should shortly perish) have with the consent of their superiors received and admitted D. Robert Sadler of the diocese of Peterborough, and D. Edward Maihew of the diocese of Salisbury, Englishmen, priests and professed monks of the Cassinese congregation, otherwise known as that of St. Justina of Padua, as brethren and monks of the aforesaid monastery; and at London, on November 21, 1607, granted, communicated, and attributed to them all rights, privileges, pre-eminence, honours, liberties, and favours which the monks professed and dwelling in the said monastery have in former times enjoyed. And finally by these presents I hold the same as pleasing, and settled and ratified. I receive and admit all others as monks, brethren, converse, oblates of the said monastery, and grant, communicate, and attribute to them all rights, privileges, &c., as above, whom Dom Thomas Preston of Shrewsbury, Dom Augustine and Dom Anselm (Beech) of Lancashire, and Dom Maurus (Taylor) of Ely, (to whom, as more clearly appears by my letter, 21st November 1607, I have granted authority and power of admitting in this sort), had admitted or received as monks, brethren, converse, oblates of the aforesaid monastery, and granted them the rights, &c., as above, and by virtue of these presents as regards all and each of their parts, I hold as ratified, agreeable, and confirmed, and will so hold in perpetuity . . .

"Given at Punsholt, *alias* Ponshelt, A.D. 1609, on the 8th day of November, in presence of the subscribed notary and witnesses."[1]

A few days afterwards, on December 15, 1609, the old man wrote the following letter:—

"*To the Superior*, DOM THOMAS PRESTON.

"VERY REV. FATHER AND BELOVED BROTHER,—Since the Divine Will has so protracted my life that now to my great comfort I see the restoration of the English congregation and its recent confirmation by the sovereign pontiff,[2] and since Divine Providence seems to have kept me alive as it were for the very end that the possession of that congregation and consequently all its rights should remain in me and in the monks aggregated by me; since also I fully see all this affair by your prudent attempts and labours has been energetically promoted, and that so happily that no small hope has arisen that the

[1] *Apostolatus*, iii. 1.
[2] The aggregation to Westminster made by D. Sigebert was ratified by the general chapter of the Cassinese congregation in 1608, and was the following year, on the 18th September, confirmed by the pope, who made good anything that might have been irregular in the action. See *Ibid.* iii. 2.

same congregation will in its own time once more arise to its old vigour and splendour. But as I on account of extreme old age and bodily weakness cannot personally govern its affairs, therefore do I ask and beg your paternity, that as you are already the superior of the Italian congregation and hold the rule thereof, you will also vouchsafe to take upon you the care and solicitude of the English congregation, and, in my name, forward and carry out whatsoever shall seem necessary to your wisdom and convenient for promoting, exalting, and propagating our old and revived congregation of England. Whatsoever you do in this matter I, by these presents, do ratify and confirm, and in sign thereof, do subscribe my name (as far as can be done by a blind man) before the witnesses as below. Begging you to acquaint me at fitting times with the success of this business, and thanking you from my heart for the charitable comfort and brotherly care of me in my helpless old age, and humbly commending myself to you, I commit you to the Lord God.

"D. SEBERTUS,
Monk of the English Congregation.

"In the presence of Thomas Loveden and Anthony Norton. 15th day of December 1609."[1]

This delegation of authority over the old English congregation to the person of the Italian superior, was ratified in a public deed by the monks already aggregated to Westminster. Their consent is dated

[1] *Ibid.* iii. 4.

December 19, 1609, and is signed on that day by D. Robert (Sadler) and D. Edward (Maihew). Eight days afterwards (December 27) it was signed by D. Augustine (Baker).[1] This is valuable as showing that for more than two years after the first aggregation, there were only three members of the English congregation.

The successful issue of Baker's plans had resulted in this position of affairs. There were now nominally three congregations of benedictines in England instead of two. But the English congregation was under the superior of the Italian missioners. The aspect of things had also changed in other respects; and the continuation of the old English congregation, thus secured, presented itself to a mind of the practical, not to say political, cast of D. Preston, and perhaps others, under quite another guise from that in which it had suggested itself to David Baker and was conceived by him. Among the Italian fathers were those who saw that, whilst the Spanish monks increased and waxed many, and were founding monasteries within reach of England, they themselves were making but little progress. This was another reason which recommended to their minds an Union of all English monks as the most satisfactory remedy for many inconveniences. The Italian fathers also felt they might now enter upon negotiation with a better grace, as having something to offer to the Spanish monks as a *quid pro quo*.

[1] *Ibid.* iii. 4.

Already as far back as the summer of 1608 the Spanish monks, D. Bradshaw and D. Leander, had had a conference at Rheims on the subject of a Union, with Dr. Gifford, then a novice at the monastery of St. Remi's: "and while they were deliberating upon the means how to bring it to pass, Father Thomas Preston came in; and so came in, that while one of them said he wished Father Thomas Preston was there, he that was wished for, being exiled out of England, knocked at the door to inquire for them."[1]

A few articles were suggested to bring about the desired union of the English monks of the *two* congregations, viz. those of Italy and Spain. At this time D. Preston seems to have considered best not to say anything about the measures in progress for the revival of the old English congregation. The meeting broke up on the understanding that within a few weeks another should be held in England of the Spanish monks, and a form of union agreed upon. This was done. The authors of the *Apostolatus* had first intended to print the proposed terms of agreement in their appendix among the other documents.[2] But in fact it is not to be found there.

The immediately subsequent history must be a matter of conjecture; only one thing is certain, that between this date and the next stage in the negotiations, it fully appeared that it was now a question

[1] Weldon's *Chronological Notes*, p. 95.   [2] *Apostolatus*, ii. 17.

not of the union of *two*, but of *three* congregations. More than eighteen months passed before anything further on the subject occurs. But on February 13, 1610, a document was signed by DD. Bradshaw and Preston, and by the three monks Sadler, Maihew, and Baker, embodying certain terms by which it was thought a Union might be brought about.[1] There were ten articles in all on the following heads: (1) The necessity of a Union; (2) the laying aside of any dissensions; (3) one common superior to be chosen by six electors, three Spanish and three *Italians or English;* (4) rules for the mission to be drawn up by the unanimous consent of the six electors; (5) the giving up by the Spanish monks, into the hands of the united body of the English monks, of all claim to houses, lands, and money, and all other kinds of goods, movable or unmovable, which were or should be in their possession, or should be due to them; (6) the handing over to the body of all bequests, except those made for any specific uses; (7) the nomination of an official to look after these funds; (8) the superior of the Italian as well as the English fathers to have the power of sending subjects to the convents abroad; (9) profession in all convents henceforth to be made only for the English congregation; (10) the superior of the Spanish fathers to undertake to pro-

---

[1] *Apostolatus*, iii. 6. The F.N.F. of this document is evidently D. Augustine Baker, who, *more suo*, has effaced himself everywhere in the *Apostolatus*.

cure licence that all already clothed at Douai and Dieuleward should be professed in the English congregation.

When D. Bradshaw returned from England and communicated the terms to his brethren, they would by no means admit of them; and pointed out how difficult it would be to obtain the consent of the superiors in Spain. That D. Bradshaw recognised the force of this objection seems clear, from the fact that he now let the matter drop. From all we know of him he was a really admirable and amiable religious, but not a man qualified to conduct business. His enthusiastic nature was easily worked upon by men who knew their own affairs and had clearly defined aims, and who also felt it was not their place to represent the interest of the Spanish mission.

When, under pressure from his brethren, D. Bradshaw dropped the matter, the other side were by no means content to let the question rest. The Italians began steadily to work for and to press a Union so beneficial to themselves. The man who now, in 1612, started a plan afresh was D. Anselm Beech, the Cassinese, who was then in Rome. His project[1] was based on the same comprehensive plan as D. Preston's, and he had the same cardinal articles, viz. "that the Italian and Spanish congregation should cede all titles to houses or any goods," &c. But, it must be remembered, the Italians had no houses or goods at all to cede, and their assets

[1] *Ibid.* iii. 6.

were practically *nil*. Moreover, according to these schemes, the dozen of Italians were, as far as government was concerned, to be possessed of the same amount of power as the hundred Spanish fathers. The duty of the first was to supply superiors, while the other had to find subjects, houses, and goods. If at this date D. Preston had, thanks to D. Baker, strengthened his position, so also had the Spanish monks. Their troubles at Douai were at an end, and Caverel had built them a monastery. Dieuleward, too, had started well; and new foundations at Paris and St. Malo were in view. They had also shown themselves to be men hardly in need of such extraneous help as the Italians could offer, and were altogether now less inclined than ever to barter their independence for, what many must have thought at that time, but a sentimental benefit.

D. Beech had, however, one great advantage. He was on the spot at head-quarters, in Rome itself, where the business would have ultimately to be settled; and there he could speak and act directly. This advantage he used to the full.

These attempts were witnessed by the Spanish fathers with concern, especially as their own vicar was now again taking part in and countenancing them. D. Leander Jones and D. Rudisind Barlow, conventuals of Douai, and both men of weight and experience, brought the matter before the Spanish general, representing that they, and the greater part of the English monks, were too warmly attached to the Spanish congregation, who had dealt so generously with its English subjects, not to view with alarm such a project as the vicar was then supporting. It would not, they felt, merely result in loss to the congregation, but would also be injurious to the Apostolic mission itself; for even their own existence was in the last degree precarious, and their houses were still struggling with the difficulties of first beginnings. As they could not as yet stand alone, it seemed folly at that time to cut themselves adrift and start a third and independent congregation. The vicar was called to Spain in 1612,[1] leaving D. Leander as prior of Douai, and made his report, which was not favourably received.

At this time, while D. Beech was putting forward his projects at Rome, means had been found to interest persons of great influence in favour of the little body of the English congregation. The agent in the matter was doubtlessly Arthur Pitts, who had been active at the time of the foundation of Dieuleward; the great personages in question were the princes of the house of Lorraine; the person through whom pressure was brought to

[1] The following extract from a letter written by Champney to More, October 23, 1612, on the occasion of D. Bradshaw's journey to Spain, is interesting from the friendly tone it shows as existing between the secular clergy and the benedictines: "Fr. White (Bradshaw), who hath written to you his occasion of going to Rome, and of whom we here desire you should testify to their procurator that we are very sorry for his absence hence, as being a special friend of our clergy, assureth us that the college of Douai is to be visited, and that the provincial of the Jesuits must be employed therein." (Tierney, vol. v. pp. cxix.-cxx.)

bear (though unwillingly) was D. Gabriel of St. Mary. So strong was the pressure that no alternative remained to the Spanish fathers but to yield to the demands of the few English monks. "We were compelled" (say the authors of the *Apostolatus*, at this point D. Leander, in words which betray the sense of undue pressure)—"we were compelled, after some treating of the matter between us, who were then of the Spanish congregation, and the monks of the English congregation, for the sake of peace, which would otherwise have been endangered, and for our own safety, to allow them an equal share of all the goods in the convent of Dieuleward, which convent the Spanish alone, through Fr. Augustine and Fr. Gabriel of St. Mary, had erected at the cost of much toil, and had alone for some years possessed in peace."[1]

Occasion was taken, lest this sharing should become a cause of future misunderstanding, to propose another form of Union between the Spanish and the English alone (signed at Douai by both the interested parties), known as the "Union of the Four Articles." It was proposed (1) that as long as England was separated from the holy see, the fathers of the English congregation should compose but one body, which should be, and should be called during the schism, the Spanish Mission or Congregation; (2) that within this body there should be twelve members in whom should be vested all the rights

[1] *Apostolatus*, ii. 18.

of the old English congregation; (3) vacancies in this number were to filled up by monks of the said Spanish mission; (4) when the schism was healed, all the monks of the Spanish mission (in England) who did not wish to return to Spain should *ipso facto* form the English congregation, but that during the schism they should be really of the congregation of Spain.[1] The Spanish general chapter had agreed to this on May 5, 1613, and appointed D. Leander as vicar in place of D. Bradshaw. The chapter also ordered that the vicar should take D. Maihew as one of his official assistants, and appoint D. Sadler as his deputy in England.

D. Preston now resigned his office of superior of the English monks, some of whom had now repudiated the late agreement. He was succeeded by D. Beech. It is not necessary to pursue the details of the proceedings of this latter.[2] It may be sufficient to say that for the moment he succeeded in carrying through in Rome an arrangement on the lines the Spanish monks had already refused to accede to.[3] Orders were issued to the nuncios at Paris and Brussels to notify the fact to the Spanish monks, who had been all unaware of what was going on over their heads

---

[1] *Ibid.* ii. 18.

[2] Nor were these operations of D. Beech looked upon with favourable eyes by all his colleagues in England. D. Augustine Smithson, writing to him from Paris (December 4, 1612), says: "I long to see you in England, where you would do much good, while in Rome you do little, to judge from what I hear from many sides" (*Spicilegium Benedictinum*, p. 18).

[3] *Apostolatus*, iii. 37-40.

in Rome. A moment came when they were actually threatened with expulsion from the houses they themselves had founded; and this even had some measure of execution.[1] But the decision come to by the Roman authorities had been based on representations which not merely gave ample grounds for an appeal, but necessitated one; and this appeal, made under the guidance of D. Leander and D. Gabriel Gifford, issued in a reversal by the authorities of their recent decision.

Wearied out with these contests, the Spanish monks, with a very few exceptions, now requested that, so far as they were concerned, they might be allowed to withdraw from all projects of union and carry on their own work. But here the holy see intervened in a manner as decisive as unexpected. The ancient succession of the English episcopate had, as we have seen, been allowed to lapse. But now the pope resolved that the succession of the English benedictines, so wonderfully preserved and handed on after the lapse of nearly half a century from the date of the schism, should continue. He insisted on a Union. The first step was to require the Spanish monks to submit their own proposal; and D. Leander with his brethren, so directed, now took the matter in hand themselves. At a meeting held in London on June 11, 1615, they supplicated the pope to put an end to all by ordering under censure the professed of the three congregations to

[1] This event is alluded to, *Apostolatus*, ii. 4, 5.

choose by vote nine definitors to arrange the terms of a Union acceptable to all parties.[1] Shortly afterwards D. Leander, in the guise apparently of a letter to the nuncio at Brussels, Bentivoglio, signed by himself and the convent of St. Gregory's, Douai,[2] explained at length the terms of union proposed. The proposal, both generous and peaceful, was accepted by the pope; and in the second half of the year 1615, D. Benet Jones and D. Sigebert Bagshaw, as procurators for the Spanish and English congregations respectively, went to Rome to arrange a basis for agreement among all parties. But the Italians, or rather D. Beech, held out stiffly against any such accommodation.

The experience of the "Union of the Four Articles" in 1612–13 pointed out to the authorities a solution of the difficulty. Left face to face with each other, the monks of the Spanish and English congregations had then found means to come to terms. Though warmly attached to their congregation, the Spanish monks had shown themselves reasonable in the midst of much provocation, and there were men in Rome at that time, intimately acquainted with the circumstances of the case and solicitous for the interests of the English congregation, who could testify that the Spanish had put up patiently with much that was trying and disheartening. As D. Beech would not listen to the "sweet reasonableness" of the others, cardinal Bellarmine, in a letter of March

[1] *Ibid.* iii. 15.   [2] *Ibid.* iii. 16–20.

26, 1616,[1] to D. Leander, proposed the cutting of the knot, and suggested that as the Italians were now the only obstacle they should be left out altogether, and the definitors chosen only from the Spanish and English congregations. The hint was taken, and on May 19, 1616, the pope issued a brief[2] ordering the *two* congregations to proceed to elect nine definitors, who were to be chosen irrespectively from either body. The details of the election were placed in the hands of Ubaldini, the nuncio at Paris, who by letters dated August 24, 1616, sent round notice to all concerned to send in to him within three months the names of those they elected as definitors: he would then appoint the time and place of meeting. While the election was proceeding the nuncio was succeeded in his office by Bentivoglio (since 1607 nuncio at Brussels), who was well acquainted with the monks of Douai. After a delay necessarily caused by the changes in the nunciature, he was able, March 16, 1617,[3] to announce that six Spanish monks and three English, truly representative, had been duly declared definitors. The election was practically unanimous, and there were only five or six votes from the two congregations that were missing. Bentivoglio appointed June 1, 1617, as the day of meeting, and Paris as the place.

When the definitors met, the first and most essential work was to secure the continuance of the old English congregation. They did not intend to make

[1] *Ibid.* iii. 21.   [2] *Ibid.* iii. 21, 22.   [3] *Ibid.* iii. 23.

any new congregation, but only to revive what had existed in England since the thirteenth century. It was only to secure this continuation that the Spanish fathers, to their own loss and inconvenience, entirely in obedience to the holy see and against their own wishes, entertained the idea of any union at all. But now, the continuation of the historic English congregation being forced upon them, they took the matter seriously; and (as subsequent history shows) resolved that, on their part, there should be no mistake about it, and that it should be no dead letter. It was now better known than in 1604 what this congregation really was. Investigations had been silently proceeding, and history had also been playing its useful part in educating minds receptive of its lessons.

The problem before the definitors was to provide for this continuance and at the same time to devise a form of government adapted to the present abnormal circumstances, viz. the existence of the monasteries out of England and of a body of monk-missioners in England pursuing their apostolic work under the terrible hand of a hostile and cruel government.

It was evident in the first place that the government of these latter could not be carried by the superiors of the monasteries to which they belonged by profession. Special superiors must be appointed on the spot. In the provision made to meet these circumstances we have at once the key to the resolution, in the minds of the definitors, of the two discordant elements of the present situation. Looked at in itself, the simple adoption of the Cassinese system, the working of which for obvious reasons was perfectly well known to all the definitors, would have been altogether the most proper and efficient if the purposes of the mission alone had to be considered. By this system, although the monks were professed in different monasteries, they did not belong, by their profession, to any particular house, but to the general body of the congregation, and they were to be esteemed as members of any house in which they might happen to be placed.[1] The general chapter, composed of a body of superiors and delegates meeting every three years, was the supreme governing body, and had authority to delegate power to certain select members in whose hands was placed the appointment of all superiors whatever, even of the inferior officials. As all property in the Cassinese congregation was considered as belonging to the body as a whole and not to the various houses of which it was composed, they could dispose of everything as was deemed best for the general interests. This Cassinese system obviously would lend itself naturally to the modifications required by the special circumstances of the present case and to the appointment of superiors in England without monasteries.

But, on the other hand, in the Cassinese system it is obvious that the monastery as such had no

---

[1] Gasquet, *Introduction to "The Monks of the West"* (ed. Nimmo), i. p. xlvii.

independent life or existence; and by no possibility of means could it be made to square with even the pretence of continuing the old English congregation.

The way in which they solved the problem before them was, in a few words, this: to leave each monastery as a definite entity and corporation, with its own property, rights, and burthens, together with its independent existence and superiors; to borrow from the monasteries monks for the Apostolic mission in England, placing them there under a new kind of superior specially created for the purpose, as required by the anomalous circumstances of the times. Perhaps a sentiment dictated the choice of only two, to bear, with the name of Provincial, the time-honoured names of Canterbury and York.

It is easy to perceive how the interests of the two kinds of superiors of the monasteries and the mission might not always coincide. Under the old familiar title of "President," but with altogether new attributes, a higher authority was constituted, to reside out of England, whose business it should be, whilst forbidden to interfere in the government by priors or provincials of their monasteries and provinces, to transfer monks from one to the other. He was, moreover, endowed with the rights of visitation, and, subject to a two-fold appeal, was also a judge of controversies. A body of five or more definitors, in whose hands was the election of the president, and three of whom formed a higher court of appeal, was appointed as the standing council of the president. Above all was the general chapter, appointed to be held every four years. This was the supreme tribunal of the congregation. In this general chapter was, theoretically,[1] vested the appointment of superiors after the communities had nominated.

The new congregation was subjected to the Spanish general only so far as to give him the title of general of both congregations, and power to visit any convent in the Spanish dominions; to give licence to receive degrees at the universities, and to choose as president whom he pleased out of two presented by the general chapter of the English congregation. The definitors declared that this their meeting had all the powers of a general chapter, and proceeded to make appointments to the various offices.[2] Their deliberations and arrangements were of course subjected to the approval of the holy see, and could not take effect until that was secured.

No one was to be forced into the union, and the rights of those on the English mission, who did not wish to enter into the union, were carefully provided for. The Spanish general gave his approval

[1] We say "theoretically," because while the monasteries were on the continent the general chapter, as will be seen, only appointed the priors of Dieuleward, Paris, and up to 1666, St. Malo's.

[2] D. Gifford was chosen first president-elect, but he never actually held the office, and, as a matter of fact, never was a member of the restored English congregation. He was made bishop before the Union had been approved at Rome, and D. Leander, the second president-elect, became the first to hold that office.

to the scheme of union on October 27, 1617, and gave orders to his procurator in Rome to use all diligence in procuring the final confirmation.[1]

But this was not to come yet. When D. Sigebert Bagshaw returned to Rome after the definitory had concluded its sittings, he found against the union an opposition so powerful and coming from so many quarters, on so many different grounds, that nearly two years passed before the matter was settled. The head and front of the opposition was the Cassinese congregation, who, through their own fault, or at least the fault of some of their members, had been left out in the cold. They complained, if Weldon can be trusted, that the union was prejudicial to their body, and was based on some misinformation given by some one or more of their own members,[2] who preferred their liberty and independence before the public good.

Other opponents were those Spanish fathers who had already given trouble; and among them was D. Francis Walgrave, an upholder of D. Beech's plan, who now opposed this other union on the unhistorical ground that there never had been a congregation in England. He gained to his side the French ambassador in Rome, on the pretext that the proposed union contained points contrary to the laws and prejudicial to his state.

The good abbat Caverel jealously watched over

---

[1] *Apostolatus*, iii. 24.
[2] Probably referring to D. Anselm Beech and his attempts.

the interests and independence of his beloved monastery at Douai, and used all the weight of his power to delay the confirmation until everything was settled in accordance with his wishes in this regard. He also took measures at Rome to secure the rights of any continental abbeys that had had possessions in England, in case their property could be restored.

The procurators acquitted themselves of their office with effect, and were able to satisfy the Cassinese, who were offered an equal share in the union if they chose to enter. The French ambassador, on becoming better informed, ceased his opposition; and abbat Caverel, having secured what affected the position of St. Gregory's, not only withdrew his objections, but assisted in securing the confirmation, which came on August 23, 1619, by a brief *Ex Incumbenti* of Paul V.[1] The Spanish general gave his consent to the publication of the brief, and within two years all was so arranged that the general chapter was summoned to meet at Douai on July 2, 1621.[2]

[1] *Apostolatus*, iii. 24. [2] *Ibid.* iii. 26.

CHAPTER XIV

DOM LEANDER AND HIS MISSION

IN the preceding chapters D. Leander had been mentioned as taking a prominent part in directing the Spanish mission and guarding its interests. It is now time to deal more fully with one part at least of the career of this remarkable man. He came to England on an unofficial mission, and reported to Rome on the state of catholicity in this country.[1] As he was here confronted with two grave questions then dividing English catholics, the oath of allegiance and the appointment of bishops, it will be necessary for us, first of all, to give a sufficient outline of the circumstances which surround these questions, and of their bearing on the state of catholicity at that time. The reader will then be able to understand the position which D. Leander took upon these controverted points. So, before dealing with the details of his life, we must go back to the last years of Elizabeth's reign, in which are to be found the beginnings of the disputes concerning the oath of allegiance.

As the queen still continued to give no serious signs of an intention to marry, and also came to an age which put all hopes of direct heirs at an end,

[1] Advantage was taken by the holy see of D. Leander's intimacy with archbishop Laud, at whose invitation the monk came, to secure an impartial report of the religious state of England.

the question of the succession became of paramount importance. Although it was prohibited by law to discuss the matter, catholics like every one else were divided on this subject. Parsons and his following continued to advocate a Spanish succession, and shaped all their policy so as to secure it; but the clergy and most of the laity, with the rest of the country, looked to James, the son of the hapless Mary, queen of Scots. When Parsons, at the last hour, saw the futility of his Spanish intrigues, James was approached by him also; and it was ingenuously pleaded that the jesuit party had only suggested another successor in order to force James to become a catholic.[1] James had a few years before made some kind of promise of tolerance for the persecuted catholics; and, we think, honestly did intend to keep it had his protestant subjects allowed. How this proposed tolerance was regarded by the Spanish faction may be gathered from a letter written by Fr. Henry Tichborne, S.J., then at Seville, to Fr. Thomas Derbyshire, S.J., at Pont-à-Mousson. The letter, which found its way into the hands of the

---

[1] Parsons had the courage to write to the king on October 18, 1603: "The principal catholic English that resided abroad and had particularly laboured for your majesty's safety and advancement, both before and after the death of your renowned and pious mother, growing into fear and despair of that which they most of all desired, concerning your majesty's inclination in religion, resolved *for the last spur* of irritation that way to cause the Book of Succession to be written, giving the name of *Doleman* thereto by allusion to *Vir Dolorum*, thereby to insinuate the grief and sorrow they felt in being forced to come to this last means, in respect both of your majesty's good and their own," &c. (*Stonyhurst MSS. Ang. A.*, iii. 36; quoted by Tierney, vol. iii. p. lxxiii, *note*).

English Government and is now in the Public Record Office, is dated February 2, 1598. The writer is alarmed at the reported "liberty of conscience at home," for this he considered will cause "the expulsion of the society," and will, he says, disanimate princes "from the hot pursuit of the enterprise." "Our rejection will leave us hopeless and helpless, and will fall out with us like the sheep that made peace with the wolves on condition they should remove the dogs. So that the circumstances and conditions necessarily implying the removal of the company (which by their rule may admit no like conditions), and are our dogs, we shall be left as a prey to the wolves, that will besides drive our greatest patron to stoop to a peace which will be the utter ruin of our edifice, this many years in building." [1]

When James came to the throne he was assured of the allegiance of catholics. But the events which culminated in the Gunpowder Plot, struck such terror into the heart of the king that he looked upon all English catholics as plotters against his life, and as bound by the opinions of a school who magnified the temporal prerogatives of the papal see. One of the measures taken for securing his safety, and, as it was meant by its originators, a fresh excuse for persecuting the adherents of the ancient faith, was the framing of an oath of allegiance to be sworn by all under penalty of death.[2]

[1] *S.P. Dom Eliz.*, vol. cclxii. n. 28.
[2] The terms of the oath were as follows: "I, A. B., do truly and sincerely acknowledge, profess, testify, and declare in my conscience before

Its origin is interesting and is twofold. After the appeal against the arch-priest to which we have

God and the world, that our sovereign lord king James is lawful and rightful king of this realm and all other his majesty's dominions and countries; and that the pope, neither of himself, nor by any authority of the church or see of Rome, or by any other means with any other, hath any power or authority to depose the king, or to dispose of any of his majesty's kingdoms, or dominions, or to authorise any foreign princes to invade or annoy him or his countries; or to discharge any of his subjects of their allegiance and obedience to his majesty; or to give licence or leave to any of them to bear arms, raise tumults, or to offer any violence or hurt to his majesty's royal person, state, or government, or to any of his majesty's subjects, within his majesty's dominion.

"Also I do swear from my heart, that, notwithstanding any declaration or sentence of excommunication or deprivation made or granted or to be made or granted by the pope or his successors, or by any authority derived or pretended to be derived from him or his see, against the said king, his heirs or successors, or any absolution of the said subjects from their obedience, I will bear faith and true allegiance to his majesty, his heirs and successors, and him and them will defend to the uttermost of my power against all conspiracies and attempts whatsoever which shall be made against him or their persons, their crown and dignity, by reason or colour of any such sentence or declaration or otherwise, and will do my best endeavour to disclose and make known unto his majesty, his heirs and successors, all treasons, and traitorous conspiracies which I shall know or hear of to be against him or any of them. *And I do further swear that I do from my heart abhor, detest, and abjure as impious and heretical this damnable doctrine and position—that princes, which may be excommunicated or deprived by the pope, may be deposed or murdered by their subjects or any other whatsoever.* And I do believe and in my conscience am resolved, that neither the pope nor any other person whatsoever hath power to absolve me of this oath or any part thereof, which I acknowledge by good and lawful authority to be lawfully ministered unto me; and do renounce all pardons and dispensations to the contrary.

"And these things I do plainly and sincerely acknowledge and swear, according to these express words by me spoken, and according to the plain and common sense and understanding of the same words; without any equivocation, or mental evasion, or secret reservation whatsoever. And I do make this recognition and acknowledgment heartily, willingly, and truly, upon the true faith of a christian. So help me God" (Tierney, vol. iv. pp. cxvii.–cxviii.).

referred in the previous volume, Elizabeth, to remove the fears of the puritans, who had heard of her aid to the secular priests, on November 5, 1602, by proclamation, banished from the kingdom all catholic missionaries. The jesuits and their party were banished absolutely, and at once; but those secular priests who would "acknowledge sincerely their allegiance and duty to her," were promised such treatment as their case merited.[1] Thirteen of the appellant priests signed an address, drawn up by Dr. William Bishop, to the queen (January 31, 1603); in which, while professing all allegiance, they drew clearly and sharply the distinction between the pope's power as head of the church (which they upheld to the utmost), and those ascribed to him as political and temporal chief of Christendom.[2]

This address, carefully worded, never reached the queen, for she was stricken with her mortal illness the very day it was signed; but it made the basis of the first part of the oath. The clause denying the deposition or murder of excommunicated princes was the work of Bancroft, archbishop of Canterbury, helped by an apostate jesuit, Sir Christopher Perkins. This latter knew well the teaching affected by the society, and their reasons for extolling the political prerogatives of the Roman see. All recent events had shown that an effort was being made to retain these powers; and so, in a cunningly worded denial of such a doctrine, Bancroft and

[1] *Ibid.*, vol. iii. p. clxxxvii.   [2] *Ibid.*, vol. iii. pp. clxxxviii.–cxci.

Perkins foresaw "a rock of scandal, and a stone of offence."

They had judged rightly; for a development of thought in the church was making itself felt, and a new spirit was beginning to work, and there was sure to be a collision between the old and the new.[1]

The pope was between two fires. The fathers of the society in Flanders had been urging him no longer to treat James with such forbearance as he had hitherto shown; and on the other hand, the king of France was counselling patience and gentleness, lest the lot of catholics should become aggravated. While the parliament, which passed the bill concerning the oath, was sitting, a secret messenger was sent from Rome to the king; but this mission met with only discouraging results. At the same time that the emissary returned to Rome announcing the failure of his mission, two fathers of the society, sent from Brussels, also arrived. They were charged with the duty of stirring the pope up to energetic measures against

---

[1] As Mr. R. Simpson so well puts it: "There are two kinds of movements and apparent growth always going on in the church; one is the fermentation of a moribund school—for a religious school never cries more loudly than in its agony, never flings more strongly than in its death-throes; the other is the secret under-growth, the silent advance of thought, discomforting and ousting the old opinions, which in their unsteadiness cry so loudly for protection, and employ the relics of their force at the dictation of their terror; for the artificial faith in a dying doctrine becomes fanatical, because passion is substituted for reason" (*Edmund Campion*, p. 489).

king James.[1] Paul, a Borghese, after the rebuff he had received, was no longer in a disposition to resist this repeal. After a short struggle he yielded to the clamours by which he was assailed, and on the 22nd of September 1606 signed a brief which was communicated to the arch-priest by Fr. Holtly, the jesuit superior, in which he pronounced the oath to be unlawful, "as containing many things contrary to faith and salvation." This declaration became, while it remained in force, a mere question of obedience; and it is difficult on this ground, however we may sympathise with them on the theoretical question, not to blame, and to blame greatly, those who refused obedience to the supreme pastor. It must also be remembered, on the other hand, that the oath contains a clause denying not only the power of the pope to depose princes, but also (and this seems to be "impious and heretical," and altogether "a damnable doctrine and position") that such princes may be not only deposed but also murdered by their subjects or by any other whatsoever. In the disputes upon the oath of allegiance this latter seems to have been forgotten.[2]

When the oath was first published, catholics were divided into three parties. Some admitted

---

[1] Tierney, vol. iv. p. 74, *note;* also De la Boderie's *Ambassade en Angleterre,* tome i. pp. 150, 200, 284, 300, 327.

[2] It is only fair to the memory of James I. personally to say, that when in the proposed draft of the oath he found a claim repudiating the pope's right to excommunicate princes, he struck it out, as he was satisfied with the claim about the rejection of the deposing power, and

the oath as it stood, others with qualifications, while others set their faces steadily against it in every particular.[1] At first Blackwell, the arch-priest, vehemently opposed it. But at a conference of clergy held early in June 1606, he announced a change in his opinions, and considered the oath might be lawfully taken. As this opinion was opposed among others by D. Preston, the Cassinese,[2] the matter was

the murdering of excommunicated princes. To quote from the Premonition of his Apologie for the oath: "So careful was I that nothing should be contained in this oath, except the profession of natural allegiance and civil and temporal obedience, with a promise to resist to all contrary uncivil violence."

[1] A piteous appeal went up to the pope (Paul V.) from eight priests, prisoners in Newgate, on account of this oath, imploring him to say what was the part which was contrary to faith and salvation. "To this appeal, so touching, so just, so reasonable, no answer was returned. But it is likely the pope never got the petition. For Parsons, through whose hands all English affairs passed, never scrupled to suppress inconvenient documents. James was still left to upbraid the pope for a silence as unwise in regard of the government, as it was injurious to the interests of the catholics: 'In this rescript,' says the monarch, 'he had dealt both indiscreetly with me, and injuriously with his own catholics—with me in not repeating particularly what special words he quarrelled with in that oath; which if he had done, it might have been that, for the fatherly care I have not to put any of my subjects to a needless extremity, I might have been contented in some sort to have reformed or interpreted those words, &c.' ... Whatever may have been the insincerity of James, it is painful to reflect on the truth of these remarks" (Tierney, vol. iv. pp. 78, 79, *note*).

[2] D. Preston is often accused of having written books under the name of Roger Widdrington in favour of the oath. Against this are three facts: he never took the oath; he died in the Clink prison (April 3, 1640), and ever disowned the authorship. So says Weldon (p. 180). It is often held that "Roger Widdrington" was the Mr. Howard referred to in D. Leander's correspondence, that is to say, a son of Lord William Howard of Naworth, commonly known as "Belted Will." But in view of the part D. Preston plays in Panzani's corres-

referred to the pope, who was already undecided what to do; and so far as Rome was concerned, the difficulty was there allowed to stand.

Now we must turn to the other point which occupied the attention of D. Leander, viz. the appointment of bishops.

We have mentioned the desire to have bishops as rulers which was animating the clergy, and how Parsons thwarted this by the appointment of George Blackwell as arch-priest. When it was found that the arch-priest, on considering the question of the oath no longer in the abstract, but as a matter of everyday politics, not only changed his opinions and publicly announced that catholics could lawfully take it, but went even so far as to take it himself, his former friends deserted him. He was deposed[1] (February 1, 1608), and George Birket

pondence with cardinal Barberini, and his endeavour to get the commands of the archbishop of Canterbury to print together with Mr. Howard a book against Courtney (see *Clarendon State Papers*, vol. i. pp. 303, 304), it is evident that he changed his mind on the question, and was rightfully accredited with being in favour of the oath. The part which Fr. Parsons took in this question, and the curious motives which seem to have influenced him, may be seen in Tierney, vol. iv. p. cxxxv.

[1] Blackwell was already imprisoned when he was deposed from his office, and in the examinations he had to undergo he made some strong remarks. When Allen's "Admonition" was brought up against him, he said he could not choose but confess from all his heart that he did dislike and disavow all the arguments published in that book. And after some passages had been read, expressed his humble desire "that he might be no more troubled with these uncatholic and bloody novelties" (*A Large Examination of M. George Blackwell*, p. 140).

appointed in his stead. When the latter died in 1614, another arch-priest, William Harrison, was appointed. At last, after much negotiation, Dr. William Bishop, one of the former appellant priests, and a favourer of the oath, was appointed bishop of Chalcedon (1623); on the one hand with ordinary jurisdiction as bishop of the English and Scots, on the other by a curious anomaly, with powers revokable at will.[1]

There was no suggestion that he was merely a vicar apostolic. He was treated and addressed as

---

[1] How often the clergy had attempted to secure episcopal superiors, and how often they had been thwarted by their opponents, have been already referred to. When John Bennet, a secular priest, was sent in the autumn of November 1621 to obtain bishops for England, the pope was at last inclined to grant the petition and proposed to send four bishops. The jesuits took the alarm. They employed Toby Matthews (a son of the archbishop of York, and a convert of Fr. Parsons) to communicate the project to the government. This he did to his personal friend Lord Bacon, on August 4, 1622, who on the same day wrote off to Buckingham (*Letters of Francis Bacon*, ed. 1874, vol. vii. pp. 378, 379). He at once told the lord-keeper, who had an interview with Gondomar, the Spanish ambassador, and acquainted him that the king would not allow such bishops as Toby Matthews suggested would be sent. Buckingham, in the letter from which we gather these facts, says: "But I am afraid that Tobie will prove but an apocryphal and no canonical intelligencer, acquainting the state with this project for the jesuits rather than for Jesus' sake" (see *Cabala*, ed. 1654, p. 291). "At last, instead of four bishops (the pope) appointed only one; and that the new prelate might be less objectionable, he selected for the office Dr. Bishop, who had formerly signed the celebrated protestation of allegiance in the last year of Elizabeth. Still, as it was doubtful how far the king might yield, or the bishop himself might form connection with the French prelates (the French bishops, and particularly the archbishop of Rouen, were proposing, if the pope would not move, to take upon themselves the duty of providing bishops for England), to make him revokable at will" (Lingard, ed. 1849, vol. vii. appendix, p. 552).

an ordinary. For instance, certain articles of agreement and concord,[1] drawn up between the bishop and the superiors of the benedictines, were signed by "William, bishop of Chalcedon and ordinary of England." D. Leander, prior of St. Gregory's, and D. Barlow, president, also wrote him, in June 1623, congratulatory letters as to the ordinary of England.[2] The latter writes:—

"Being it hath pleased Almighty God to make choice of your lordship's person to be the ordinary bishop of our nation, by this, in the name of our whole body . . . I do promise unto your lordship all due respect and reverence, all filial love and correspondence, and assure your lordship that all ours shall endeavour and labour by themselves and friends to persuade all the catholics of our nation to yield due obedience unto your lordship, and to oppose ourselves against any one who shall impugn or withstand your lordship's place and authority."

That the first intention was that he should have ordinary jurisdiction, seems a conclusion warranted by a perusal of the documents. A vicar apostolic was not asked for, and Dr. Bishop certainly did not so consider himself, but always acted as possessing the ordinary jurisdiction which appertains to a bishop in his own diocese; moreover, Rome did not interfere, but recognised the chapter he appointed. On

[1] Sergeant's *History and Transactions of the English Chapter*, p. 43.
[2] Tierney, iv. p. cclxxv.

his death, in 1624, he was succeeded by Dr. Richard Smith, who began to inquire into the faculties the regulars enjoyed, and insisted that, being the ordinary, by the common law as laid down in the Council of Trent, his approbation was necessary for their exercise.[1] This brought the question of his position and jurisdiction to the test. Advantage was taken, by those who had always opposed the appointment of bishops, of the clause in the bulls of both Bishop and Smith appointing them *ad nostrum et sedis apostolicæ beneplacitum*, to deny that they were anything else but vicars apostolic, and that their jurisdiction was limited and did not include those who, like themselves, were dependent upon the will of the holy see. The bishop insisted on his position. His enemies gave out that he intended to introduce not only the internal jurisdiction of an ordinary, but also to erect a tribunal for the external exercise of his authority in such matters as appeals, probate, &c., &c. Some of the less scrupulous of his opponents succeeded in again bringing the presence of a bishop in England to the knowledge of the Government. He was obliged to fly to France, 1629, where he died in 1655.

The claims of Dr. Smith to be ordinary were at last denied at Rome; and, as it was impossible for him to return to England, the question of a successor was raised. Some wanted a vicar apostolic; others a bishop with real ordinary jurisdiction.

---

[1] *Canones et decreta Concil. Tred.*, Sess. xxiii. cap. 15.

Practically parties stood this way: the jesuits were opposed to any episcopal superior,[1] but if one were to be appointed, they wanted him to be only a vicar apostolic, with faculties so limited as not to be able to interfere with them. To this plan the clergy were strongly opposed. They demanded a bishop with ordinary powers, or nothing at all. The benedictines as a body were in harmony with the desires of the clergy in their opposition to a vicar apostolic, for not only were the powers of such a functionary abnormal and arbitrary, but they considered that they themselves would be safer under the common law of the church exercised by an ordinary bishop.[2]

In this controversy D. Rudesind Barlow, who was evidently a man of unyielding character, took advantage of his position of president of the English benedictines, to print a book on the subject, which, if the account of Panzani[3] written some few years

---

[1] Panzani, in a letter to Barberini (July 13, 1635), writes: "Your eminence must not be surprised that I complain so much and so often of the jesuits, because I see plainly they are the only persons that cannot bear a bishop, and questionless they will excite all their penitents against him. Every day I have new complaints of them and their equivocations, and yet I have given them more encouragements and tokens of confidence than to any others, which they requite with spreading idle and personal reflections, casting my horoscope and pretending to be privy to the particulars of my life" (*Memoirs of Panzani*, p. 175).

[2] It was this simple instinct of following the common law of the church as the safest way, which prompted the late venerated archbishop Ullathorne, O.S.B., on the day of his consecration (1846) to vow he would never rest till the regimen of vicars apostolic was done away with.

[3] *Add. MS.*, 15,389.

later can be trusted, was communicated by the jesuits to the council (contrary to all the intentions of the writer), and was thus the direct cause of bishop Smith's exile. From the detailed account given by the same writer of the origin of the difficulty existing, it must be allowed that the question of jurisdiction was not raised by the benedictines; and it was raised moreover in a most unfortunate manner. At the same time it would seem not improbable that D. Rudesind was influenced by ideas that the former possession of cathedral chapters left some ordinary jurisdiction inherent in their representative *sedibus vacantibus*. This clinging to what events have shown to be a mere phantom of rights, caused the benedictine authorities on more than one occasion to swerve from that attitude of friendliness to the clergy, of which D. Rudesind was, only a few years previously, himself the exponent.

These two questions were agitating and dividing the unhappy and much-tried catholics in England when Urban VIII. was elected pope. He had the wisdom to see that the world had changed, and that the zealous advocates of the former policy were not the wisest of his counsellors. He was more inclined to conciliation than his predecessors, as will be seen from a reply he made, in an allocution, to the demand of cardinal Borgia and the Spanish court for the excommunication of the kings of Sweden and France. He said:—

"We know that we may declare protestants excommunicated, as Pius V. declared queen Elizabeth of England, and before him Clement VII. the king of England, Henry VIII. . . . But with what success? The whole world can tell. We yet bewail it in tears of blood. Wisdom does not teach us to imitate Pius V. or Clement VII."[1]

This pope desired to have an unbiassed opinion on the state of England; and in the early part of 1634 D. Leander was sent over at the suggestion, it seems, of Laud, archbishop of Canterbury. He was followed at the end of the year by Gregorio Panzani, an ex-oratorian, who came over, evidently at the request of Leander, as one formally accredited from Rome.[2]

D. Leander of St. Martin, otherwise known as John Jones or Scudamore, was born in London 1575,[3] of protestant parents. His family was Welsh, and came from Llanwrinach, near Brecon. After learning his letters at a small preparatory school he was sent to Westminster School, and then to the newly established Merchant Taylors' School. Among his school-mates were Lancelot Andrews and Juxon, both of whom became Anglican bishops. About the age of sixteen he was elected a scholar of St.

---

[1] *S.P.O. Charles I.*, Italy, 24; quoted by Mr. Simpson in *Bishop Ullathorne and the Rambler*, p. 42.

[2] He arrived at Dover December 22. The reports of this latter throw a great deal of interesting light upon passages in D. Leander's mission.

[3] Boase's *Oxford Register*, vol. ii. p. 185.

John's College, Oxford, and went to that university (October 15, 1591), where he had as companion in his room William Laud, the future archbishop of Canterbury. Jones and Laud became bosom friends, and their mutual love never grew cold, although their paths in life were to be so different. Jones acquired fame as a dialectician; and in a public theological disputation proposed some questions which none of his fellow-students could answer. When the professors came to the rescue, they, too, were silenced, and had nothing to say to the objections raised by the young man. This led to his being accused to the university authorities of being a catholic in disguise. In spite of his denials he was expelled his college. This naturally drove him into that church where he found answer to his theological difficulties; and so, shortly afterwards, he was received by Fr. Gerard, S.J., and then set out for Spain, on December 20, 1596, to take up his quarters in the seminary at Valladolid.

The story of his vocation and the part he took in the affairs of the Union has been already told in the previous chapters. The date of his mission (1634) found him for the second time president of the congregation. After having completed his third term of priorship of St. Gregory's, advantage was taken by Laud, now archbishop of Canterbury, of his old friend, to see whether there was any chance of bringing about a reunion of England with Rome. Already there had been some kind of negotiations.

Laud, in his journal under the dates of August 4 and 17, 1633, writes that on those days he had been sounded whether, under conditions, he would accept a cardinal's hat. This offer he had reported to the king, together with his answer of refusal, "till Rome should be other than she is." But many persons thought there were serious grounds for a hope of reunion. The queen, Henrietta Maria, was a catholic, and had a public chapel to which crowds flocked to hear the sermons and attend the services. As we have seen, conversions of late had been numerous. In Holy Week 1632, as many as 10,000 people visited the sepulchre in the queen's chapel. At the same period upwards of 1000 used to attend the service every Sunday at the chapel of one of the ambassadors. In 1635, at the opening of the queen's new chapel in Somerset House, there was exposition for forty hours, and 2500 people went to holy communion; the decorations were kept up for a month, that the crowds who came to see them might be satisfied. Between 1632 and 1636 the French capuchin fathers serving it received 670 protestants into the church, besides reconciling a number of catholics; in 1636, on the feast of the Rosary, over 2000 persons signed the Rosary Roll at this chapel.[1]

Among the State papers collected by Lord Clarendon for the purposes of his history, are a number of documents concerning D. Leander's mission.[2]

---

[1] *Downside Review*, vol. xii. p. 189.
[2] *Clarendon State Papers*, vol. i.

From them, and from Panzani's correspondence[1] with cardinal Barberini, the nephew of pope Urban VIII., and protector of English catholics, we are able to trace the various stages of the negotiation. Laud, who had undoubtedly a great desire to bring about a reunion between Rome and England, partly from religious and partly from political motives, had bethought himself of D. Leander as one likely to deal with the preliminaries in a large and open-minded manner. He petitioned the king for a licence for the monk to return to England. This we know from the rough draft of the actual letter[2] sent by secretary Windebank to Leander with the leave; altogether in the actual copy sent Laud's name is not mentioned.[3] It seems from the subjoined letter, addressed to "Mr. Leander at Douay," that he had been told to apply for a licence :—

"SIR,—His majesty hath lately seen a letter of yours under the name of B. Leander, *alias* John Skidmore, alias Jones, now a poor benedictine monk,

---

[1] *S.P.O. Roman Transcripts* (Stevenson's) *Barberini Library*, ii.
[2] *Calendar of Clarendon Papers*, vol. i. p. 41. '
[3] Windebank, whose name figures so much in these negotiations, was a protégé of Laud's, with whom he had been at St. John's, Oxford. He therefore most likely would have been also a friend of D. Leander. When Laud became bishop of London he recommended his friend to the king as secretary of state in place of Sir Dudley Carleton (June 15, 1632), evidently to serve some such purpose as he had now in view. Windebank was impeached at Westminster, November 3, 1640; but escaping, went to France, where he died September 1, 1646. He was reconciled to the church before his death.

once a fellow of St. John's College in Oxford; wherein you are a suitor that his majesty should be graciously pleased to give you leave to come into England to see your friends and kindred without molestation for religion; and although his majesty does not like to give way to a dispensation so directly repugnant to the laws of this realm, yet in regard to your solemn promise to carry yourself warily and without offence, his majesty hath commanded me to let you know that he hath given you leave to repair hither into England to see your friends and kindred whensoever you think fit; and that it shall be lawful for you to stay and remain here (by virtue of his majesty's said permission), without trouble or danger of the laws, you carrying yourself peaceably and without scandal. This I have in charge from his majesty to assure you of; and therefore, whensoever you shall come into these parts and address yourself to me, I will take order for your protection and security.—And so I rest, your loving friend,

"FRAN. WINDEBANK.[1]

"FROM THE COURT AT WHITEHALL,
  Dec. 1, 1633."

Occasion did not offer to visit England until the spring of 1634, when, on giving notice of his coming, special precautions were taken at Dover to assure D. Leander's safety, and also to keep his arrival secret.

[1] *Clarendon State Papers*, vol. i. p. 72.

Laud and Windebank arranged together for the removal, without any judicial process, of Rooks, the searcher of that district, and put in his place two professed recusants, Turbeville Morgan and Charles Powell.[1] But when he came over, the spies were soon on his track. In an undated letter to Windebank, but which was evidently written soon after his arrival, he complains that "Here is one Gray, and a boy of his, who sometime was a pursuivant, but now out of commission, as I guess, and some other of that sort of men, who do beset and watch my lodging with some molestation to my quiet, and seize upon such as I employ in my small business of providing me books and other necessaries. I cannot demand any general remedy against such diligent molestators, who have the law on their side; but my

---

[1] *Cal. S.P. Charles I.*, vol. cclxxxi. No. 60, is a petition of George Rooks to the king, praying for a trial for the recovery of his office, of which he is kept out of possession by the power of his adversaries. It was, says Prynne, "F. Price (otherwise known as D. Bennet Jones à S. Facundo) who procured the searcher's place at Dover, and put papists in it for the more secure passing of priests, jesuits, and popish agents the easier into England, conveying English men and women to foreign monasteries, and intelligence to and from Rome and other parts, by the assistance of Windebank, Canterbury, and others" (see *A Complete History of the Tryal and Condemnation of William Laud, late Archbishop of Canterbury*, pp. 448 and 559). D. Price appears in a list of 261 priests who were in London and its neighbourhood, March 26, 1624, as "superior of the benedictines" (see Gee's *The Foot out of the Snare*). D. Bennet Jones, otherwise known as William Price, was at one time procurator in Rome, during the affairs of the Union, and was afterwards superior of the mission. He was chosen president, but did not take the office. He was also agent for the nuns at Cambray. He died in London, October 19, 1639.

fear is they will proceed further to the molestation of Mr. William Price, whom I recommended unto your honour as my confident friend, in whom I repose all trust to supply my absence (when it shall happen) in performing those honest and loyal offices which I have promised your honour, and by God's grace will endeavour to perform. In which cause, if it be not too much presumption to request so much, I humbly beseech your honour that the said William Price may have such a protection that he may not be molested by any such means; since, as upon my conscience I have signified to your honour, you shall even find him a faithful, loyal, discreet, and well experienced man, and most sincerely willing to do all such offices as I have spoken of, and a man of my own intentions and desires, as I have now these thirty years experienced."[1]

D. Leander took his time, and evidently had several interviews with Laud personally, and his intermediary, Windebank. The result of his experiences are contained in a letter to cardinal Bentivoglio, the old friend of the English congregation. A copy of this document was sent to Windebank, August 26, 1634, with a letter in which Leander says: "Being to go down into Wales to see my friends, I went to Croydon first, to take leave of my lord of Canterbury, and receive his commands. . . . I have included in this letter the copy of the letter which I wrote *verbatim* to my

[1] *C.S.P.*, p. 106.

lord cardinal Bentivoglio; the original I have sent faithfully to Rome to our procurator to deliver; with whom, if your honour vouchsafe to keep correspondence, I have commanded him to be diligent and careful; and I dare promise he will be faithful and loyal. The inscription to him, if your honour should write to him about any business, may be, '*Al molto Riverendo Padre, il Padre Giovanni Wilfrido Redo, Procuratore de la Congregatione de i Monachi Inglesi de S. Benedette.*'"[1]

But already D. Leander was beginning to feel the unkindness of those who had been always opposed to his order. In this same letter he refers to it, and begs Windebank to continue his favourable opinion. "Yet, because I am much noted in England, being of some estimation (above my deserts) among catholics, as having been many years superior of my order, the freeedom which I now enjoy being not altogether unknown, especially by reason of the ancient friendship, which many have understood in times past was between my lord's grace and me in our younger years, I do much fear lest the various surmises of men (who use to speak by their conjectures of men's actions which they do not well comprehend) may do me some harm, either in magnifying my favours received, as if they were due to my endeavours, or in mistaking my endeavours, as if I performed but weakly the part of a good catholic. But this second I pass not much, because I refer my

[1] *C.S.P.*, p. 128.

conscience to God alone; but for the first, I must crave your honour's favourable judgment of my modesty that I give no occasion, neither by word nor deed, to any such matter, but that they be but conjectures of curious brains, who many times speak such things that they may seem to know what indeed they are ignorant of."[1] The "conjectures of curious brains" were to pursue him all during his stay in England, and did not hesitate after his death to take the form of calumny.

The letter to cardinal Bentivoglio, written on July 12, is a long Latin document, and we here extract the salient passages:—

"MOST EMINENT LORD AND ILLUSTRIOUS CARDINAL, —I now do what I lately promised your eminence. I tell you about our affairs which, being now in England, I see with my own eyes and, as it were, touch with my hands; and I will do it with the sincerity and fidelity which I have always been accustomed to use with your eminence. I know there will be others who will also write on these matters, but I am not ashamed to say of myself that no one will do so with greater fidelity, or with more certain truth. There are some who, occupied with their pretensions and undoubtedly look to the greater glory of God,[2] give to all their actions and information that colour which these very pretensions seem to

[1] *Ibid.* pp. 128-129.
[2] *Ad majorem Dei gloriam indubie respicientes.*

demand. There are others, wandering men,[1] and but little versed in English affairs, who, I hear, are destined hither to report to you how the state and people are affected about certain businesses. But neither of these can satisfy you. Not the former, on account of the lust of their pretensions, which overmaster their judgment; nor the latter, on account of their inexperience of our affairs, which take a long time to be fully understood. The first may, perchance, give an insincere account; the latter an imperfect one. I (unless my heart deceive me), being moved by no motive of private pretensions, and being somewhat instructed by a long study of English affairs, and being also desirous of ecclesiastical peace, and at the same time compassionating the miserable quarrels of my catholic fellow-countrymen, will attempt to set before your eminence a true account of our affairs, so that his holiness, rightly informed about all things, can opportunely determine whatever may heal our evils.

"There are two points which particularly disturb us: one is the oath of allegiance, and the other is the question of sending one or more bishops to England. Concerning the oath, two books have been lately written; one, printed and published with the royal licence, contends for a lawful sense of the oath, according to which it can and ought to be taken by subjects. The other, against the tenor of the oath, has not yet been printed, but has been

[1] *Peregrini homines.*

passed about secretly in many manuscript copies. The authors of both books are reputed to be two noble laymen. The one against the tenor of the oath has greatly displeased his majesty, and not altogether without cause, for since the book in favour of the oath was brought out with his approval, it seems an act of contempt to follow it with another which is more vehement and bitter than is fitting.[1] . . . The writer seems to me (I have carefully read the whole of his little work) to defend his cause weakly; hence it happens that not only is the king offended, but, by so poor a defence, the very cause is betrayed. And it is also to be remembered that it is presumptuous and against ecclesiastical rules for laymen to undertake a disputation upon matters of faith, a matter which is hardly allowed to most learned ecclesiastics."

D. Leander goes on to say: Fear was expressed lest on account of these books the puritans should drive the king on to another persecution, although he was favourably disposed towards his catholic sub-

[1] This is the book by Mr. Courtney, who, posing as a layman, was really Fr. Edward Leedes, S.J. (Foley, vol. i. p. 251, *seq.*). The book contained propositions highly offensive to the idea of the Divine right of kings, such as—*The king alone is not the legislator in his kingdom, but when he is together with the parliament;* and, *the commonwealth in certain cases can depose their king and resume the authority and majesty which at a former time they had transferred to the king; and therefore make the throne an elective one.* Such nowaday commonplaces were the politics advocated by the puritans. This explains Windebank's remark to Panzani: "If we had neither jesuits nor puritans in England, I am confident an union might easily be effected" (*Panzani's Memoirs,* p. 163).

jects, and inclined towards the pope. By the advice of many prudent and moderate members of the nobility, he suggests to the pope a means by which the tempest may be averted. Since the king professes that in this oath he only requires a true, civil, natural obedience and loyalty, and not that any spiritual power due to the pope should be denied; and, moreover, admits all explanations of the oath which makes it more tolerable for catholics, all go to show that the oath, as now intended and declared by the king, is very different from that which the apostolic see forbade. It is expected that his holiness would be pleased somewhat to modify the prohibition in favour not only of English catholics, who "have suffered more in times gone by for the authority of the holy see than all the rest of the faithful," but also as a favour to the king, who deserves so well of his holiness. These nobles say that as the pope writes to the pagan kings of India in the hopes of converting them, and to the schismatical kings of Abyssinia in order to reunite them to the church, why does he not do the same kind office to our king? The pope tolerates in France the rejection of the deposing power, why should he not—as a kind and indulgent father—tolerate equally the rejection of it by the catholics of England, who are much more in need of gentle handling? It is also suggested that the pope should write to the king a letter in which his right to the throne should be acknowledged, and, at the same time, expressing regret that so many indiscreet publications should have been issued against the oath, and also undertaking to suspend the prohibiting decree.

"Such are the suggestions of some of our best and most intelligent men; and with all due respect I suggest it will bring about a great beginning of good if his holiness will write such a letter to the king or to his devout consort, but preferably to the king. It is not unworthy of his holiness to conciliate and make advances to a son so great, in order to gain him—as Gregory the Great, by kind letters and paternal entreatments, induced our king Ethelbert more attentively to give ear to St. Augustine's preaching. Nor is our king altogether unworthy, neither is he a heretic, although he be not fully instructed in some doctrines; neither did he ever quit the bosom of the church, but having had none but protestant teachers, he remains in that belief in which he was educated, a devout worshipper of God according to the measure of his knowledge, &c., &c.

"About the question of bishops: From those upon whom I can depend, I find that the most reverend bishop of Chalcedon is personally obnoxious to the king and the State on account of his excessive officiousness while he was in England, and on account also of some things he is supposed to have done in France, where he now is. These have deservedly offended the king. To send him back to England will mean his own execution and the increase of persecution. I am also informed that it would be very unsafe to send into England any bishop or bishops with the power of external jurisdiction; and that such a proceeding will displease the king, his ministers, and especially the State bishops. And why should all these be offended and irritated? . . . Then, although many of the catholic laity, indeed almost all, who are under the secular clergy desire the government of a bishop, many others, almost all of those who are under the regulars, are averse to it on account of the laws and the danger. The number of these latter, though not equal to the others, is, I know, still of such weight that it ought not to be passed over by his holiness, nor should a petition be easily granted which will pain and offend so important a part of the catholics, and which will most certainly bring about a greater dissension and stir up a greater conflagration. . . . Therefore, I am sure that to send bishops with external power will be both dangerous to us and displeasing to the king."

He suggests that the Irish bishops be instructed to visit England and Scotland for the purposes of confirmation.[1]

This letter, D. Wilford, *alias* Read, *alias* Selby, the procurator in Rome, handed to cardinal Barberini. In a letter to D. Leander, dated October 23, 1634, he says he did so: 1mo, because he is protector of the nation and order; 2do, because he governs all, and therefore they are more properly to be given

[1] *C.S.P.*, pp. 129–133.

to him."[1] He then goes on to inform his correspondent that some adverse reports, "the conjectures of curious brains," had reached Rome, and expresses his concern at hearing the person and honour of D. Leander attacked. In another letter, bearing date of November 18, 1634, D. Wilford mentions that he had spoken to cardinal Barberini about a letter Leander had written in the previous September, and that the cardinal had said that both he and the pope were gratified at the king's dispositions. But there was evidently something, however, about his remarks on the question of the oath which did not please, and he was assured that at Rome the idea of suspending the oath would not be entertained. On the margin of this letter D. Leander makes the following note: "It is not demanded that the brief should be suspended, or recalled papally; but to be declared not to condemn the king's meaning of the oath, but only the meaning ill-applied."[2]

In a letter of November 13, to Windebank, Leander recurs to the reports about him: "For being by some cardinals loved for my plain dealing with them, and not wanting many eyes that look here upon my actions, it is likely that many conjectures are there buzzed into their ears con-

[1] *Ibid.* p. 152.
[2] *Ibid.* p. 164. The bull deposing Elizabeth had been suspended. But this particular brief, as is clear from the rest of D. Wilford's letter, was looked upon by the Roman officials as a declaration of Faith, and therefore never to be suspended.

cerning the favour which I find here of his majesty and my loving patrons, especially by those who are ignorant of my moderation and sincerity in matters of disputable questions. This makes (me) supplicate to your honour, that information which I have and will give, may be so accepted and used as may not be prejudicial to my credit at that court where I am of some esteem; not that I fear much though they and all the world knew what I do inform, since I will, by God's grace, inform nothing against truth and good conscience; but because the continuance of that good opinion which there they have of my sincerity, may be more to that honest and harmless service which I do desire and purpose to do for God and my sovereign and country according to my innocent vocation."[1] He ends by asking leave to go to Douai, and return as often as may be necessary, as his duties sometimes require him there.[2]

The next step taken was to write a letter, dated December 16, 1634, to cardinal Barberini, the pope's nephew, which before it was sent was corrected by Windebank. In it D. Leander refers to two letters he had received from the cardinal; one

---

[1] *Ibid.* p. 167.

[2] In a letter unsigned of November 22, 1634, evidently, by its contents, by one of D. Leander's subjects, and which is full of personal affairs, the writer says: "The only reason why they thought of your person was from your indifferency and independency and honesty;" and he advises him to "confound your enemies who labour at Rome to persuade the cardinals that you have taken up your abode there (in England)" (*C.S.P.*, pp. 171, 172).

recommending to him some English capuchins who had come on the mission, despite Richelieu and Fr. Joseph's attempt to have only French capuchins in England,[1] and the other the grateful news (being a mark of esteem) of his appointment, by the congregation of *Propaganda*, prefect of the whole benedictine English mission, together with the instructions how the prefecture should be administered. In accordance with his new office he sends a general detailed account of the state of the whole English mission, together with some observations of his own, which he submits to the approval of the ecclesiastical authorities. He refers to his former letter upon the oath, and says that he hears he is traduced at Rome as one who looks at the interests of the State rather than to those of God and the Church, and that some declare he favours the oath or is cogitating a *via media* which will mitigate its vigour. When questioned about the oath he

---

[1] See Leander's letter to Windebank of November 13, in which he says: "Some months past two English capuchins and two Scottish capuchins sued for their mission into England unto his holiness in Rome, but the French ambassador there opposed himself, showing his holiness his instructions from the cardinal of France, that in any case he should be careful that no English or Scottish capuchins should be suffered to go into England or Scotland, but only French capuchins; and they, too, only under the command of Fr. Joseph, the cardinal's inspirator. . . . These good men of a poor and humble spirit coming into London, have complained unto me that they have been mightily opposed by the French capuchins here, who by their agents have procured to disgrace them in all places of the city where they had any access; so that they were forced to leave the city and go to the north and to Scotland," &c., &c. (*C.S.P.*, pp. 167, 178).

is accustomed to say simply and with reverence, whatever others' consciences may decide upon questions on which doctors disagree, that as a monk and a man of fearsome conscience, he respects the opinion of his supreme pastor; and that therefore he cannot without wounding his conscience take the oath in that manner, and in that sense in which heretofore it is commonly supposed to be offered by the civil authorities. Wherefore he is falsely accused by those who were jealous of him, and who strive to make him suspected at Rome. As regards the *via media*, if such can be found whereby the obedience due to Cæsar may be reconciled with the duty to the pope, this is not a matter of accusation. Whatever he thinks about this he openly has said to their eminences whose place it is to decide. And then he adds: "Permit me, most illustrious lord, my pastor and protector, to speak freely and without offence. What have you effected by following the counsels and opinions of those who have recommended severer measures, and have extorted the prohibitory decrees which have so much exasperated the king? He and his friends are in astonishment that doctrines are condemned here which are at least tolerated in the catholic kingdom of France. What else have our nobility and leading men gained by these decrees, when it is believed that the doctrines on which they are founded countenance the malefactors and those engaged in that most wicked conspiracy which planned the destruction of the sovereign and all the nobility, inasmuch as such doctrines prohibit the condemnation of the principles on which those men relied to justify their attempt? I know that this cannot be justly inferred; but I also know that our countrymen make this inference. If they had seen that the pope had published any decree which condemned both that detestable attempt and the principles on which it was endeavoured to be justified, they would have passed a very different judgment on that most unfortunate deed. They would have thought that it proceeded wholly from the criminality of the persons engaged in it, and not from any opinions of catholic treatises. Hitherto you have believed these advisers who, not not knowing of whose spirit they were, or whose they ought to be, have called down upon England the thunders of excommunication and the lightnings of prohibitions; the only result of which has been the load of suffering by which the much enduring catholics have been almost quite oppressed. Yield, I beseech you, at length to those who advise the way of mildness, and who tell you (as it is said in the vision of Elias) that it is not in the whirlwind nor in the storm, which breaketh the rocks, that the Lord appears; but it is in the whisper of a gentle breeze, that is in the spirit of meekness. I am perfectly convinced that mildness and condescension are more likely to obtain, in a few months' time, from our king and his ministers that relief which for so many years has not been obtained by other means."[1]

In the letter in which he sends the corrected copy of this report to Windebank, Leander refers to some changes the secretary had insisted upon:—

"Now my humble suit to your honour is, that, since you perceive how sincerely willing I am to do all such good offices as an honest poor catholic man may do *salva conscientia*, you would please so to order matters that in performance of my duty no more be expected of me than my religion permits me; and to give me leave to write as bescems a catholic of my profession, and to uphold my credit and estimation as well in that court of Rome as with his majesty, lest otherwise I should be made unable to do any good service to God and my king—for I want not many emulators and adversaries that write and inform against me; but I trust my sincere intention and innocent endeavours will keep me blameless; and howsoever I hope his majesty will accept of my loyal intentions, though perhaps the event correspond not to my expectation through opposition of others."[2]

Together with this document he sent to Rome a carefully drawn up paper upon the oath, so as to explain more fully what he had already written, and which he understood had met with considerable opposition. He considers two stages in the controversy; one the oath as imposed by parliament,

[1] *C.S.P.*, pp. 185-187. [2] *Ibid.* pp. 184, 185.

and the other as interpreted by the king after the prohibitory brief. The former was rightly condemned; for it was drawn up in hatred of the catholic faith. He then takes the text of the oath, and gives in parallel columns, clause by clause, the presumed sense and the really intended sense. He has but little difficulty in showing the hollowness of the objections brought against the oath as interpreted by the king.[1] He ends up by suggesting that all controversy should be prohibited on either side; and again advises that the decree should be either suspended (he refers to cases where such decrees have been suspended), or that the pope should send some one to the king to ask that the oath should be either abolished or a new one drawn up, which would secure to the king all he requires, and be at the same time acceptable to catholics.

Either with this letter, or soon after, he sent a lengthy paper on the state of the Apostolical Mission in England. It is full of interest. It is divided into three sections. The first part is intended to give the cardinals the idea of the protestant Anglican church, which he had gained from his intercourse with that High Church section with which he was

---

[1] The defence put forward by those who championed the prohibitory brief must be judged on the ground they took. Had the rejection of the oath been based on the plea that it made for a Divine right of kings, then wisdom would have been justified. But, as a matter of fact, the great constitutional struggle was but beginning here, and was largely due to Parsons' book on the Succession.

in continual communication, and who were favouring the idea of reunion.

He says: "The church of the protestants of England retains the outward appearance of an ecclesiastical hierarchy, such as existed in the times of catholic profession. They have a certain form of ordination agreeing in great part with the forms prescribed in the Roman pontifical. Without this form of hierarchical rule our protestants in England think that not only is the glory of the Christian Church observed, but also that its very nature and substance are destroyed. Wherefore, they consider as schismatics those other protestant churches scattered throughout Europe, who have repudiated and turned away from this most ancient hierarchy.

"In the greater number of the articles of faith the English protestants are truly orthodox.... In respect to the articles on which there is a difference, this, they say, lies for the greater part either in the mode of expression (which, beyond doubt, they should rather receive from mother church and learn the form of sound expression, than presume to teach her whose children they are); or if the difference is in the things themselves, they say it is not in the fundamental articles of faith which are necessary for salvation; but in questions in which error may be tolerated and pardonable, and which do not hinder the way of salvation, nor put those dissenting outside the substance of the covenant.

"They contend they have been treated unworthily

by the Roman church as heretics and schismatics; that greater differences than theirs from the Roman church were tolerated by the council of Florence; and that the importance of Great Britain and its dependencies renders it an object of as much moment to reconcile her to the Roman church, and as much worth while to call a special council for the purpose, as it could have been to obtain the reconciliation of the Greeks; that their bishops (for they claim to have true bishops) are neither few in numbers nor are they wanting in learning, and perchance would be more easily conciliated than the Greeks, and, moreover, if once reconciled would remain firm, which the Greeks did not. If we do not consider them to be true bishops, for inasmuch as we believe there is wanting a true imposition of hands, they nevertheless contend that they have true bishops and truly ordained, by which at least they show there ought to be a true episcopate in any church properly so called."

Whilst thus expressing in fair terms the ideas of Laud and Goodman, D. Leander cannot help seeing that they were in the same position towards reunion as are some of the more advanced Anglicans of to-day. They did not represent the established church, but only a party in it, and a party whose very policy was loudly denounced by the other sections. He speaks of the puritans as very numerous and fierce, increasing in power and hostile alike to Anglicans as well as to catholics. He intimates that if they were out of the way something might be done. He ends up by saying it is important that the Anglican controversy should not be confused with the Lutheran and that of the other bodies. They are nearer to the church than the continental sects; and there is some hope of a better state of things. Missioners ought to apply themselves to the special study of the question, and especially to history and the fathers; for these are held in such esteem by the protestants, that their more learned men say they are willing to receive any doctrine that can by these be sufficiently proved to be necessary for salvation.

Having thus given a view of the Anglican church, as seen by him from the outside, he proceeds to report on the condition of catholics, and gives us a vivid light on the state of affairs :—

"Labouring at the salvation of souls there are five hundred or more secular priests; almost two hundred and forty jesuits; one hundred, more or less, benedictines; twenty dominicans; as many carmelites; fully twenty franciscans; four English and Scotch capuchins; as many minims." After speaking of the dominicans, carmelites, and franciscans, all of whom are governed by their own provincials, he proceeds to mention his own order :—

"The body of benedictines is more numerous. They have beyond the seas, four convents for men and there are four for women (besides two others, one of which is governed by the jesuit fathers and the other by the secular clergy). They number in England more than one hundred, the greater number of whom belong to the English congregation; six or seven belong to the Spanish congregation; the same number to the Cassinese; three or four to the German Scottish monasteries, and two or three to the congregation of Lorraine. The Cassinese have a superior of their own; while the others are ruled by a prefect apostolic, who is the president of the English congregation and depends upon no other external superior. In the monasteries there are almost one hundred monks and thirty-seven nuns. On the mission the monks, two by two, or often singly, live, as though in their cells in houses of the catholic nobility, intent upon prayer, the ministering of the word and of the sacraments. They do not confine their work to those dwelling in the same house, but endeavour to look after those who live within reach.

"But of all the regular missioners the most numerous are the jesuit fathers, who are thought to reach three hundred. As they have the control of the seminaries of Rome, St. Omer, Lisbon, and Valladolid, in which they bring up a great number of fathers and brothers for the use of the seminary, and also other colleges abroad for educating youths for their own order, it is easily understood how they have increased. They have also certain residences in England in which they are wont to gather together for practising the exercises of their institute. They have also schools adapted for educating young noblemen. Of the manner in which their mission is governed I have not been able to learn anything, except that they have a provincial whom they all obey. But this we do know well, that as their number is greater and they are more united, so they have illustrious, noble, and powerful patrons, and have more authority over them than the other missioners, who, hitherto, have not tried or have not been able to attach their own patrons in the manner the jesuits have done.

"The prelates, appointed by his holiness, divided the secular clergy into certain dioceses or districts under six vicars-general, eighteen archdeacons, and a certain number of rural deans. This hierarchical form being established (but let them seek by what authority they had to establish it, as they had neither diocese nor parishes, nor even any order respecting these matters from the pope), they used every means to enforce an ordinary coactive jurisdiction over all the regulars and all the catholic laity. From this violent contentions rose, the bishop and secular clergy carrying their pretension into actual execution, and obtaining the consent of many of the faithful laity who were ignorant of what was being aimed at, but were moved by the majesty of the episcopal name. But the regulars of every order, along with the greatest part of the laity, opposed them meanwhile on the ground that they were under no obligation of admitting such jurisdiction, on the ground that it had not been conferred upon the prelates, and also that by the ancient laws of England the admission of such was an offence against the crown and brought their fortunes into jeopardy. But the pope tried to put an end to this dispute by the beautiful brief he addressed to the bishop and whole body of missioners, in which he curbed the immoderate claim to a jurisdiction which had never been conferred. Still the secular clergy were not quieted, neither do they cease to urge their claims; but are still earnestly soliciting the apostolic see to appoint a bishop over them.

"This is a general view of the English mission, in which about one thousand labourers are employed. Almost all of them are men learned and skilled in philosophy, ethics, and in theology. So that if we regard learning and godly life, there is scarcely any catholic kingdom can display a more splendid set of priests."

D. Leander goes on to offer some practical suggestions which have occurred to him. One thing is evident: the missioners are too numerous. Not, of course, for the wants of the mission, but because the way they are sent or rather turn out of the seminaries, make them more a burthen than helpers in the harvest. The root of the difficulty is the dispute between the clergy and the jesuits as to who in these days ought to have the task of bringing back England to the faith. The seculars contend that this charge is theirs alone, or at least theirs principally; while the jesuits say that their order is better adapted than all others for the conversion of souls. Hence perpetual quarrels; hence also missioners are sent out too soon from the seminaries, before having gone through their course of studies or sufficiently matured for so great a work. This is specially the case in the secular colleges with those who favour the jesuits, and in the seminaries under the jesuits with those who favour the clergy. Then, again, many take up the mission not out of a zeal for souls or devotion, but for the sake of a living; hence if a fixed residence is not at once appointed them they are compelled either to wander from house to house or to beg. In this manner they bring contempt upon the priesthood; and, like hired servants, even sometimes try to turn others out of residences they have secured.

The remedies for these ends are: greater care in accepting candidates who have no patrimony of their own, or who, at least, are of good birth. A full course of study should be insisted upon in the seminaries, and no one should be sent on the mission till about forty years of age. For the welfare of the mission depends more on the fitness than on the number of missioners. Not how many, but what kind of missioners is the important point. Then, no one should be sent into England until some place had been prepared for him, and a certain district assigned to him. The number ought to be limited to keeping up the present needs. The contest between the seculars and regulars about bishops almost brought about a schism. The French in their national synod encouraged the dispute, and interfered with so great vehemence, joined with such an ignorance of the state of the controversy, that one cannot say whether they were carried away more by a headlong fervour of a sudden zeal, or by a wilful departure from the question at issue. Leander then recommends that Dr. Bishop should not be allowed to return to England, and declares that the advent of another bishop, with ordinary coactive jurisdiction, would be disastrous to the catholic cause for several reasons which he specifies. He suggests that as the regulars have their provincials, so the clergy should be governed by a dean or a prefect apostolic. He proceeds to show that in the disposition of money bequeathed for given purposes, or assisting from destitution, sufficient regard for the poor is not shown. All of it goes to enrich one religious order; every other description of persons, and the poor laity in particular, are excluded from any participation in it. He recommends that one-third, or at least one-fourth of such moneys should be given to the poor, and a temporal council chosen from all parties to decide upon all points in dispute.

Other matters, too, have attracted his attention, and ought to be brought beneath the pope's notice. For instance, much mischief arises from the differences of opinion in practical casuistry; also from the difference of rituals used—some following the

Roman, some the French, and some the old English use of Sarum. There is no uniformity of fasts and feasts. All these matters could be settled by the afore-proposed council. He laments the fierceness of the controversial tone that prevails, and earnestly recommends the pope to prohibit absolutely all public discussion on questions concerning the relations of the civil and the ecclesiastical powers.

He ends up his report by mentioning another evil. "Another defect is the mutual turning out or driving away of missioners from their residences and building on the foundation of others, a course of action which was not approved of by St. Paul. It often happens that a dominican, for example, has converted the whole of some noble family, and then a jesuit, having by his importunity driven out the dominican, takes possession of that family. I only know of one remedy, . . . that the supreme pontiff should forbid such practices under the severest censures."[1]

On the 17th December 1634, D. Leander showed his loyalty both to the pope and to his sovereign. He took an oath of allegiance to the king; not, however, the parliamentary form, but one which he himself drew up, and which begins with these words: "In the name of our Lord God and Saviour Jesus Christ. Amen.—Because I dare not in conscience, for just causes, take the new ordinary oath of allegiance as it lieth, and yet am most desirous that his royal majesty should be assured of my faith and

[1] *S.P.C.*, pp. 197–205.

loyalty, I do, of my own accord and free will, after mature deliberation, profess and protest my allegiance more plainly, fully, and (in my poor judgment) more sufficiently in this oath following, written in my own hand and pronounced from my heart, than is or may be expressed in the aforesaid new oath."[1] The substance of the oath is unimpeachable, and is thoroughly catholic in tone and English in its straightforwardness. It gives to Cæsar the things that are Cæsar's, and does not deny to God the things that are God's.

As we have seen, D. Leander had no official mission from Rome. He came at the request of Laud, who, knowing his old friend to be so highly esteemed at Rome, considered him as an intermediary grateful to both parties. Leander soon saw that not having an official position was a detriment to the cause, and also that the fact of being a benedictine did not recommend him to the party opposed not only to his order and to the clergy in general, but also to the projects he had specially come over to advance. Besides, his age and the precarious state of his health told him it would be advisable to have the help of an accredited agent from Rome, who could carry on the work if he was called away. His views and desires were laid before cardinal Barberini, and the mission of Gregorio Panzani was the result. In him, D. Leander providentially found a defender of his good fame and policy, both in life and after death.

[1] *C.S.P.*, vol. i. pp. 210, 211.

The envoy brought clear instructions to D. Leander ("a good man, and very active," so says the cardinal) that the oath of allegiance proposed by the king could not be accepted, and that the prohibition could not be suspended.[1] Panzani arrived in London on Christmas day, and was visited by the clergy, both secular and regular. We will only touch upon his mission so far as it concerns D. Leander. Having now an accredited agent in England, D. Leander was most anxious to get back, at least for a while, to Douai, where his presence was greatly needed. "I have," he writes to Windebank, "even now received so many letters from beyond sea conjuring me in any sort to come over but for one or two months, that I am enforced to prefer the matter again to your honour's consideration. The cause of their earnestness is, as you may see by the letter of the college regent hereto adjoined, that the founder of our college and convent of Douay was this Christmas upon point of death, and being fourscore years of age, feareth a sudden departure. Now, because he began that college and convent at my instigation, and useth me as his instrument in the trace of all, he will not make an end of his foundations, which are many and magnifick, until I come; by whose pen and counsel he is resolved to consummate this great work (which will come to more than fifteen hundred pounds yearly) for the good of those coun-

[1] *S.P.O. Roman Transcripts* (Barberini to Panzani, December 5, 1634).

tries and ours also, and he is so earnest of my return that he is almost impatient. My humble suit then to your honour is that, with good leave and licence of his majesty, I may make a step over, only for two months or six weeks (and if I may be so bold), that your honour would vouchsafe to write a letter to the said abbat, our founder, to let me return within the said space, or sooner, if I can sooner despatch the writings, instruments, and laws which I am to draw, for my proper desire and intention is to spend the remnant of my days in his majesty's loyal service in England, if his gracious majesty be so pleased."[1]

But Windebank could not spare him just at present, and wrote an elegant Latin letter to abbat Caverel, asking that Leander's visit might be deferred as he was doing so much good, and that the important business he was about was not yet completed. The date of this is January 21, 1635.[2] The abbat gave his consent in a reply of February 22nd, and in the course of his characteristic letter, in which he speaks of D. Leander as *vir doctissimus et modestissimus*, he says: "If I have been able to do anything in favour of men and youths of your nation, I have done it all the more willingly, as I have found them more modest and more learned, and never forgetful of benefits received."[3]

On February 19, 1635, D. Leander wrote a later letter to Panzani, in which he warns the envoy that there were rumours about that he had written in favour

---

[1] *C.S.P.*, p. 222. [2] *Ibid.* p. 222. [3] *Ibid.* p. 233.

of the oath, and that it was lawful to take it. "I have
nothing to do with other people's consciences, and
leave them to be informed by prudent directors. I
neither praise those who have taken the oath, nor do
I condemn those who from conscience have refused
to take it. I dare not judge one or the other, but
for myself, and searching my own conscience, I find
I must abstain from taking it. Therefore, I have
written nothing for the oath nor against it. For its
mitigation I have modestly advised a few things
which however I see, although not accepted, yet
have not displeased. But the rumour here has
arisen from the fact that when Mr. Edward Courtney
wrote a book against the oath, and put forward
twenty demonstrations, with which the king was
greatly exasperated, I was informed that his majesty
desired me to candidly state my opinion as to whether
his demonstrations were of such value as to make
catholics abstain from taking the oath. I did what
turned out to be unfortunate. I found the reasons
advanced to be weak, founded upon principles which
are hateful, or seditious, or false, or, at the best, disputable. Wherefore it should be shown that catholics
relied upon better arguments and less offensive, some
of which I have mentioned in another writing. I
ended my paper with this protestation: 'I have
only solved these quibbles as St. Thomas in the
Summa solved the arguments, derived from the light
of nature, for the mystery of the blessed Trinity. He
thought it unworthy that infidels should think that

Christians held so great a mystery upon such feeble grounds. And I also thought it was unworthy that catholics should refuse to obey their king's command for such trivial reasons, and should take their stand upon such hateful ones, when others, truer and more appropriate, could be given. This writing of mine gave no offence and harmed no one, but perhaps soothed excited feelings. I showed it to one person only, who is zealous for our reunion, and who commanded me to write it.[1] I know he showed it to no one, except perhaps the king. But it happened that I myself, yielding too easily to the prayers of some friends, communicated my imperfect copy to a familiar friend, with the stipulation that he should show it to no one else. But he, by importunity, allowed himself to show it to one other, by which means it came about that, contrary to my will, it passed into the hands of many others. There are two things in it which may give offence: the first, that I expressed no opinion on the power of the pope to depose princes, and the other, that in two parentheses I cast the blame of some matters upon the jesuits. The first did not concern me, as I had not been questioned on that point. The second was necessary, lest all catholics should be thought guilty of those accusations to which only a few had given consent. And all this was only written for a man who is a lover of peace and is our well-wisher, and who relieves us whenever he can. This is the whole

[1] Windebank most likely.

affair. . . . The only copy about is an imperfect one, and the one that is perfect, he for whom I wrote it does not consider it convenient to let me send it. My greatest desire is that his holiness should understand that I am a true and faithful son of the church, and that my king should acknowledge me as an obedient and innocent subject.'"[1]

But already Panzani had written to Rome that D. Leander and other benedictines were defenders of some form of oath.[2] And Leander's insistence with the envoy, about the necessity of giving all his attention to this one great point which blocked the way, was sure of being misrepresented by his opponents. "Too long," he says, "has the holy apostolic see believed the information that some zealots have given, who look more to their own pretensions and ideas than to the greater glory of God. Let it now give ear to those who counsel easy measures which are salutary and pacific and honourable to the chair of Peter."[3]

[1] *S.P.O. Roman Transcripts*, ibid.   [2] *Ibid.*, February 9, 1635.
[3] April 12, 1635, *C.S.P.*, pp. 249–256. That these reports had been persistently forwarded to Rome is clear from D. Wilford's letter to Leander, under date of April 13, 1635, from which we can also see the statements made without the slightest foundation against his character. "Some aspersions have been laid upon you . . . about what you had writ concerning Mr. Courtney and the oath. Here your good name was once more called in question as a defender of the oath, and that you had confessed so much. Some have already laid a groundwork against Panzani, and I fear they will make him come short of his count ; hence others have engaged themselves ; let them go through ; I pray you keep aloof as long as you can ; if you get the chestnuts, give others leave to burn their toes," &c. (*C.S.P.*, p. 250).

It was laid to Leander's charge in Rome that he had acted badly in writing at all against Courtney, and moreover that he had written nothing in defence of the oath. D. Wilford told Buccabella, the secretary of Propaganda, that Leander had only done what he was commanded to do, and that he had already given his reasons against the oath, and when that official demanded why these reasons had not been published, D. Wilford tells Leander that he answered: "Because it pleased them that did you service to divulge your discourse to omit the reasons against the oath, and that it was against your will that this discourse had been divulged."[1]

In the spring of 1635 it was proposed to send an agent from England to Rome to make a report on the hopes for reunion, and D. Leander drew up instructions for him so that he might "be made capable to give a sufficient relation of the state of religion in this our realm; in which point it seemeth that most of our Roman catholics beyond the seas are not well informed, and especially the court of Rome." After having spoken of the differences in doctrine, in all of which there can be no accord unless one "church yield to another," and which might be brought about he thinks "by an assembly of moderate men, without contention or desire of victory, but out of a sincere desire of Christian reunion," he goes on to suggest as a means to bring it about that, in favour of the pro-

[1] *C.S.P.*, p. 257.

testants, the disciplinary law of communion under one kind might be dispensed with, and the marriage of the clergy, together with the use of the liturgy in English, allowed; also the admittance of the English clergy (coming to agree in points of faith) in their prelatures, dignities, and benefices, either by re-ordination *sub conditione*, since their orders here be invalid or dubious, or, by way of *commendam*, as many princes ecclesiastical and other beneficiated persons are admitted. He explains the doctrine of the royal supremacy now held in the highest quarters as being different from that of Henry VIII. It is only a temporal supremacy over all people by which no " prelature or ecclesiastical benefice or state be conferred, but according to his ordinance or consent, because of the relation which such places have to points of state and temporalities. . . . Out of which it seemeth very consequent that if his holiness would condescend to this point, as it is above declared and practised in other catholic kingdoms, his majesty and the state might be easier induced to admit of the pope's spiritual supremacy."

He proposes a form of oath to be approved of by the holy see, and he ends up the instructions with these words: "Lastly, it seemeth very convenient that the pope and court be dealt withal not to vex moderate catholics by censures and disgraces, since their end is to please God and the king, and promote the union of the catholic religion, and the means employed by them are in their conscience lawful and allowed of in other catholic states. The contrary proceedings cannot but exasperate the king and state, to see none favoured or magnified at that court but over-timorous zealots, and none laid at by emulation more than peaceable and well-minded patriots; especially, this proceeding hindereth many learned and able men from declaring themselves for the king's lawful and laudable intentions, who otherwise would reverently speak what they think to be true for the greater good of the church and of their country, and without any offence of true religion."[1]

The authorities at Rome knew too well the sterling worth of Leander; and in spite of the frequent attempts of his opponents their good opinion was not destroyed.[2]

---

[1] *Ibid.*, pp. 207-209. D. Leander was attacked on all sorts of questions. He was accused of claiming that there were many priests in England with episcopal power and authority. This was on account of the erection of the old cathedral priories, in which according to common law, *sedibus vacantibus*, episcopal jurisdiction was vested. He had to give a long explanation of this simple matter to Windebank, for a paper of his on the subject had, by the advice of a jesuit, been shown to the archbishop of Canterbury as containing matter very pernicious to the State (*C.S.P.*, p. 256).

[2] D. Wilford writes, May 9, 1635: "The last week, after long insistence, I obtained the congregation to be held upon your letters and proposition about the oath. I informed the cardinal, and did what I thought was convenient and the circumstances required; the effect was that the cardinal answers you by this post. . . . I was told the answer concerning the main point would not displease you; that here they would show themselves willing to condescend to his majesty's just desires. . . . Let me entreat you by all the love and service I owe you, that you will not engage yourself further in writing of this argument of the oath. . . . I fear some other form of oath must be thought upon, whereby his majesty may abundantly and superabun-

It was suggested that a new form of oath should be drawn up. There were many propositions made. Lord Baltimore,[1] on whom the oath was pressing in the business of his colony of Maryland, drew up one form; the ever active Toby Matthews another;[2] and it was tried to induce the jesuits, the great opponents of the oath through every phase of the controversy, to draw up one of their own.[3] But the part of opposition has such decided advantages that they were unwilling to lose their position.

D. Leander began, at the request of Panzani, an apology for the paper he had written against Courtney; but illness seized him when in the midst. "I have seen Father Leander," writes Panzani to Barberini, August 15, "who is ill with fever, and have pressed him to hurry on with the *Apologia*."[4] In a month's time he writes again that the patient is not yet well. It was the beginning of the end. Gout was mastering him, and consumption was beginning to show itself. Dropsy,

---

dantly, if anything can superabound in this matter, be secured of his subjects' loyalty, and yet there be no entrenching on subjects' conscience nor the authority of this seat; which having stood for its rights so many ages in the cause of deposing princes, will be very unwilling to permit the oath as the words lie, though glossed with another intention . . . take heed of meddling with the deponibility of princes, for that article will never pass here. . . . Here they have your learning, person, and virtues in a very good conceit, only they imagine you are a little too facile and are sorry you engaged yourself in anything against Mr. Courtney" (*C.S.P.*, pp. 271–273).

[1] *Panzani's Correspondence*, December 19, 1635.
[2] *Ibid.*, November 7, 1635.   [3] *Ibid.*, October 17, 1635.
[4] *S.P.O. Roman Transcript* (Barberini Library), vol. ii.

too, afflicted him. But though borne down with disease, the old man of peace would not leave the world without making an effort to restore harmony between the clergy and the regulars.

There had been several previous negotiations, which were happily brought to an end on November 17, 1635, when a meeting was held between the representatives (with one exception, however) of the clergy and regulars, and a document was drawn up embodying their resolutions. D. Leander got up from his sick-bed to make this last effort in the way of peace.[1]

---

[1] *The Instrument of Peace and Concord between the Secular Clergy and the Regulars.*

"Because the common good of religion ought principally to be regarded by those who labour in the Lord's vineyard, and that good may be promoted with more ease and success when the labourers are united by one common principle; therefore, under the direction of the Holy Spirit, as we presume to hope, the secular clergy of England on one side, with the fathers, benedictines, franciscans, dominicans, and carmelites on the other, have resolved to settle a form of union among themselves adapted to this end, leaving their respective rights and privileges untouched. And that nothing may obstruct the progress of this desirable concern, it is first resolved that all former feuds and differences be now closed; and that the parties mutually promise to bury their animosities and to abstain from all recrimination. Wherefore on this present day, the 17th day of November 1635, being met in London, on behalf and in the name of the R.R. bishop of Chalcedon, and of the secular clergy the underwritten N.N.N., and on behalf and in the name of the fathers, benedictines, &c., the underwritten N.N.N., the same approved the following form of union intended to endure till the Lord shall restore to these kingdoms the free practice of the Roman catholic religion.

"The parties mutually promise that they will unanimously attend to the common concerns of religion, and will aid one another, as often

The joy of the day was to be heightened to Leander by another incident which Panzani relates.

as it may be wanted ; nor will they, as far as depends upon themselves, suffer his holiness to be imposed upon by false representations, or the honour and government of his majesty to be disturbed. To this end it is therefore resolved that at least every quarter, and as often besides as may be occasion, deputies from both sides shall meet for the purpose of deliberation.

"But as his holiness has deputed hither the Rev. Gregory Panzani, it is our desire that he be requested to meet our deputies, in order that our reconciliation be made more firm and solemn. And if the members of other orders be disposed to join our union we admit them to it.

"In testimony of which the said deputies have signed three copies, one of which remains with the secular clergy, another with the aforesaid religious, and the third is given to the reverend Gregory Panzani to take to Rome.

Previous Promises made verbally.

"The deputies of the religious orders promise that neither they nor their brethren will, directly nor indirectly, from this time forward oppose themselves to the establishment of episcopal authority in England ; not impede the bishop or bishops there established, or to be established, in the free and peaceful enjoyment of all rights, privileges, and faculties granted to them by the see apostolic. The secular clergy on their part promise that neither they nor the bishop or bishops, established or to be established, will, directly or indirectly, impede the said religious in the free and peaceful enjoyment and exercise of whatever rights, privileges, and faculties which have been hitherto conceded by the see apostolic. Both parties promise that as soon as the clergy have an immediate superior residing in England, they will treat of more special terms of union.

(Signed) GEORGE FISHER, JOHN SOUTHCOTE, THOMAS WHITE, of the secular clergy ; LEANDER of St. Martin, BENEDICT of St. Facundo, PAULINUS GREENWOOD, benedictines ; THOMAS of Media Villas, LEWIS of St. Ildefonsus, dominicans ; FRANCIS of St. Clare, GILES of St. Ambrose, franciscans ; ELIAS of St. Michael, FRANCIS of the Saints, carmelites (discalced).

(Dodd, vol. iii. pp. 132, 133). To this agreement there was one dissenting party—the jesuits. "When the parties were met to sign the articles of agreement, one Father Roberts, a jesuit, desired to be admitted. His

On the conclusion of the agreement, an apostate priest came to him, all contrite, and asked to be received back. D. Leander was the one he chose to reconcile him.[1]

Just a week before the signing of the agreement, D. Leander wrote to Windebank to beg the king's protection for his brethren: "Although the mercy of God and the careful attendance of my skilful and charitable physicians do put me in hope of recovery, yet the disease, being joined with a consumption, is so uncertain that it maketh me look homeward to heaven every hour, and to think principally thereof; which also emboldeneth me, in all humility, to request two things of your honour. The one is to recommend unto his royal majesty my poor brethren the benedictines, whom I doubt not but he shall find

---

business was to expostulate with them why Panzani was called to the assembly. He was assured that Panzani was not present at their conferences, but was in a room near at hand, that he might be ready to confirm the appointment and congratulate them on the happy conclusion of their differences. He was assured, moreover, how agreeable it would be to them all if he or any other, in the name of the jesuits, would appear and subscribe, as the other deputies did, and that there was a blank left in the writing for the purpose. Father Roberts was far from being satisfied, though they acquainted him with every particular. He even exposed the meeting, representing it as a conspiracy against his society. . . . Soon after Panzani made it his business to find out Richard Blond, provincial of the jesuits, whom he pressed very hard to join the other orders. But he declined it, which so irritated the other deputies that they advised Panzani to importune him no longer, for that it made him put too great a value on his concurrence" (*Panzani's Memoirs*, pp. 219-221, and *Panzani's Correspondence*, December 5, 1635).

[1] *Panzani's Correspondence* (December 5, 1635).

always trusty, loyal, and so obedient unto him that none of them will ever be disobliged from their loyalty to his sacred majesty; the other is a special favour for my brother, Mr. W. Price, whom your honour sufficiently knoweth to be a most loyal subject and a very able man. My desire for him is that your honour would vouchsafe to procure for him, under his majesty's hand and signet, the protection of his person, and of that small means which he hath to maintain himself, with which hitherunto he hath also in a manner maintained me. These two petitions being granted, if I live I shall endeavour truly to deserve them; if God calls me in His mercy, I shall then be mindful of them, and pray for his majesty and for your honour's eternal felicity."[1]

Having provided for the welfare of his own and for the peace of the clergy, his work was done. There were others left to carry on in his own spirit the work he had begun. Rome had sent Panzani, and just a little while before his death, an English envoy, Captain Arthur Brett, had been sent to Rome. This last had instructions from the king to put the matter of the oath in its proper light; to let the pope know the pitiful state catholics were in on account of the prohibition; to procure exemplary punishment of Courtney; to show the impossibility of accepting a bishop; and lastly, to ask for the recall of the jesuits, lest the law should have to

[1] *C.S.P.*, p. 360.

take its course in their regard. Brett was further ordered by the king to take for his adviser D. Wilford, "a moderate man, and of good affection towards our service, and one whom you may trust."[1]

Death came to the monk very soon after. Abbat Caverel died on the first of December (1635), and on the twenty-seventh of the same month D. Leander followed his father and friend. He was buried in the grounds of Somerset House, in a small cemetery which had been consecrated only four days previously for the use of the queen's household. He was the first of them that slept there.

While alive he had only defended his character to his superiors for the sake of the credit of the work he was engaged upon. But now, when death was before him, and knowing that enmity would follow him to the grave, he took all precautions to secure the good name which belonged to his order as well as to himself. Panzani says:—

"Father Leander being in great danger, in order to secure his good fame, made the profession of faith in the presence of many witnesses, and declared his wish to hold, even in detail, whatsoever opinion concerning the oath shall be determined by the church.[2]

---

[1] *C.S.P.*, pp. 354–357.

[2] Among the Clarendon State Papers is one (by some unknown hand, but endorsed by Windebank) to this effect: "That his majesty is informed that here, and at Rome also, it is reported that Father Leander, but ten days before his death, in the presence of Signor Gregorio and another man, friend to Father Leander, did retract what he had taught

And he asked me to send to your eminence a long letter, in the shape of an *Apologia*, which he has written and signed in the presence of three witnesses. And since the jesuits have spread about that the recent agreement (between the clergy and regulars) was directed against them, he asked me to send and bring him any jesuit, so that in my presence he might justify himself, to the intent that after death, which is not far off, his good name may not be slandered." [1]

Writing again on January 2, Panzani says that many protestants called to see Leander before he died, among them a bishop, who particularly wanted to have an interview with the dying monk. But his brethren who were with him, in view of the interpretation that might be put upon the visit, would not approve of it. And as soon as it was known that D. Leander was dead, the provincial of the jesuits came to Panzani, with signs of all possible concern, and asked if it was true that good Father Leander had justified his opinion concerning the oath. Glad of the opportunity of removing all pretext of ignorance, Panzani tells his correspondent:[2] "I told him all that had taken place, not only about the oath, but also about the declaration or held concerning the oath, that the king desiring to know the truth thereof, would have Mr. Secretary Windebank to send for them both, and to require of them a declaration of the truth on this point under their hands; of this point only, I say, simply and plainly, without glosses or circumlocutions" (vol. i. p. 711).

[1] *Panzani's Correspondence*, December 26, 1635.
[2] *Ibid.*, January 2, 1636.

he made of not having in any way worked against the jesuits, nor entered upon the agreement with any sinister view."[1]

Thus lived and died D. Leander Jones, whose days were spent in seeking peace. His name will ever be illustrious in the annals of the English benedictines as one of their greatest men—one who was a lover of his brethren and of his country.

[1] *Panzani's Correspondence*, ibid.

CHAPTER XV

CHRONICLES OF THE CONGREGATION. II

BEFORE carrying on the history of the monasteries, it will be well to treat of such affairs as affected them in common and in as far as concerned their congregational aspect. The real life, however, is to be found in the records of each monastery, and in the unhappily very scanty records of the missioners, and not in the results of periodical meetings.

The second general chapter (the *first* after the Union) met at Douai on July 2, 1621. It had a difficult work to do; for this was the first time that the prelates of the congregation were the appointment of chapter. At the meeting held in Paris, things had been left pretty well as they were found. But one noticeable change had been made; D. Maihew was not included in the number of priors, evidently as an impossible man. It must be remembered in his favour that he had never had the advantages of a real novitiate. The only one of the old English congregation who was a properly trained monk was D. Augustine Baker. D. Maihew had spent his life on the mission, where he was a most zealous missioner. But his religious life had begun at a time of general conflict, in which much heat was engendered—and this was not calculated, in a man of a somewhat absolute cast of mind, to produce on his entry upon conventual life and government, that serenity of spirit and evenness of temper which are of so much value in community life in general and in superiors in particular. D. Maihew's first experience of monastic life was at Dieuleward, where shortly after his arrival a general chapter of the few members of the old English congregation was held, February 28, 1613,[1] and he was nominated president, and in this capacity took upon himself to act in the place of the prior, D. Foster, who had also been a secular priest, and received, whilst on the mission, into the old English congregation. With the exception of a short period of exile, D. Foster does not seem to have lived out of England. D. Maihew having therefore the full practical control at Dieuleward, had shown that capacity for ruling was not one of his qualities, and so was therefore not appointed to any office by the chapter. All the nominations made were from the Spanish monks, with the exception of the Paris house, which had D. Sigebert Bagshaw of the old English congregation. The other prominent member of the old English congregation, D. Vincent Sadler, who had been provincial of Canterbury, died ten days before the chapter met. He too had spent his life on the mission, and had never been a conventual.

There was a difficulty at this time which had to be

[1] *Apostolatus*, iii. p. 38.

contended against. Two of the Spanish monks, D. Francis Waldegrave and D. John Barnes, began a vigorous campaign against the Union, and were led into many extravagances in their opposition. Among other points they raised was the plea that the papal approbation had been obtained by false representation. It professed, they said, to be a restoration of the old English congregation, and they denied that there ever was such a thing as an English congregation in pre-Reformation days. Assuming that a congregation necessarily implied some such centralised form of government as that obtaining among the Cassinese, they contended that the only example of congregation in England was that of Cluni, and that all benedictines had been either subject to them or had been wholly independent. Their position was simply due to their own ignorance of monachism in England during the Middle Ages.

This was a point to which D. Baker for the last fifteen years had been directing his attention; and his vast stores of learning were now of use to put the idea of what the English benedictine congregation really was on the right basis. He was at this time living in the west of England, and was ordered to perfect his collection of historical materials for the history of the order in England, a task much to his liking. In his gradual accumulations of materials he got access to many of the ancient records, and travelled up and down England ransacking libraries. This made him acquainted with many of the leading historians and archæologists of England, and his correspondence shows the intimate terms he was on with the famous antiquaries and historians, Sir Richard Cotton, Sir Henry Spelman, John Seldon, and William Camden, from all of whom he received help and in return gave them also much assistance.

Whilst he was so engaged he had to leave England. Though not perfect according to his mind, the result of his researches, as applied to the question under dispute, is embodied in the *Apostolatus benedictinorum in Anglia* which passes under the name of D. Clement Reyner. This book, despite its form, and though published more than two centuries ago, shows an accurate insight of English mediæval monastic antiquities which successive generations of antiquarians have completely failed to attain.[1]

About this time "the Emperor (Ferdinand II.) having recovered a great tract of ground from the heretics, on which stood many monasteries of the order of St. Benedict, the English fathers knowing the Bursfeldian congregation to want monks to put into them, petitioned them to consider fraternally the case of their affliction and exile, and charitably to stretch their arm to help them."[2]

Their petition was backed by abbat Caverel, and

[1] That D. Baker's views, based as they were on documentary evidence of first-hand authority, were correct, may be gathered from a decree of the Roman congregation of the Council, dated May 23, 1626, declaring that the organisation on the basis of the Lateran council of the English black monks previous to the dissolution, constituted a true congregation. [2] Weldon, 157.

the German congregation lent them (May 18, 1628) the abbey of Cismar upon conditions, among others, that all the rights of the house should be maintained; and in the next year the house of Rintelen. The German monks lent to the English, besides the houses mentioned above, Dobran, Scharnabeck, Weine, with Lambspring and Stoterlingbough, for their nuns, which houses, in the then condition of things, were of no use to them, and had to be recovered from the protestant occupiers. But with the exception of Lambspring they were all given up. An attempt was made at setting up a seminary at Rintelen, but came to nothing. The superiors of these houses were to be chosen for life by the members of their own communities, and were not, like those of Dieuleward, Paris, and St. Malo's, nominees of the chapter, nor like that of Douai, whose prior was chosen by the house, and received his confirmation from the abbat of St. Vedast's.

In 1634 "the president of the congregation was empowered from Rome to give all the faculties for missioners that used to be given to the subjects of the king of Great Britain, and to lessen and augment them as he saw convenient. Also all benedictine monks whatever, who laboured in the mission of England, were to labour under his presidentship, excepting those of Monte Cassino."[1]

[1] Weldon, p. 172. This was the appointment of D. Leander as prefect of the benedictine mission in England, which has been mentioned in the last chapter; and is a point D. Weldon does not seem to have understood (*Chronological Notes*).

A college at Rome, instituted by abbat Cajetan on the plans of the present universal college of San Anselmo, was given over at this time into the hands of the English monks. The general chapter was chary about accepting what had been a failure in the hands of its founder, and only gave leave to the English procurator at Rome, D. Reade, to see what he personally could make of it. It soon proved to be an unwise experiment, and cost the congregation a large sum of money.

About this time also Urban VIII. issued what has been always looked upon as the great charter of the English congregation, the bull *Plantata in agro Dominico*, whereby he confirmed everything his predecessors had done, and gave to the monks all the rights and privileges enjoyed by their predecessors in time gone by. Foremost among them is the right to all the cathedrals, nine in number, which had belonged to them together with the three abbeys of Gloucester, Chester, and Peterborough, made by Henry VIII. into cathedrals.[1] He appoints to these cathedral monasteries, priors, and with the monks assigned to them, declares these communities to be, now and henceforth, the actual

---

[1] Clement VII. by a bull (June 4, 1529) had sanctioned one of the schemes of Wolsey, which was to create, out of certain abbeys, new cathedrals. This had been done formerly, as in the case of Ely (1109). The papal leave, however, was not used. But in 1541 Henry, now the supreme head, by his own authority created six new sees, Westminster, Oxford, Gloucester, Bristol, Peterborough, and Chester. This was only, however, a part of a much larger scheme which never took effect.

capitular bodies of these sees, with all the rights of their predecessors. He forbids most strictly any attempt to dissolve or annul the aforesaid monastic cathedral chapter.[1] These and other provisions of the bull were obtained on the expectation of an immediate return of England to the holy see, an idea which lies under the missions of D. Leander and Panzani mentioned in the preceding chapter.

But we have already seen that from the necessities of the times, and the circumstances of the case, a certain duality of aim had arisen among the benedictines. On the one hand the ancient English congregation had to be continued, on the other the monks were engaged in carrying on a mission in England under stress of the penal laws. Hence it will not surprise any one, in perusing the chronicles of the restored congregation, to find as it were a double current; one making for centralisation according to the Cassinese model, the other for freedom according to the English pattern. The former tendency expressed itself, at times in an exalting or extending the power of the president or that of the general chapter, both representing the same idea, viz. the preponderance of a central authority. Although D. Maihew was not appointed to office at the chapter of 1621, he remained at Dieuleward till

---

[1] As events turned, the cathedral chapters have long since been given up, though the title of "Cathedral Prior" survived, and gave, up to within a recent date, a seat in the general chapter.

1624, and before that date had already seen, as prior of that house, D. Lawrence Reyner his most faithful disciple, and the inheritor of his idea. It is curious to observe the development of the ideas these men had inherited naturally enough from their association with the Cassinese, and the new congregations of Lorraine and France, which were organised on the same model. The unfettered rule of a general was more to their mind than the tempered constitution accepted by the definitors at the time of the Union. Moreover, the missionary work of the congregation became to them the one important end of English benedictines. From scattered references to the general chapter of 1625, the acts of which are lost, this view was then put forward, but evidently it met with no general support. In 1633, the matter being again urged, a commission of seven was appointed by the chapter to discuss "the nature and substance of the congregation," and to present a report. Three priors, three ex-presidents, and two influential missioners, who afterwards held the office of provincial, represented every interest. In their report they say :—

"It seems to us that this congregation is an assemblage of the distinct convents and prelates of the order of black monks of St. Benedict in England, continued by an unbroken succession from the time of Innocent III., which prelates have ordinary powers to rule the monks of their own convents under an aristocratic form of government, prescribed by the church, consisting of a general chapter to be summoned at stated times, one or more presidents, the prelates of the convents, and a certain number of definitors, with authority to reform and correct, according to the rule of St. Benedict, the sacred canons of the church and approved customs; moreover, various privileges of exemption, mission, &c., accrue to their assemblage and belong to it (*accidunt et competunt*) . . . The *end* [of the congregation] is that the convents and monks be kept in regular discipline according to the ordinances of the rule, the canons, approved customs, and laws canonically passed. The *accidents* seem to be chiefly exemption, faculties for the missions, and the various privileges and laws suitable to the aforesaid end. . . . And our intention in establishing this congregation was and is that we might be stable in the mode and form of government and of regular life, according to the rule and canons of the church and the rights legitimately acquired to each convent."

It is worthy of note that nothing is admitted into this definition but what squares with the condition of the old English congregation before the Reformation. This clear and definite statement was adopted by the chapter and confirmed by the succeeding one in 1639, and by every chapter till 1661.[1]

It was some years before the ideas of D. L.

---

[1] *Notes on the Origin and Early Development of the Restored English Benedictine Congregation*, pp. 45, 46.

Reyner were once more formally brought forward. He had in 1649 become provincial of the missioners in the north. On the close of his term of office in 1653, he proposed at his provincial chapter and secured assent to a series of proposals affecting, among other things, the general government of the congregation. These he forwarded to D. Claude White, whose term of office as provincial of Canterbury was also expiring, with a view to obtain the assent of the southern missioners. The following were the principal propositions :—

"(1) That the president's authority be rather enlarged than diminished, and his place and person be had in great honour and veneration, according to the rule of St. Benet, and that it be not lawful for every prior or inferior to contest against him if he doth not carry himself well; let him be then censured when he is out of office, not before.

"(2) That the president should be outed of his office at the beginning of the general chapter, and another preside therein, seemeth a thing unto us not to be suffered.

. . . .

"(5) That the portions of novices be here [*in England*] detained, to wit, the principal thereof, and an annual pension only allowed them during the time of their abode there [*in their convents*]."

Moreover, it was further proposed, among other points, that "the judges of causes," who were a court of appeal from the president, should be abolished, and that the various restrictions requiring the residence of the president and definitors in the convents abroad should be done away with, and that the domestic powers of the conventual priors should be curtailed.[1] To some of these propositions the missioners of the southern provinces agreed. The outcome of the matter is thus stated by Weldon: "The fathers hitherto had been very rigid in exacting of the presidents that they should neither be installed in England nor live there during the time of their office, but on the continent, either in Flanders, France, Lorraine, or Germany. The first with whom they dispensed with on this point was R. F.

---

[1] Add. MS. (Sloane), n. 4156, f. 8. The text of these further propositions is here given in the original:—

"*Ut in posterum non sint judices causarum, sed si contigerit aliquam appelationem fieri, debet esse ad præsidem et a præside ad capitulum generale.*

"*Desideratur quod omnes definitiones limitantes residentiam in Anglia præsidis sint abrogatæ. Et si contigerit eum esse in Anglia eo tempore quo debere installari, sit potestas penes provincialem et suos definitores ad eum installandum; et ut ibi remanere possit quamdiu rerum necessitas suam presentiam postulat.*

"*Desideratur quod missionarii nostri (quamvis in Anglia residentes) sint capaces officii definitorum Regiminis et si contigerit aliquem definitorem Regiminis in Angliam mitti, possit gaudere suo officio (non obstante sua residentia in Anglia) et dum præses in Anglia resideat possit habere provincialem (?) cum duobus definitoribus ejusdem provinciæ in qua residet, pro suis consiliariis qui gaudeant equali potestate cum definitoribus.*

"*Quod omnes professores in tota nostra congregatione nominentur per capitulum generale qui obligabuntur ad legendum per totum quadriennium nisi aliter statuetur a præside et regimine, et nullo modo licitum erat prioribus conventuum eos a suis studiis evocare, nec ad chorum frequentandum tenebuntur.*"

The copy in the British Museum is the original acts of the provincial chapter, and has the autograph signatures.

Claude White (elected president) in 1653; but now (in the chapter of 1661) not only the president but even the definitors were left free to live in England or out of England.[1]

At the chapter of 1661 the dependence upon the Spanish general of the English congregation (now firmly established) was done away with. The delay caused in obtaining the confirmation of the election of the president by the Spanish general was found inconvenient, especially as in practice no purpose was served thereby.

Charles II., who had received great help and kindness from the benedictines during his exile, on his restoration determined to have a body of monks for the chapel royal at Somerset House, lately set apart for the use of his queen, Catherine of Braganza. D. Paul Robinson, a monk of Dieuleward, whose acquaintance the king had made when on the continent, was now in England and was made use of by his majesty to arrange the foundation. Stuart d'Aubigny, the queen's high almoner, wrote to the chapter sitting at Douai in 1661 telling them that all D. Robinson had to propose concerning the projected foundation had been sanctioned by the king. The next year D. Benet Stapleton, a gregorian, was appointed sub-almoner and first chaplain to the queen, and six other priests and two lay brothers took up their residence at Somerset House. The king provided handsomely for their

[1] Weldon, pp. 196, 197.

support, giving £100 for each priest and £50 for each lay brother. This establishment came to an end in 1679, on occasion of the Titus Oates' plot, when the gentle lay brother, Thomas Pickering, a monk of St. Gregory's at Douai, was executed on the false charge of having conspired with jesuits to murder the king.

In 1667, at a chapter held at St. James's Palace, a proposal was made by those who advocated a closer bond of union, that the college which St. Gregory's had carried on for nearly half a century at Douai (the source to them of many subjects) should be made common to all the houses. What was offered in return was that Dieuleward should be made a common novitiate. For eight years St. Gregory's taught humanities to all-comers, while the arrangement at Dieuleward of a common novitiate did not last even for four years, and the former system of each monastery having its own novitiate was resumed.[1]

When James II., in 1685, succeeded his brother, the benedictines took advantage of the prospect of more peaceful times to establish communities. One of the king's first cares was to found at St. James's Palace a royal monastery of fourteen monks, choir monks, and two lay brothers, with D. Augustine Howard as prior. A "pretty little convent," at St. John's, Clerkenwell, was set up in 1687 by D. Corker, monk, and afterwards abbat of Lambspring,

[1] Allanson.

and mass was said there publicly.[1] Some of the old abbey property at Bury St. Edmunds was on the point of coming back by sale into the hands of its old owners, as represented by the monks of St. Edmund's monastery at Paris. But representations were made to the king, who personally advised them to forego the purchase. For sake of peace, the monks withdrew till a more favourable opportunity. But soon after the place was bought up by the jesuits, and a mission and school started.[2] It was also proposed to establish a monastery within the precincts of St. Mary's abbey at York. In a letter dated York, December 22, 1687, it is said: "Mr. Lawson and several other benedictines are come to this town, and

[1] During the short reign of James there was a wonderful outburst of catholic life, which shows how strong it must have been in spite of the years of persecution. Besides these benedictine monasteries mentioned in the text, the franciscans opened a house in Lincoln's Inn Fields, January 1687; the next month the dominicans followed suit in Great Lincoln's Inn. In March the earl of Salisbury was reported to be building a popish chapel at Hatfield. D. Corker had leave to open a church in the Savoy, which he did in the upper part of a house. His opponents, seeing his success, took the lower part, and started their services a little while before his, and otherwise so inconvenienced him that he had to move off to Clerkenwell. The jesuits opened a public school (May 23, 1687), which was so successful that in a short while their pupils numbered over 400, one half of whom were protestants; and in the July of the following year, bishop Ellis, O.S.B., held a confirmation in the chapel of the college, and confirmed some hundreds of youths. The carmelites opened a church in the city, and in 1686 some secular priests opened a public church in Lime Street, which after a month they were compelled to relinquish on a charge of Jansenism. Six months after the jesuits reopened the chapel. See Gillow's *Biographical Dictionary*, vol. ii. pp. 451, 452.

[2] Weldon's *Life of James II.*, Add. MSS. 10,118, f. 394.

have the manor, anciently St. Mary's abbey, resigned to them. Whether the mansion-house, without the large appurtenances of a mitred abbat, will satisfy them, you, that are a far-seeing and skilful man, can best tell."[1] But the Revolution brought all these undertakings to an end.

In the monastery at St. James's, from July 30th to August 10th of 1685, a general chapter was held under the presidency of D. Joseph Sherburn, a monk of St. Edmund's, Paris. The capitular fathers waited on the king to receive his commands, and he desired that they should not elect for their president D. Maurus Corker, who had been condemned to death during the Oates' plot. The king was afraid that, were he elected, it might give offence to his protestant subjects, and thus draw down enmity upon the monks.

James II. having secured the appointment of four vicars apostolic, one of whom was D. Philip Ellis, the old questions of jurisdiction broke out again as soon as the king had abdicated. The bull of *Plantata* complicated matters considerably, as it confirmed the benedictines in possession of all their old rights as holders of the jurisdiction during the vacancies of the sees. To this had to be joined the pope's express command that no attempt should be made to abrogate this position. A letter from D. Augustine Walker, though written during a later dispute on similar grounds, gives so clear a *résumé*

[1] *Twelfth Report of the Historical Manuscripts Commission*, Appendix vii. p. 208 (Rydal Hall Collection).

of the arguments used by the monks in defending their rights against the vicars apostolic that we here give extracts therefrom :—

"The Roman catholic bishops, only temporary missioners from Rome, without any hereditary right or jurisdiction, seem to fix their hearts too much on becoming ordinaries and in some measure independent of the disposition of the pope; who having sent them only for a time, with a limited jurisdiction, can recall them at pleasure as he sent them. They seek to have their power enlarged, and in a word to have all the jurisdiction of bishops in their proper diocese. But above all they seem desirous to gain an absolute command over the regulars; the inferior secular clergy join with the bishop in endeavouring to bring it about. . . . On the other hand, the regulars, jealous of maintaining their privileges, did all in their power to put a stop to what they thought an encroachment of the bishops. The last pleaded the canons and laws of the church for the submission of the regulars to them in all that belonged to the administration of the sacraments and other missionary duties. The regulars, on the other hand, pleaded that they derived their mission equally from the same source that made the bishops missioners; and that their missionary faculties were of a much older date, having laboured in the English mission long before any missionary bishops set footing in England; and consequently that they did not want any authority from the bishops for the exercise of these offices of which they had so long acquitted themselves without the assistance of the bishops.

"The benedictines, above all the regulars, pleaded another motive of exemption founded on the canon law, in virtue of their having kept up a succession of canons since their expulsion from Canterbury and other cathedral churches [1] of which they were possessed at the time the Reformation began. . . . Hence the benedictine monks seem to have some reason to say that, as there are no Roman catholic bishops of the old sees in England, all right and jurisdiction is devolved upon them, as they are the only ones who have kept up a succession in their churches; according to which the missionary bishops themselves ought rather to have this authority from the said chapters of benedictines. But though the benedictine monks, for the sake of peace, have always been willing to waive the last part of the question, they think it hard to be deprived of what regards themselves." [2]

The real value and weight to be attached to these pretensions is, perhaps, best estimated by their history, which is a record of continual retreat. The point of canon law was referred to the pope, who in 1696 decided that while the *regimen* of vicars apostolic existed, all other jurisdiction ceased.

When the Revolution took place, the little monastery at Clerkenwell was one of the first to be

---

[1] This assertion of fact will not bear scrutiny.

[2] *Downside Review*, viii. pp. 155-156. This letter, written (June 5, 1762) to Mr. L——, was occasioned by a passage in Hume's History of England relating to St. Dunstan.

destroyed. On November 11, 1688, "the rabble assembled in a tumultuous manner at St. John's, Clerkenwell, there, on a report of gridirons, spits, great caulderons, &c., to destroy protestants, they began some outrageous acts, till the horse and foot guards were sent to suppress them; 'tis said they killed some first." [1]

At the general chapter held in London in 1697, under president D. Gregson, a measure was passed to the effect that no one should be elected to the office of president, provincial, prior, or abbess for two successive terms. This rule, which must evidently affect the stability of the monasteries, was abolished in 1717. The number of professed fathers in the congregation in the year 1705 was 124, divided among the houses as follows: St. Gregory's at Douai numbered 39; St. Laurence's at Dieuleward, 17; St. Edmund's at Paris, 32; and the abbey of Lambspring, 36.

The reaction against the narrowing policy of 1697 was brought about by D. Laurence Fenwick, who in 1717 became president. He was determined to make a bold stroke for liberty; but instead of setting to work in a constitutional way, he essayed violent measures. It is useless to attempt a fundamental reformation before men's minds are prepared and, so to say, educated up to it. The French Revolution never would have succeeded had it not been for Rousseau's *Contrat*

[1] Pink's *History of Clerkenwell* (ed. Wood), p. 310.

Social, which taught the people their right and gave them power to use it. Like so many other reformers, quick enough to see the evils but not to see the true means of remedying them, D. Fenwick went to an extreme. He wanted to be president for life. His instinct in a certain sense was right. Stability is a benedictine principle. But he applied it to the office of president, in which there is not the like necessity. His fate was sad. He was deposed, and died in disgrace, though treated with great kindness by his brethren. As a matter of fact, the next president, D. Thomas Southcott, a prudent man, remained in office for twenty years (1721-41).

In the chapter of 1725 it was proposed to erect two schools in England, one for each province, for the purpose of providing subjects for the houses. Douai had its own college and was not in need of any extraneous help. A beginning was made at Redmarley in Gloucestershire in 1731, under D. Edmund Cox of the Paris house, and he was succeeded by D. Cuthbert Hutchinson of Douai. But the school did not answer and was soon given up. The other school, for the province of York, never got beyond the realm of proposal. At this chapter the fathers gave to bishop Ellis[1] the right to sit in chapter, with a deliberative vote; and it was decreed that, for the future, any English benedictine pro-

---

[1] D. Ellis was publicly consecrated in the chapel royal, St. James's (May 6, 1688), bishop of Aureopolis and vicar apostolic of the western district of England. He followed James into exile, and died bishop of Segni in Italy, 1726.

moted to an episcopal see should have the same rights. A stricter bond of union was advocated by the president, D. Southcott, who had been opposed to D. Fenwick's ideas. But the abbat of Lambspring, D. Augustine Tempest, seeing it would prejudice the rights of his abbey, which he was bound to maintain, opposed the motion so successfully that before the next chapter was held the project had been abandoned.[1] The influences dominating under the presidency of D. Southcott are indicated by the fact that during the thirty ensuing years (1721 to 1753) the general chapters, which since 1661 had been held alternately in London and in one of the monasteries abroad, were now held regularly at Douai, as being the monastery most convenient for the attendance of both missioners and conventuals; in fact, his rule seems to have been a sort of *remora* on tendencies, the development of which the circumstances of the times now rendered inevitable.

Up to the accession of the House of Hanover there had been hopes, if not of reunion at least of establishing a *modus vivendi* between England and the Holy See. With the firm establishment of the new dynasty all hopes of a return of the monks, except in the guise

---

[1] So Allanson in his manuscript history, but he gives no details as to the nature of the proposal. Abbat Tempest died in 1730. It is of interest, as perhaps bearing on this matter, that president Southcott in his correspondence with cardinal Gualterio, the protector of England, signs himself "General of the English benedictines" (*Add. MSS.*, 20, 309).

of solitary missioners serving the diminishing needs of a dwindling sect, seemed over. No one could anticipate the marvellous series of events which was to bring back the monasteries to their native soil. In these circumstances, the views which prior Laurence Reyner had advocated seemed now to be the only ones which, in practice, could recommend themselves to sensible men desiring to be of service to their fellow-countrymen : viz. that the members of the congregation must be missioners, and that the monasteries existed only as seminaries for the education of these missioners, and a place of refuge and retreat in time of danger and old age. These views must have had the more weight, inasmuch as with the exception of Douai, which had its school, the monasteries had no external work.[1] The predominance of this idea is again shown by the simple fact that from 1757 the general chapters were henceforth, with one exception (1785), held in England.

During this period the Jansenist controversy was raging in France, and "the charge of Jansenism was often used as a convenient means of attack (says D. Allanson) in order to serve a party purpose or to gratify the malevolence of the human heart." Without the slightest grounds of probability, the English congregation of benedictines had to undergo the same imputations that had been charged against the whole body of the English clergy. In

---

[1] Lambspring, too, had at one time a small college for English boys, while Dieuleward taught boys from the neighbourhood.

the chapter of 1745 the assembled fathers indignantly repelled the charge and solemnly accepted the constitution of Clement XI. (the *Unigenitus*) and his bull, *Vineam Domini Sabaoth*. They made a simple and entire acceptance of all the decrees which had emanated from the holy see, and condemned all appeals to a future general council. In order to make their protest as solemn and as public as possible, an instrument to this effect was drawn up and was signed by all in the presence of a public notary, and the great seal of the congregation was thereto attached.

In 1753 Benedict XIV., by his bull *Apostolicum Ministerium*, generally regulated all the affairs of the mission, which, as can be seen by the letter of president Walker quoted above, were again in dispute.

In 1766 Louis XV. issued his famous *Commission des réguliers*, which was to take cognisance of the affairs of all the monasteries in his kingdom. The commission, against which the pope protested in vain, among other articles of inquiry ordered that all religious bodies should submit their constitutions for its approval and for the purpose of legalising their existence in the country.[1] When the English

---

[1] They even went so far as to lay down laws for the validity of monastic vows. The result was disastrous to the orders. Taking the benedictines as an example, in 1770 they were 6434 in number, and in twenty years' time had fallen to 4311. The commissioners report highly in favour of the English benedictines, and say they need no reform.

benedictines sent in their constitutions in order to save their monasteries, all of which except Lambspring were now in French territory, the Latin in which they were written did not please the French purists, who accordingly sent them back.

The general chapter (1773) therefore appointed a committee for revising the constitutions and for making certain alterations demanded by the commission, such as the abandonment of a custom of abstinence on Christmas, Easter, and Whitsunday.[1] When the newly worded constitutions were sent up, they were again rejected, for some ambiguities in the wording and the retention of laws which had become obsolete. In the chapter of 1777 nine monks were appointed with full power to correct, change, add, or omit any law to which two-thirds should agree. Their work was presented to the following chapter of 1781, and in 1784 the new constitutions were finished and laid before the royal commission, who were good enough to confirm them; on which the king granted letters-patent for the civil existence of the monasteries, under the condition that the superiors should be bound to take care that the doctrine contained in the well-known declaration of the Gallican Church of 1682,[2] touching ecclesiastical power, be taught in all their convents.

In the chapter of 1781 a liturgical change of great

---

[1] It does not seem that St. Gregory's observed this custom, as their internal life was regulated by abbat Caverel's charter.

[2] The jesuits in France in 1707 and again in 1761 had already accepted this doctrine.

value was made. A new calendar which had been in project since 1753 was accepted, with the notable feature that all Sundays were to be kept as doubles, giving place only to the greater feasts.

About this time, as will be noted elsewhere, the president fell back upon a former project of having one common novitiate and one common alumnate. This time Dieuleward was to have the school and Douai the novitiate. But hardly had this been set on foot and the revised constitutions confirmed than the French revolution broke out. It was God's opportunity for bringing the monasteries to England. How it affected each house will be told in the subsequent chapters.

A general chapter was held at Acton Burnell in 1794, where the laurentian community had found a shelter offered by Sir Edward Smythe to the gregorians (by whom he had been educated and for whom he entertained the strongest affection), who were unable to accept it for the moment as they were in prison. The relative numbers of the professed fathers of the congregation at this time were: Douai, 22; Dieuleward, 28; Paris, 12; Lambspring, 25. Chapter decreed that the monastery of St. Lawrence should be reconstituted at Acton Burnell. When the gregorians were released and were able to accept the generous offer of the owner to settle at Acton Burnell, a proposal was made by the laurentians that the two communities should amalgamate. This was not carried into effect, and the latter moved elsewhere.

In 1818 D. Bede Slater, a monk of St. Lawrence's,

who had just been appointed vicar-apostolic of the Cape of Good Hope (East), obtained from the holy see, as a favour for his brethren, the right of appointing titular abbats with the names of the old English monasteries. Some time before this (1725) it had been decreed that the president should enjoy the title of abbat of St. Augustine's monastery at Canterbury.[1] This incident shows how faint had become by this time the knowledge and apprehension of the past which had been so notable a feature in earlier days.

In 1829 and the succeeding years an anxious period set in for the congregation. We refer here to bishop Baines and his attack on the canonical existence of the congregation. A fuller treatment of the subject will naturally come in the account of St. Gregory's monastery, which bore the brunt of the attack. Suffice it here to say that judging the proceedings with that larger and calmer view which time gives to every question, we can only look upon his actions, regrettable though some of them were, as proceeding from the instinct that the monasteries, to do their work fully, must be independent. Though hampered by existing circumstances, what he really seems to have wanted was to remove one of the monasteries from the control of the congregation and put it in the same state as most of the old English abbeys had been. It is, however, not improbable that his immature

[1] Allanson.

scheme would have ended in secularisation altogether. The whole incident is to be regarded, we venture to think, as only another ebullition of the old spirit making for independence.

But bishop Baines was before his time; nor indeed does he seem to have had a clear perception or firm grasp of the principles really underlying his action. This is but in accordance with his character, which was greatly moved by exterior show. He succeeded in raising questions too, whereby the real point at issue fell quite out of sight. Indeed, one of his most strenuous opponents said in after years, that had he realised the issues actually involved he would have acted otherwise than he did; and within twenty years after the dispute the same monk, then become bishop, desired to do in his own district much what bishop Baines had proposed.

In 1858 the former project of having one common novitiate, this time on the ground of a much-needed return to the common life which had been disturbed by the necessity of the times, was again started; and in 1859 a general novitiate for the three existing monasteries was opened at St. Michael's monastery, Belmont, near Hereford. Mr. Wegg Prosser, a recent convert, gave over into the hands of the congregation a church which he had begun to build whilst still an Anglican. This, together with a property in land, a generous benefaction, enabled the congregation to erect a monastery adjoining the church for the purposes of a novitiate and house of studies for the juniors.

The church in 1863 was appointed the pro-cathedral of the diocese of Newport and Menevia, and is the only catholic cathedral in which the divine office is daily celebrated by canons of a regularly constituted chapter. The pope wished in the new hierarchy to give a mark of his veneration for the English benedictines, and a recognition not only of their work in the mission but of their old right of holding the greater part of the former cathedrals. He formally ordained that the chapter of the diocese of Newport and Menevia should henceforth be a monastic chapter[1] with a cathedral prior at their head. By a recent decree of the present pope, the prelate has the same rights of *pontificalia* as were enjoyed by some of the cathedral priors in olden days.

As time went on and the monasteries became firmly established in England, many provisions, made when they were abroad, became useless, and impediments in the way of development of the monastic institute. On one hand a house established in Scotland at Fort Augustus made a precipitate movement for independence, and, acting

[1] Unfortunately, the chance of restoring a monastic chapter as it always had been in England was not made use of. A chapter was formed on the plan of the secular chapters, with resident and non-resident canons, but, unlike them, with no fixity of tenure. The old monastic chapters consisted, as is now known, wholly and entirely of the monks belonging to the cathedral monastery, who, as a community, formed the chapter.

under foreign advice, severed itself from the congregation. But others began to see and to think, to compare notes and ideas, to study more deeply their own history, and to work out the whys and wherefores of things. A process which weighs each step and profits by experience has the best promise of producing a true solid work, and such has been the recent history of the English benedictines.

Two bulls have been lately issued from the holy see, ever watchful, and intent upon the truer interests of that order which has so special a claim on the pope as to need no other head than the abbat of abbats himself. One in 1884, the *Romanos Pontifices*, deals with the new relations introduced into missionary life by the restored hierarchy of bishops; and the other (1890), the *Religiosus Ordo*, concerned with the monks' own domestic government. By this important document the provincials are abrogated as no longer necessary, and the monks on the mission are now under the immediate jurisdiction of the superior of the monastery of their profession. This bull is a great step in restoring the English congregation to the state when Glaston, St. Albans, Westminster, St. Edmund's, York, and Chester, with many another fair and stately abbey sent its deputies to a chapter truly representative of all English benedictines. And here we must leave our chronicles of the congregation.

CHAPTER XVI

ST. GREGORY'S MONASTERY

THE reader is already acquainted with the first foundation of this monastery. We will now resume our sketch of its history from the finishing of St. Gregory's by abbat Caverel in 1611.

It was fortunate not only for the temporal prosperity of the house but also for the formation of its inner life, that men like D. Leander Jones and D. Rudisind Barlow presided over its destinies and were themselves, in many ways, guided and trained by their munificent founder, abbat Caverel. His own monks at Arras were in a model condition. There was nothing fussy or "faddy" (if we may use the word) about their spirit. A broad, generous view of things, keeping zealously to what they could do and not trying to make themselves models of austerities beyond their strength and work; these, together with the wholesome determination to be masters in their own house, were qualities which reigned at Arras under Caverel and found their counterpart at Douai.

The new foundation of St. Gregory's had at first no fixed allowance for its support except about £20 a year from the abbat and a certain quantity of corn. A petition from the monks, signed by D. Barlow, the prior, D. Leander, the Spanish general's vicar, and D. Benet Jones, was presented to the abbat on the 14th of September 1616, in which they asked for some secure means of livelihood. He at once allowed them a certain sum as an experiment; and began to consider the steps necessary for placing his foundation on a sure basis. But while the affair of the Union was pending, it was unwise, considering the temper of some, to risk endowing an establishment for a purpose other than what the founder had in view. So Caverel waited; and when, in the scheme of the Union of 1617, his attention was called to certain parts adverse to the interests of St. Gregory's, he instituted such a vigorous opposition to their confirmation that nothing was sanctioned that could harm his beloved monastery. There is something quite touching in the paternal care he showed on every occasion to St. Gregory's, and in the way he fenced it round about and made such stringent conditions effectually to prevent any attack on its rights. And not only was it the abbat himself, but the monks of St. Vedast, too, showed the greatest affection for their brethren at Douai, and willingly gave consent to all the measures D. Caverel took. And their interest remained a fixed tradition in that illustrious house.

When the affairs of the Union were arranged, and the abbat had secured the exemption of the monasteries from episcopal jurisdiction,[1] and for St. Gregory's the vital point that the election of prior should not depend upon chapter, but be a house election to be confirmed by him and his successors; he proceeded to give a permanent foundation to the monastery of 2000 florins a year, making the condition that every new prior on accession should ask the abbat of Arras for a continuation of the right to live in the monastery. D. Leander, however, pointed out that the condition was one-sided; it did not oblige the abbat to grant it, and, moreover, another prelate might refuse to renew the gift. At once a new clause was added to the effect that as long as the English monks kept to the conditions of the foundation according to what "a sincere, prudent, and pious judge might determine," they were to be left undisturbed. A subsequent clause stated that it was "inserted to oblige the said religious to remember the respect and friendship due from them to those of Arras, and that there might be for ever a right understanding betwixt them, with love of regular discipline and learning, especially a serious study of philosophy and divinity."[2]

---

[1] It was necessary, both under the circumstances then existing on the continent and also in England. But the old English tradition is that the abbeys should be under the jurisdiction of the diocesan, an arrangement consonant with the rule and conducive to harmony between the monks and the clergy. The cathedral priory was necessarily subject to the bishop; and all other houses, great or small, with the exception of five, were likewise under the bishop of the diocese, whose power is for edification and not for destruction.

[2] Weldon, p. 151.

The abbat's foundation was for twelve monks. In token that he and the convent of St. Vedast were absolute lords of this rent and dwelling, and likewise in token of gratitude, the president of the congregation, or the prior, with the convent, had annually to celebrate a solemn mass, during which they had to offer to the abbat or to his deputy a wax candle of 2lb. weight, with a declaration that this was done as an act of gratitude for his bounty; and the same had to be done in the monastery of St. Vedast on the same day. And all priors on taking office were obliged to send a petition to the abbey for the confirmation and renewal of the bounty. The monks of St. Gregory's were to engage to add at their profession the vow of the mission at the will of their superior. The abbat then laid down rules for the solemnising of the divine worship; and the particular regulations show that he was determined that St. Gregory's, like St. Vedast's, should cultivate a great love for the liturgy. He prescribes their mode of life, their food and fasts. Everything is regulated on a large spirit, and bears the mark of wisdom and discretion. He ordains that there must always be some qualified to teach philosophy and divinity in the neighbouring college of St. Vedast; and these professors were to be entirely at the disposal of the abbat, and could not be sent away unless there were others he should approve of as capable. If at any time no such capable men were to be found in the community, a reduction of 50 florins for each vacancy was to be made in the grant. By this wise regulation the spirit of learning was kept up in the monastery, and the community not allowed to dwindle down in number.

There were two ways recognised in this charter for electing a superior. The house was to vote, and the abbat chose three names out of the number, one of whom the general chapter had to select; or else they (the capitular fathers) were to present him three names chosen by the convent, and he made his choice. He was free to choose whichever plan he considered best for his foundation. By this important condition the prior of St. Gregory's never was the nominee of the chapter, but of the community. The powers of the capitular body were confined either to selecting one of three elected by St. Gregory's, or of sending the names chosen by the convent to the abbat of Arras, who made the selection. As a matter of fact the last was the course always pursued. The house elected, the chapter forwarded the names, and the abbat selected. And, as the interests of St. Gregory's and that of the abbats were identical, the election of prior was confined practically to the house.

Although the foundation was only for twelve, the prior could take in as many more as he liked, provided they were not a burthen to the house. And when any of the twelve places became vacant, the persons to be admitted were to be presented by the prior to the abbat. Every one admitted to live in the monastery had to take an oath that he would " maintain the honour of the said abbat, and that he will not by any means seek to extort upon the accompt of the said foundation anything from him or his monastery further than what is established. Moreover, he must promise not to disturb the peace of the convent, or seek to change to work the laws of it, or seek absolution from the said oath or take it if offered." [1]

By this provision D. Caverel enabled St. Gregory's to maintain its own family life.

He further ordains there were never to be less than nine in the convent, so that the divine office might be carried out with due solemnity. During his own lifetime he reserved to himself the powers of visitation; and also stipulated that he could send to live among them, paying a proper pension, any of his own religious from Arras, either by way of penance or for recollection, or for any other cause. These visitations were a source of great benefit to St. Gregory's, and brought it more closely into touch with the wise, firm spirit which obtained at Arras.

As regards the administration, the founder ordained that every year the prior should present the accounts to the abbat of Arras; and, in case of debt, neither the abbey of Arras nor the income of 2000 florins were to be called upon for payment. Any money received from Flanders went to the

[1] Weldon, p. 154.

foundation, and so with any money from England. But with this difference: when England became catholic again, and the community could return there, they had to give up, together with the possession of the buildings, all moneys of the foundation which came from Flanders; but were free to take that which had come from English sources.

The monks of St. Gregory's engaged to say a certain number of masses every year for D. Philip Caverel and his successors, and when it pleased God to make England catholic again, they promised to receive at their house at Oxford (Gloucester Hall) whomsoever the abbat of St. Vedast might send for purposes of study.

The original deed of acceptance of this noble gift is a magnificent parchment roll which has been lately discovered among the archives of the Pas de Calais. It is tastefully illuminated, and has portraits of the gregorian martyrs, to whom we shall refer.

There was only one thing needed now, and that was to get the deed of foundation sanctioned and confirmed by the supreme authority of the pope. On June 3, 1626, Urban VIII. published the bull, *Copiosa sedis Apostolicæ benignitas*, in which are embodied all the particulars of D. Caverel's foundation, and which now received the vicar of Christ's approval: *Ad perpetuam rei memoriam.*

We mentioned that one of the objects of the foundation was to supply a certain number of professors to the college of St. Vedast's. It was caused by the following circumstances. As soon as St. Gregory's was finished, the abbat thought he would like to build for his own monks a college in the university of Douai, and the plan he now proceeded to carry out. As a result, his foundations at Douai were, as the benedictine travellers Martène and Durand tell us a century later, "the most famous in the university."[1]

The opening of the college of St. Vedast's happened about the time when the opponents of the benedictines succeeded in depriving them of the professorship they held in the college of Marchienne.

"The following year (1621)," says Weldon, "the abbat of Marchin put out of the college of Marchin his own religious and the English fathers, where they had so long supported the honour of their nation and order, as being inferior in learning to none in the whole university; and their ejection (not for any demerits, but to make way for the jesuits, to whom the abbat would give that place), had been much lamented had it not been so timed by Providence that the new college of St. Vedast was ready to receive them with open arms, whither they returned by the abbat Caverel's orders and drew a great number of their scholars after them, though the schools of St. Vedast were not opened without great resistance of the university."[2]

This new college of St. Vedast necessitated an

---

[1] *Voyage Littéraire*, ii. p. 76. Attached to the college of St. Vaast was a school of some four hundred boys. [2] Weldon, 150.

arrangement of the houses to keep each community distinct. In his deed of foundation, the abbat, in his love for the monastery, charges the college with the repairs of the whole building. The church was to be common to the two communities. It was for the purpose of securing a constant supply of professors for this college, and also to make up to them for the loss of the lectureships at Marchienne college, that Caverel made the stipulations mentioned in his deed of foundation.

To this period also must be dated the foundation of the English college of St. Gregory's. It was already in existence in October 1622, and would very likely have been started before the foundation of that of St. Vedast. This school was evidently in a separate part of the building from that which the monks occupied. In 1626 the informer, Lewis Owen, tells us a little about it :—

"They have many other benefactors in that country, and withall they read a divinity lecture in their cloisters and have many scholars which are beneficial to them, and many gentlemen's sons (which are their friends and benefactors in England) do diet in the cloisters, but not in the same part where the monks live,[1] but in the other side of the cloister; for they, and all other monks and friars, will not have any secular man to know their private knavery."

[1] P. 94. In the inventories made for the visitation of St. Gregory's held in 1622 there is a mention of a "Schollers' Refectorie." The school does not seem to have been a large one; on the average some forty boys.

Having thus told the story of abbat de Caverel's foundation, it is necessary to dwell for a time on the fruits the monastery brought forth after so much tendering. First and chiefest of all is the large number of martyrs belonging to this monastery. On the illuminated parchment roll referred to above, are portraits of venerable Mark Barkworth (1601), the first of the Spanish monks to suffer for his conscience; George Gervase, 1608; John de Mervinia (John Roberts), the founder of St. Gregory's, 1610; Maurus Scott, 1612; and Thomas Tousta (Tonstall), 1616.[1] A noble contingent, in truth, of the "white-robed" army. And to these must be added, after the Union, the names of Ambrose Barlow, 1641; Philip Powell, 1646; and Thomas Pickering, 1679. Few monasteries now existing can look back on such a list. Surely it must be a good tree that could produce fruit so good and fair to the Master's eye as were these monks—true martyrs of obedience.

The pope had forbidden the Oath of Allegiance. Rightfully or wrongfully, mattered not to them. The abbat of abbats had spoken, and they obeyed. So to these "martyrs of the Oath" a halo peculiarly appropriate to monks has been given, and from them reflected on their monastery of St.

---

[1] Thomas Tonstall, a secular priest of Douai, publicly stated at his death that he had made a vow of becoming a monk. As there is a baptism of desire, so is there also a profession of desire. The second, third, and fourth were conventuals of the house.

Gregory's. The whole benedictine order counts them as gems in the *Corona fratrum* which stands before the throne of God; but St. Gregory's claims them as sons and her especial glory and joy.[1]

The renown of these martyrs would go far to deepen the spirit of St. Gregory's. We may consider as one of the fruits of the first martyrs which resulted in the others, was the coming of the great ascetical master D. Augustine Baker to St. Gregory's. Together with the early members of the old English congregation, he had been designed for Dieuleward when a share of that house was given to them by the Spanish fathers, its founders. But D. Baker never became a conventual of St. Lawrence's, and, as far as can be found out, never even set foot in it. His life, since his profession by D. Sigebert Buckley, had been passed in retirement, far away from the turmoil which sorted not with his nature. He set himself to cultivate that gift of prayer he was afterwards to teach to others. He was probably acquainted with the community for some time past, and knew some of them intimately during the business of the Union. His reputation also had won him friends there, and,

---

[1] The news of a martyrdom was the occasion of great rejoicings. "Instead of dressing the church in black and singing of requiems we put on all the best ornaments, and with the greatest solemnity possible we sing the most joyful hymn *Te Deum*, and invite all the faithful to partake in our joy for such great triumphs" (Weldon, i. 26). Bound up in the MS. of Weldon's *Life of James II.* (in the British Museum) are some of these public invitations.

moreover, one of his spiritual children was a member of that house. The president, D. Barlow, after the chapter of 1621, was anxious to secure his services for St. Gregory's, so that by word and example he might train up the community in the monastic method of prayer, of which he was so great an exponent. But D. Baker had for some time longer to remain in England collecting material for the *Apostolatus*. In 1624, after having been several times invited with great kindness by D. Barlow, he came to Douai. But his stay was not then to be for any time. He had not finished his work; and "not finding a convenience suitable to his mind" he went on to Cambrai (July 1624), to the newly formed convent of English nuns, where, as we shall tell in its place, he trained them in the spiritual life.[1] The ordinary of this house was the prior of Douai, of which monastery D. Baker was henceforth a conventual.

Among his spiritual children had been the future martyr, D. Philip Powell. A fellow-townsman, at the age of sixteen he was sent from Abergavenny to London to study law (1610) under the care of D. Baker. He remained with him nearly four years, and was sent by him on business into Flanders, and "coming to Douai he was so inflamed with a great desire of being a monk among the English benedictines of St. Gregory's in that town."[2] This

---

[1] D. Maihew was that year the chaplain to the nuns, and he died the following September.

[2] Challoner, *Memoirs of Missionary Priests* (ed. 1878), vol. ii. p. 196.

would be another tie between D. Baker and this monastery.

During his stay at Cambrai, D. Baker's system of spirituality, which is so different from the discursive method, excited a good deal of opposition, not only among his brethren, but outside also. To put his system (it is only that of the old saints) in a few words, it consists in the active work of putting oneself at the disposal of God, and trusting to the Author of all holiness to perfect the work of sanctification. The soul has to *co-operate* with God and to follow His leading, not to go before nor to hurry on. She will use all the means He provides, and in the way He suggests to her. In fact, D. Baker teaches that sanctification is an individual work, and that God deals with us each one separately.[1]

For the perfection of his work God allowed it to be called into question and to be severely criticised. The vicar of the nuns at Cambrai, D. Francis Hull, a laurentian, caused him very great trouble,[2] and many others took up the question in a spirit adverse to D. Baker. The superiors of the congregation in-

---

[1] "A certain religious priest who was a person of note in the mission asked him the difference between his spirituality and that of others. He answered that the difference was not between spirituality and spirituality, but between spirituality and no spirituality; for his adversaries did neither teach any spirituality nor require any in their subjects or disciples, only they did forbid and hinder anybody to withdraw themselves from under their *magisterium*" (Anthony à Wood's *Breviate*).

[2] When D. Hull died at S. Malo (1645), Weldon says: "He sorely repented himself on his death-bed" (p. 186).

stituted a rigorous inquiry into the system. During this trial his great help was the staunch advocacy of D. Leander, who, as president, in 1633 brought the investigation to an end. A solemn confirmation of his teaching was passed, in the course of which it is said :—

"That the Divine calls, inspirations, inactions, influences of God's grace, joined with the humble frequent use of the sacraments of Christ, are the most noble and sublime means to spirituality; without which, to endeavour after contemplation and perfection were to fly without wings. And that these calls or holy lights and inspirations are always to be regarded, but chiefly in prayer and conversation with God. And that whosoever neglecteth his interior, nor hearkening to the interior voice or allocution of the Holy Ghost, nor labouring to direct his external observances, to taste God more sweetly, to see Him more clearly, to love Him more ardently, and to enjoy Him more intimately in his soul and spirit, can never attain to purity of intention and the spirit of contemplation, though he be never so exact in external observance and austere in corporal mortification."

Although D. Baker had been vindicated, the opposition did not cease when, after nine years, he left Cambrai and returned to his monastery at Douai.[1] Here he lived in the strictest solitude

[1] In the Rushworth papers at the Bodleian are a number of documents on this controversy which show how strong was the opposition.

compatible with conventual life, but his holy conversation bore much fruit.

"He brought many religious from a tepid life to a fervent practice of prayer, and drew many secular youths from their sinful excesses to a life of devotion, and some also to a state of religious profession."[1]

With the younger portion of the community[2] he had a great deal of influence, and under his guidance their love of prayer emulated that of the dames at Cambrai. Even, as we see, with some of the college youths he did a great work, and two of them—Francis Gascoigne and Joseph Errington—died in their youth with the reputation of sanctity. Nor was his influence for good confined to St. Gregory's. He was in high repute at the secular college, where he formed many to virtue and to a habit of prayer. At Douai he remained about five years, and then, in his old age, was sent out on the mission. The exact reasons have not fully appeared. But the opposition which had sought to condemn his spiritual teaching would not see with favour his success at Douai. When it was known that he was again to be sent on the perilous English mission there was a great outcry. Dr. Kellison, the president of the secular college,

---

[1] Anthony à Wood's *Breviate*.

[2] At the chapter of 1633 the community at St. Gregory's consisted of 19 priests, 5 choir religious, and 1 lay brother, the lowest number it has been since the Union. In 1621 there were 29; in 1625, 40; in 1629, 34; and now in 1633, 25. At this time, this single monastery had to bear, by far, the greater share of supplying new members for the mission in England.

made many efforts to have him kept at Douai, were it only for the sake of his own students. But it was of no avail, and in 1638 he went to England for the last time. But he left behind him a living influence which carried St. Gregory's through many trials. His eminently benedictine spirit, learned at Padua and ripened at Douai, is much needed nowadays. Amid the perpetual rush and hurry of modern life, and the multiplicity of occupations imposed on one, a simple, quiet, straightforward spirit of prayer such as D. Baker taught is necesssary to escape the evils about us, and to do thoroughly and steadily the work to which we are called.

While D. Baker was living at Cambrai the dispute with bishop Smith concerning jurisdiction broke out, and D. Rudisind Barlow, prior of St. Gregory's, took the part we have mentioned in the preceding chapter. He felt deeply what he considered the ungrateful conduct of the bishop, whom he had so warmly recommended to the authorities in Rome. In the beginning of December 1624, before the dispute began, shortly after the death of Dr. Bishop, D. Barlow wrote a letter to Propaganda, the salient passages of which we here give, as they show how loyal the benedictines were to the cause of their secular brethren :—

"MOST ILLUSTRIOUS AND MOST REVEREND LORDS OF THE MOST ANCIENT SENATE OF THE CATHOLIC CHURCH,—Peradventure we do a new thing and hitherto unaccustomed—yet, as we hope, neither ungrateful nor unpleasant to your piety—monks endeavouring to promote the cause of secular priests, although truly howsoever the abusive speech of the vulgar distinguisheth the clergy from the regulars, as if the secular priests should only constitute the clergy, but the regulars should by no means belong to the body of the clergy. Yet we benedictines were always of a far other opinion, esteeming even ourselves to be some part of the clergy, although not a ruling part, yet an assisting part, out of the most ancient privileges of the see apostolic. We do not, therefore, a thing different from our profession if we suffer together in the difficulties of the English clergy, since we judge the same in part to extend to ourselves. Verily we should not deserve to be under Christ, the Head of the clergy, if we should not suffer together with the body, especially with the body of the English clergy, of which we remember the greater part by far in the primitive church of the English to have been of our fathers, the monks of St. Benedict. . . . Hence it is that under the best and most prudent old man of pious memory, Dr. William Bishop, the most reverend ordinary of England and bishop of Chalcedon, the pious foundations of a wholesome concord were laid[1] between the seculars and regulars, the workmen of the mission, we benedictines agreeing. . . .

"For we have received (not without great dolour

[1] The benedictines were always ready to meet his wishes in every particular.

of mind) from two chief men, Master Matthew Kellison and Master Richard Smith, ancient priests and old doctors of divinity, who among others were nominated to our most holy lord to undergo the episcopal charge, that many things are objected by some, only out of a show of the zeal of God, but in truth out of a hope of retarding that business, than which *there is none more necessary for the advancement of religion and piety in England.* . . . But we, emulating the humanity and sincerity of our fathers, and seeking the glory of Christ, not our own honour, desire the peace, profit, and increase of the secular clergy as much as our own tranquillity. . . .

"Therefore we benedictines, your humble servants and sons, beseech you that, rejecting their accusations (which denegate the same of the best priests only that they themselves alone, in a clergy without a head, may shine, as it were, by an *Antiperistisis*, that they may seem hierarchical, and by a division of minds in the clergy, may think that the best way to greatness lieth open to them), you would be pleased to grant a bishop to our England, seeing that no province of the catholic world hath more need of one." [1]

In reply to this, D. Barlow was ordered to recommend, in his own and brethren's name, one who should succeed Dr. Bishop; and he recommended, among others, Dr. Richard Smith, who was consecrated in 1625. How another gregorian, D. Leander

[1] Prynne's *The Popish Royal Favourite*, p. 60.

Jones, brought about a second reconciliation has been already told.

Among the visitors, or even perhaps postulants, at Douai at this time was the famous Chillingworth, who had (1631) become a catholic. In that interesting book *The Lady Falkland, her Life*, in which there are many details of benedictine missioners, there is the following reference to Chillingworth and his stay at Douai: "Also, Mr. Chillingworth (who, having been a fellow at Trinity College in Oxford, and there, by reading, became a catholic) went to Douai, to the benedictine college, where, not shining so much as he expected, for there he found young students able to do that which gave him matter to admire ever after, he returned to Oxford a protestant—at least no catholic."[1]

In 1634 a gregorian died, about whom there is a strange story told by Prynne, which illustrates the progress of the benedictines on the mission and the friends they made.

"Lewis Cooke, general of the benedictines, dying without issue at Temple Cowly, in Oxfordshire, where he had purchased divers lands and goods, his brother, a civilian in Ireland, learning of it, comes over and claims his lands as heir, his goods as administrator to him. The benedictines withstood his claim to both, alledging that he had purchased both goods and lands with the money of the order, and for their use and maintainance only; and by

[1] Page 56.

Sir William Havard and their court friends there made such a strong party against the heir that, despairing of his own right, he made his addresses to Sir John Bankes, the king's attorney, and procures a commission of inquiry, with a *fiat* under his hand, dated 2nd January 1635, to entitle the king to the lands and goods as a mortmain purchased for the use of the monks, whereupon they compounded with the heir and gave him £300, as I am creditably informed by Mr. Bernard, who drew up the commission, whereupon it proceeded no further."[1]

Another monk, D. John Huddleston, should be here mentioned.[2] His name is known in connection with the conversion of Charles II. After the battle of Worcester, when Charles was hiding in Mr. Whitgrave's home at Moseley, where D. Huddleston was the chaplain, the king spent a great deal of his time with the monk, and, taking up a MS.

[1] *The Popish Royal Favourite*, p. 64. The Lewis Cooke here referred to was D. Justus Edner, *alias* Rigge. The little that is known of him is as follows: A Londoner, of good rank, he went in his fifteenth year to Valladolid. Although his parents were catholics, he does not seem to have been brought up one, for, before his admission to the English college, he had lived for a year at the college of St. Omers, where he was reconciled to the church by Fr. "George," S.J. He was received into the English college January 10, 1600, and took the mission oath in the following December. In the September of 1603 he was one of a body who left the college and joined the benedictines at San Benito. After his ordination he went on the mission. He must have been a man of great worth and ability, for he was chosen, in the chapter of 1625, as president, but would not accept the office. His election to the presidency, perhaps, led Prynne to describe him as "general of the benedictines."

[2] He was professed in the mission.

treatise, *The Short and Plain Way to the Faith and Church*, written by his uncle, D. Richard Huddleston, a Cassinese monk, the king read it attentively and then said —

"I have not seen anything more plain and clear upon this subject; the arguments here drawn from succession are so conclusive, I do not conceive how they can be denied."

The friendship begun under these circumstances ripened; and when the monastery at Somerset House was started in 1662, D. John was one of the community, and when the king was dying (February 5, 1685), while the ante-chamber was thronged with courtiers and Anglican clergy, he was smuggled up by a back staircase, and there reconciled Charles to the church and gave him the last sacraments.

Another of fame was the learned D. Serenus Cressy. Once a prebendary of Windsor and dean of Leighlin, and a great friend of the Falklands, on his conversion he intended to join the carthusians, but was attracted to St. Gregory's by the reputation it enjoyed for literary pursuits. He was professed in 1649, and is well known for the compilation he made of D. Baker's treatises under the name of *Sancta Sophia*. He began also, mostly from materials collected by D. Baker, a *Church History of Great Britain*, which, unfortunately, never got beyond the first volume. He died at West Grinstead, 1674, where he was chaplain to the Caryll family, a member of which, D. Alexius Caryll, had been with him at Douai and was at that time prior of St. Gregory's.

In 1675 St. Gregory's was honoured by a visit from cardinal Philip Howard, then on his way to Rome. He stayed at the secular college the day of his arrival, and the following day visited St. Gregory's, where he was received by the whole community and led into the church in solemn procession, where the *Te Deum* was sung and the ritual for such receptions fully carried out. From the church he turned into the cloisters, and was regaled with a splendid banquet. A panegyric was there addressed to him by Richard (B. Wilfrid) Reeves, a religious student of the college, which was afterwards printed. "All which," says Anthony à Wood, "was so well performed that viscount Stafford was pleased to say that it was the only fit reception his eminence had met with in all his journey."[1]

We will now take a glimpse at the daily life at St. Gregory's up to the time of the Revolution. Ecclesiastical studies held a high place; and from the *Voyage Litteraire* of DD. Martène and Durand we learn that the fathers taught St. Thomas', as being the surest and most solid method. They had a library of their own, some 5000 books, and access to the larger library of St. Vedast's.[2] To give an idea of the "lazy" monk's

---

[1] Father Palmer, O.P., *Life of Cardinal Howard*, p. 162.
[2] *Voyage Litteraire*, ii. p. 76.

day, we give the *horarium* observed at St. Gregory's: 3.45. A.M. Rise. 4 A.M. Matins and lauds, recited; half-hour mental prayer; prime *sung;* prime B.M.V., recited. 6.30 A.M. Private study; masses; breakfast for those who had permission. 8 A.M. Lectures and disputations. 10 A.M. Little hours B.M.V., recited; tierce, mass, sext, *sung.* 11.30 A.M. Dinner. 12 noon. None *sung;* vespers and compline B.M.V., recited. 12.30 P.M. Siesta. 1 P.M. Hebrew or Greek lecture. 2 P.M. Vespers *sung.* 2.30 P.M. Lectures and disputations. 4 P.M. Private study. 6 P.M. Supper. 6.30 P.M. Recreation. 7.30 P.M. Public spiritual reading; compline *sung;* matins and lauds B.M.V., recited; half-hour mental prayer. 8.45 P.M. Retire. From this busy day we gather that all the day-hours were sung; matins and lauds were recited, except on feast days, when the whole or parts were sung according to the solemnity; tierce, vespers, and compline were sung *morosius;* the rest *rotundius;* but the *Benedictus* and the *Magnificat* always *valde solemniter*, except on the great feasts, when they too were sung. The bells chimed at the *Te Deum.* During the meditation the monks knelt, facing their stalls and having their hoods up. The little office of our Lady was recited every day, till Benedict XIV., in 1748, released them from the obligation. The conventual mass, sung every day, DD. Martène and Durand tell us, was celebrated *avec beaucoup de majesté.* This, coming from monks fresh from the liturgical glories of French and German abbeys, is praise indeed. It shows, too, that the liturgical spirit is one of the fundamental characteristics of St. Gregory's, and is one of the sources from which the community has drawn its life. A chapter was held on every Friday. Only one hour was allotted to recreation in the day; but there were most likely periods, such as vacation time, when the religious had a longer rest from their work.

This life of prayer and study, together with the solemn recitation of the Divine office, was the counterpart of the old English benedictine life which the monks of St. Gregory's aimed at. It was an ascetic life; but the austerities were tempered with a wise discretion. The use of the discipline and other bodily mortifications were practised as conventual acts, and did much to nurture the manly Christian life.

The good monks in their peaceful cloister were not without feeling the effects of the stirring times.

In 1667 the siege of Douai by Louis XIV. forced the monks to take up a new character. Owing to the smallness of the garrison, the citizens, the professors, and even the clergy were armed, and had posts assigned to them on the ramparts. From the *Chroniques de Douai*[1] we learn the duties put on the monks:—

"The company of William Caudron was destined to defend the Porte d'Ocre with the dominicans, the professors, and students of St. Vedast, the English benedictines, and the religious of Furnes."

[1] Vol. ii. p. 356.

On the morning of the 1st of July 1667, the French army invested the town, and all were ordered to their posts. On the 5th the king summoned the magistrates to surrender. The next day the capitulation was signed.

"In the year 1667, on the 2nd of July, Lewis the Great besieged Douai, and entered it on the 7th. He did our fathers the honour to hear mass in our church, when some one boldly laid on his prie-dieu the famous book written against benefices *in commendam;* but D. Hitchcock was adroit enough to get the book before the king came." [1]

In 1710 Douai was again besieged, this time by the allies. Marlborough began the investment on 22nd April, and planted his chief batteries in such a position that St. Gregory's was fully exposed to their fire.

"Some of our religious sheltered themselves as they could in neighbouring monasteries; the rest with the prior abided the siege. R. F. Pullein took their boys with him to Cambrai, that from thence he might get to speak to the duke of Marlborough, who recived him very civilly and promised he would favour the house; and so, though all the force of the batteries was opposite to it—the house was more frightened than hurt." [2]

Two of the monks of St. Vedast not only went

---

[1] Weldon, ii., *in loco.*

[2] Weldon, p. 253. Marlborough told D. Michael Pullein that he had received special instructions from queen Anne upon the subject.

to prince Eugene and Marlborough, with letters of recommendation, but managed to visit the besieging batteries which menaced their colleges. "D. Hurtrel," writes D. Ignatius in his Memoirs, "addressed himself to an artilleryman from Mons, and begged of him to spare the two colleges, which were in full view, and which he pointed out." On the man's promise, D. Hurtrel wrote in the trenches a note by which he engaged to pay this man and his company a certain sum if he kept his word.

"The artilleryman kept his word, and when the town was taken he went to the college and presented the note to the regent, who paid him on the spot. In fact, during all the siege (over two months) neither ball nor shell touched either college, except when they were destroying the steeple of St. Albin's. Then the college which was behind the church received a few balls.

Towards the end of the century they rebuilt their school, little thinking for how short a time it was to serve their turn.[1] Before the final crash came the gregorians were looking far afield, and there was a great chance offered of a settlement out in America. Already, in the early days of the Maryland Settlement, St. Gregory's had sent out there one of her sons, D. Ambrose Bride, and the tie had been strengthened by a Marylander, D. Paul Chandler, who came to Douai in the early part

[1] This building still exists, and forms the main part of the college of St. Edmunds.

of last century, and was professed there in 1705. When bishop John Carroll, the founder of the American hierarchy, was consecrated at Lulworth, it was an English benedictine, bishop Walmesley, who laid hands on him.[1] Shortly after he had settled in his vast diocese, one of his first thoughts was to secure English benedictines to help him. He wrote (September 19, 1794) to D. Benedict Pembridge, a gregorian missioner at Dorking, saying: "I said that your letter was a precious favour, but nothing can be more pleasing to me than the prospect of having in my diocese a settlement of English benedictines. . . . If, therefore, your venerable chapter has encouraged *your* idea, I promise, as long as God grants life, to give the undertaking every encouragement in my power."

The monks were not to go out as missioners only, but as a monastery. For the bishop proposes Pittsburg "as the properest place for a settlement and school." But unfortunately the French revolution, the effects of which we have now to trace, prevented the bishop's offer being accepted.

The thunder-cloud which for a long time had hung over France at last broke, and drove the monks of St. Gregory's away from their old house at Douai. A rapid sketch of the events of the time, as far as they affected the monks, must here be given.

---

[1] Thus the flourishing American Church of to-day date sits succession from one of the English sons of St. Benedict.

We can trace some of the events from a printed statement (in French) entitled " A Brief Memorandum of what has happened from 1790 till the present treaty to the establishments founded in France by the catholics of the three united kingdoms; with some observations on the papers printed by M. Ferris." It was evidently written between 1815 and 1816, and is signed by John Brewer, doctor in theology of the faculty of Paris, and superior-general of the English benedictines; Henry Parker, superior of the English benedictine house, Rue St. Jacques, Paris; Richard Marsh, formerly superior of the English benedictines of St. Lawrence's, Dieuleward.

The first law affecting the monasteries, dated November 7, 1790, confirmed all the foreign establishments in possession of the property with power to administer. The religious were no longer recognised as such, and were forbidden to appear in public in their habits. A dispensation was got from Rome, August 30 of the next year, allowing them for the time to put aside their religious dress, and to receive novices without the usual publicity. This decree was followed by another of March 8, 1793, which declared that all French colleges belonged to the nation. But the property of the foreign establishments was specially exempted. When the revolutionary party had worked the iniquity of the king's death, and had proclaimed war against England, and the decree of October 10 ordered the arrest of all British subjects and the seizure of their property, the benedictines still thought themselves safe, as the exception made in their favour by the law of March 8 had not been revoked. But those who undertook to execute this latter decree arrested them as a measure of safety, so they said, and did much worse than sequestrate their goods.

In Monsieur Dechristé's interesting work, *Douai pendant la Revolution*, we find a list of the gregorian *familia* taken from the *Archives Départementales*. We give it as it stands :—

"P. Jérôme Sharrock, prieur, 50 ans; P. Anselme Lorymer, sous-prieur, 49 ans; P. Georges Johnson, procureur, 40 ans; P. Laurent Barnes, prêtre, 40 ans; P. Pierre Kendalt (*Kendall*), prêtre, 32 ans; P. Augustin Lawson, prêtre, 32 ans; P. Jacques Higgnison (*Higginson*), prêtre, 26 ans; P. Henri Lawson, prêtre, 26 ans; P. Jean Culshaw, sous-diacre, 23 ans.

"*Novices.*— Frère Jean Moris, 21 ans; Frère Guillaume Allan, 20 ans; Fr. Thomas Barker, 20 ans; Fr. Georges Turner, 19 ans.

"*Frères Convers.* — Guillaume Starrock (*Sharrock*), 73 ans; Guillaume Quince, 45 ans; Thomas Herdness (*Br. Francis Holderness*), 25 ans; Guillaume Wilson, 36 ans.

"*Pères en Mission.* —P. Jean Warlmal (*Warmoll*), 72 ans; P. Thomas Barr, 52 ans; P. Michael Pembridge, 66 ans; P. P. Eowland (*Rowland*) Lacou, 46 ans; P. Jean Walkensonn (*Watkinson*), 62 ans;

P. Edmund Hadlet, 46 ans; P. Guillaume Calwel (*Caldwell*), 52 ans; P. Guillaume Digby, 46 ans; P. Arclubald Magdonald (*Macdonald*), 53 ans; P. Thomas Bennett, 67 ans; P. Jean Naylon, 52 ans; P. Richard Butler, 41 ans; P. Joseph Hadley, 51 ans; P. Guillaume Allan, 40 ans."[1]

The *familia* of St. Gregory's, therefore, at the time of the revolution consisted of twenty-two priests, one sub-deacon, four choir novices, and four lay brothers; thirty-one in all, if the above list be correct.

The effect of the decrees was soon felt at Douai. From a manuscript narrative of one of the victims we learn some particulars of the suppression of St. Gregory's. On 8th August 1793 an order reached the town that all persons suspected of ill-will to the convention were to be expelled within twenty-four hours. There were, of course, many English in Douai, and the benedictines, as monks, came under the more immediate attention of the authorities. Only a few hours were allowed them to pack up as much of their personal property as they could carry; and with the hope of some day returning to their old home, they hid part of the rest. On the afternoon of the 9th, the monks bade a sad farewell to the house which had sheltered them for so long. They went to their country house at Esquerchin, two or three miles out of Douai, and there for some weeks remained under strict guard. The authorities, in the name of

[1] *Douai pendant la Revolution*, p. 278.

liberty, were determined to keep for themselves whatever the monks possessed, and had no intention of allowing the rabble to share in the plunder. So they ordered D. Jerome Sharrock to remain in the town to protect the monastery from pillage.

"It was during their stay at Esquerchin that a plan was concocted to effect their escape out of the country, and was attempted to be put into execution. They left their country house at night in parties of two or three together, and agreed to make for a certain farmhouse where they knew they would be safe, as the farmer had been in his youth a student with them at the college. Here they arrived safely, and were entertained while they were resting. They left in a body under a trusty guard. By midnight they had got to within half a mile of the Austrian lines. But they fell in with the French sentinels and were fired upon. One half of them got back to England, the rest were seized, and in the morning were taken to headquarters at Monsen, thence to the prison of the Annonciades. Here they remained till they returned to Esquerchin. At the beginning of October they received orders to return to Douai."[1]

Any gleam of hope given thereby was dispelled upon their arrival; for they found they were being recalled to a prison. Their cloisters were in the hands of soldiers, who now became their jailers, and kept them under watch for about a week of

[1] Allanson.

terror and uncertainty. They knew not when the order might come to lead them out to the guillotine, which was then busy with its bloody work of regenerating France. But at last orders were received to remove them, together with all other English prisoners, to the citadel at Doullens.

On Wednesday, 16th October 1793, the benedictines, together with their friends from the secular college, bade adieu to Douai and steadfastly set their faces towards their future prison. The departure of the monks was witnessed in silent sympathy by many of the inhabitants of the town, who had grown to love the English sons of St. Benedict. Of the monks there were only half-a-dozen;[1] some had, as we have seen, escaped, and others had been sent over to England by their superiors with the college boys when the storm was about to break. Two lay brothers, whose age and infirmities made it impossible to travel as far as Doullens, were allowed to remain behind; one of them died soon after, broken-hearted at the desolation which had overtaken his home. Together with the monks were forty-one members of the secular college, and those who together had laboured for the conversion of England were now to hasten on that event by their companionship in suffering and imprisonment.

[1] In a list given in Monsieur L. Dechristé's book the names of the benedictines at Doullens are given as Jerome Sharrock, A. Lorymer, S. Lord, J. Barker, J. Eldrigh, Barker (*Barber*).

As night was fast closing in, the prisoners arrived at Arras, and were at once huddled into the barracks for the night. Early the next morning, though footsore and weary, they were marched off to Doullens, which was reached that evening. The forty-seven prisoners were thrust for the night into a dark underground passage, and in this "Black Hole" had to shift as well as they could. Next morning they were taken up to a garret which was to be their home for some time to come. Here, half famished and in hourly fear of their lives, these holy men began to lead lives as regular as if they were still in their monastery or college. The prior comforted them with holy words and gave them heart. By his advice, old habits of prayer, study, and recreation were resumed.[1]

They rose between six and seven o'clock in the morning, cleaned up their garret as tidily as possible, stowed away in a corner, till it was required for the next night, the straw upon which they had slept, went to a trough for their morning ablutions, to the great astonishment of the French guard who were among the "great unwashed," then had public prayers and meditations; after which followed a scanty meal on dry bread and very diluted milk by way of breakfast. Then came time for study, broken by a quarter of an hour's exercise under the care of the guards. Dinner was at noon; but this was irregular, as they had to wait the convenience

[1] *Downside Review*, vol. ii. p. 8.

of the soldiers. Recreation succeeded dinner, lasting till two o'clock; then studies till half-past four, then recreation again. The evening was spent in reading. Supper-time followed, irregularly; and at nine o'clock the straw was prepared for the night's rest. Night prayers were said publicly, and praying for "a quiet night and a perfect end," the forty-seven, with as much ventilation as they could contrive and as was compatible with screening themselves from the cold of the night, forgot the sorrows of one day and prepared themselves to rest to meet the hardships of another.

It was an edifying picture, this harmony of the benedictines and seculars; and it is touching to read the narrative of these latter, and to see in what terms they speak of the monks their companions, nay, true messengers of comfort, in this day of common distress. The picture thus drawn suggests, too, another thought; and causes a pang of regret as we think of the dissensions that reigned at Wisbeach; and reflect how much bitterness and misfortune would have been spared the English Church had the spirit at Wisbeach been that which filled the hearts of all at Doullens.[1]

[1] We cannot resist giving here an extract from an account from the pen of a priest and professor of the English college, who was one of the prisoners. After giving details of the hardships endured and of the manner in which they spent their day, the writer proceeds:—

"Mr. Sharrock's family shared with us all the rigours of confinement, and by their company, conversation, example, and courage, helped and edified us in every change of scene and distress. They were but six in number, consequently it was easier for them to find

Faculties had been got from the bishop of Amiens, in whose diocese they were, and thus they had also the consolation of the sacrament of Penance. Christmas, Lent, Easter, and Whitsuntide came and found them still prisoners. And as time went on the severity of their treatment was increased. An unfortunate guard, who had been found guilty of

a regular meal at a fixed time. This they did at the licensed alehouse (cantine), if anything like ale can be found in France, which was for one part of our time within the narrow precincts of our enclosure. In this alone they may be said to have fared better than ourselves. But bad was the best. Their finances, like our own, were limited and precarious. French fare, at the time when the laws of *maximum* and *réquisitions* had nearly shut up shops, shambles, and markets, was very poor doings for hungry stomachs, at any price that their poor pockets could afford. We found more than sympathetic friendship at their hands. Their extraordinaries were liberally extended to many of us. A cup of coffee was a luxury, and the writer of these lines and others have often received it from their generous hand. A glass of unadulterated and generous wine, since the time that the law of *maximum* had frightened all wine into vinegar and had poisoned all brandy with vitriol, was a very scarce boon indeed. Some friends, however, supplied them with some of a very choice and valuable quality, and this their liberality poured out to the sick, for the use of the altar, and to individuals, with the hospitable charity of the benedictine religious. Greater cordiality and union could not exist between brothers than existed between the English benedictines and us. And at this day I and others cherish the recollection of the Black Hole, the garret, and other circumstances of our confinement, with a soothing satisfaction for the acquisition of six such friends as Mr. Sharrock, Mr. Lorymer, Mr. Lord, Mr. Barker, Mr. Eldridge, and Mr. Barber. *Animas candidiores nusquam tulit tellus.* To them we were indebted for the great happiness of being able to say mass. They had just time enough before the arrival of the gens d'armes at Esquerchin to secrete a chalice, an altar-stone, about a hundred unconsecrated hosts, wax, and one complete set of green vestments. Providentially the whole arrived safe and unknown to our persecutors. Even in our garret we ventured to say mass; and showing them too much kindness, was for that very reason sent off to the scaffold. It was news of no uncommon occurrence in those days to learn that one or other of their aristocratic fellow-prisoners had been called out to the same fate; and the holy confessors, whose numbers had been lately increased by the inmates of the college of

thrice at least was the Holy Sacrifice offered under circumstances as extraordinary as history records of the days of ancient persecution. Our garret was directly above the bed-chamber of the sub-commandant and sergeant Oliver. To have risen at an earlier hour would have displeased or perhaps given room for suspicion. For how could forty-seven individuals rise without some noise? We were at a loss for a table on which to place our altar-stone and altar-clothes. Necessity, the mother of invention, erected an altar-table of a new construction. We had brought with us the baker's bread-basket. This we placed on the wide side. To lift it as convenient a height as possible, we set it upon boxes behind the chimney which I mentioned before. We then took one of the windows from its hinges and placed it upon the basket. A blanket was spread to hide the whole, and answered the purpose of an antependium, and by covering the pane of glass in the middle made it more convenient for placing the altar-stone. The altar-stone, the altar-cloths, the chalice, crucifix, missals, cruets, vestments, and wax tapers were soon in readiness. Each man dressed as quietly as could be done, knelt on his own bed to prevent noise, and thus mass was said at least on one Sunday on All Saints and All Souls. Only one French gentleman, a fellow-prisoner from Doway and a man of great piety, was privy to our devotions, and was admitted to assist. On Sunday, 3rd November, we celebrated the last mass in this place, for on Monday morning our accommodation was changed. From the garret we descended to the ground floor. In the corner (of one of the two rooms in which the English prisoners were henceforth confined) was a brick hob, with two convenient charcoal fire-places, to warm and dress our ragouts, or to keep a second course hot till ordered on the table. To us indeed it did not answer that purpose, but a much more noble and necessary end. It was our altar; and on it every Sunday and holiday for many months was offered the Holy Mass (*The Catholic Magazine* for 1831).

St. Omers, lived in daily expectation of receiving a like summons. How cheerfully it would have been met, and how gladly they would have laid down their lives for Christ's sweet sake, had He asked it of them, can well be imagined by the peaceful and religious behaviour of these men during such a prolonged imprisonment. They were truly martyrs in all but deed.[1]

A year had already passed in this state, and then at last hope began once more to revive. Robespierre had followed his victims, and the thirst for blood had been satiated. A petition was now drawn up by the prisoners, and leave was asked to return to Douai. Monsieur L. Dechristé gives us in his book a copy of the letter from the Commission for the Administration of Civil Affairs, dated Paris,

---

[1] Soon after the monks were taken to Doullens a search was made in their garden for supposed treasure. On November 9th the Mayor of Douai had the following notice from the District Directory : "DOUAY, *19th Brumaire, Year II. of the Republic.* We are told that some valuables have been hidden in the garden of the English benedictines. Could you not preside at this operation ? I would very willingly accompany you, as there is question of so interesting a discovery. Health and fraternity. D., *Vice-President.*" There is no record that they found anything ; but it is likely that the few things that had been smuggled away to Doullens were noticed when the inventory, taken by order of the Government as far back as April 1790, came to be examined. According to this inventory the church plate at Douai comprised four chalices, a monstrance, a ciborium, a processional cross, two acolytes' candlesticks, and two thuribles, all of silver. What became of this plate is clear from the minutes of the general council of the Commune for December 3, 1794 : "On the motion of a member, resolved that all the silver plate lying at the Hotel de Ville be sent to Paris to be cast into the national melting-pot." See Dechristé, *Douai pendant la Revolution,* p. 344.

10 Vendemiaire, An III. (1st October 1794), to the citizen-administrators of the district of Douai, ordering the benedictines at Doullens to be transferred to Douai and there confined in some building. When the transfer was accomplished they were also ordered to furnish the monks with necessary clothes, firing, and sufficient furniture, and the sum of two francs a day per head for their food. The council at Douai demurred and made excuses. They could find no proper place for the monks. But on the 6 *Frimaire*, An III. (26th November 1794), a notification from the citizen-administrator was received to say that the monks were already on their way back, and were to be confined in the Irish college.[1]

They left Doullens on the 24th of November, after more than thirteen months' imprisonment. But how changed they found Douai.

"The abomination of desolation had been in the holy places. The goddess of reason had been for a time worshipped there, where had dwelt the Holy of Holies.[2] The church, in which the daily office had been sung for more than a century and a half, had been used as a receptacle for bells, which had been plundered from the churches and were to be melted down and cast into cannons. The monks were still to consider themselves as prisoners, but were enabled to perform their conventual duties with some degree of regularity. Not in the church alone had impiety and vandalism done its ruinous work. The

[1] *Ibid.* pp. 366-371.   [2] In the Church of St. Pierre.

splendid libraries, the slow and sweet growth of years, were scattered; some of the books had been torn up for cartridges; others had been claimed as national property and had been transferred to the public library of the town, where many of them are to be seen bearing the old stamp of the monastery."[1]

It was clear Douai was no longer a safe shelter for them. Eyes were turning wistfully towards England, and the monks began to talk of returning home. The times seemed propitious. The penal laws had been relaxed; there were rumours of catholic emancipation; and England had opened her arms with generous sympathy to receive the *emigrés*. Would she not do the same for her own sons? Thus they argued, and at last made up their minds to make the venture. They sent in a petition for passports, and asked leave to return to their native land. On the 21 *Pluviose*, An. III. (9th February 1795), the Committee of Public Safety allowed the passports to be made out and gave leave for their departure. All was ready by the 2nd March, and early that morning the monks left for Calais and took passage on board an American vessel, and arrived that evening at Dover. Just a

---

[1] *Downside Review*, vol. ii. p. 10. A little detail of the state to which they were reduced is afforded by the following circumstance. The Directory of the district of Douai on the 18 *Nivose* (7th January 1795) gave orders that each monk should have two pocket handkerchiefs and an extra shirt apiece given him in the name of "the One and Indivisible Republic" (*Dechristé*, p. 370).

hundred years ago did they return and "take root amid an honourable people." Persecution had driven the monks away from England, and persecution had brought them back from exile.

Before they had been imprisoned at Doullens an old student of their school, Sir Edward Smythe, had invited them to come over to England and stay at his family seat of Acton Burnell, near Shrewsbury, which he generously placed at their disposal.[1] So,

[1] The following letter, written by prior Sharrock to Dr. Poynter, the vice-president of St. Edmund's college, where part of the old secular college at Douai was reformed, is not without its interest:—

"ACTON BURNELL, SHREWSBURY, *October* 3, 1795. DEAR SIR,—After different inquiries after yourself and the rest of our Doullens friends, I hear that you and Mr. Stapleton, with some others of our acquaintance, have taken up your quarters, at least for a time, at Old Hall Green. Our former friendship, so well cemented by our common adventures and a long captivity, makes me particularly curious to know what is become of all our fellow-prisoners. I have often regretted that our various avocations when we arrived in London allowed us to see so little of one another, and since our separation, though I have been in different parts of England, scarce have I met with one of the celebrated *Trente-deux* or their associates. I hear that several are with you; others in London, others in the North, &c. God be thanked, I do not yet hear that any one is yet dead. For my part I am settled, at least for the present, at a seat of Sir Edward Smythe's, my former *élève*, with nearly all my former family. The situation is pleasant, and healthy and retired. We see a newspaper about thrice a week, and have full leisure to contemplate at a distance the extraordinary circumstances and progress of that awful revolution of which we were once too near spectators. Shall we ever see Douai again? is a question which as naturally as frequently mingles itself with our reflections. No doubt the same very difficult problem often presents itself to your thoughts. . . . Our property may possibly enough be restored at the peace; what then to do with it will be another puzzle. One Mr. Higginson, who was confined with the Coutrai nuns at Compiègne, tells me that soon after we came over, there appeared another decree concerning us, declaron arrival in England, the travellers made their way to Acton Burnell, where they found installed some of the Dieuleward monks, to whom Sir Edward had for a time extended a welcome, until such time as his friends from Douai could come. The gregorians, together with some of the vedastine monks, soon settled down in their new quarters; and their generous benefactor did not seem able to do enough for them. He gave up a part of his mansion to their exclusive use, and buildings were added for their better accommodation. The school was resumed under the name of "Acton Burnell College," and some names which live in the history of our church are associated with that place. Thomas Brown, first bishop of Newport and Menevia; John Polding, first archbishop of Sydney; and William Morris, bishop of Mauritius, were schoolboys at Acton Burnell.

"Under this good confessor for the Faith, D Jerome Sharrock, monastic observance began once more to flourish on English soil, and until he died in 1808 he spent himself in forming his community in piety and learning. Humble and full of merit, he

ing that our property had been only sequestered and not confiscated. I wish Monsieur Despres may have seen the decree. I am told he is Mayor of Douay. He might avail himself of it in case our houses should be put up to sale. . . . If you are building, I presume you and your friends sometimes collect no little quantity of *mundanus pulvis*. Acton Burnell will be an excellent place to shake it off. Come then, by all means, to see us in due time. Remember me in the kindest terms to Mr. Stapleton and all our friends.—I am, dear Sir, and ever shall be, most sincerely yours, J. SHARROCK.' See Mgr. Ward's *History of St. Edmund's College*, pp. 150-152.

constantly refused the dignity of the episcopal office which was offered to him,[1] for he loved more to work for the good of his monastery, which was the very apple of his eye.

This settlement was from the first considered to be of a temporary nature. With innate delicacy of feeling, the monks felt they could not impose upon the liberality of their good benefactor for one day longer than was necessary; and the superiors for a long time were on the look-out for a suitable place. After some search, this was found at Mount Pleasant, Downside, a property situated upon the Mendip Hills, about twelve miles from Bath and eight from the cathedral city of Wells. On March 25, 1814, the property was transferred by purchase to "the reverends Richard Kendal, Thomas Lawson, and James Higginson, clerks," for the sum of £7338. But D. Kendal was never to see his community settled at Downside; for after completing the purchase, and on his way back to Acton Burnell, he suddenly was taken ill at Wootton Warwen, and there he died.

D. Augustine Lawson succeeded him as prior; and a month after, on Wednesday, April 28, 1814, the little party of monks and boys left the shelter of Acton Burnell and set out for their new home at Downside. Travelling was slow in those days, and inconveniences had to be accepted as cheerfully as

[1] His brother, D. Gregory Sharrock, prior at Douai, 1775-80, was consecrated vicar-apostolic of the Western District, 1780.

could be by those on a journey. But, still, travellers' tales, if full of adventures, were also often spiced with the humorsome. It was so in this case. The party was under the command of D. Leveaux,[1] an old maurist monk who, on his escape to England, had joined the gregorians at Acton Burnell. When they arrived at Worcester they spent the night at the Star Inn, where, as soon as supper was served, D. Leveaux astonished the waiters by intoning the monastic grace used at Acton Burnell. Upon their arrival next day at Downside in cold, dismal weather, they found a large bare house awaiting them—no furniture (it was still on the way), and no fire. But the superior did not consider the difficulties of the first few days sufficient to excuse him from seeing the ordinary routine of a conventual establishment carried out in detail. Choir was observed and the ordinary hours of study kept, although this latter (it is recorded) was difficult, as the books had not yet arrived. However, books are

[1] D. Martin Leveaux, a disciple of Montfauçon, a maurist, found a home with the gregorians when they settled down at Acton Burnell. He formally joined the *familia* of St. Gregory's by renewing his religious profession among them, August 22, 1798. He was made novice-master, and taught philosophy and theology. Subsequently he became sub-prior. In 1815 he kept his jubilee, and, with leave, resigned his offices and returned to France to take part in the hoped-for restoration of the maurist congregation. Upon the failure of the attempt, he still had hopes of rejoining the gregorian community in Douai. The old man ultimately withdrew to Senlis, where he lived like a hermit on the alms of the faithful, and never left his hut save on Sundays, when he would totter down to the parish church and assist at mass as sub-deacon. He died June 3, 1828.

not always essential to study, and the hours devoted to that purpose were probably not lost.

Meanwhile how had things been going on in Douai? The town, after the wild delirium was over, began to reflect, and missed the advantages the benedictines and other English establishments had brought. St. Gregory's always had had a good name, and the English custom was a consideration; and so, in 1801, we find an attempt was being made by the town to bring back the English establishments, or at least the benedictines. The authorities began to institute inquiries as to the state of the properties and buildings. And the following year a hint was given by a member of the government to the mayor, to press the matter as "the English guineas" would come in very useful.[1] But nothing was done, and St. Gregory's remained in the hands of the military till 1805. In that year Napoleon, the emperor, united all the religious foundations hitherto held separately by English, Scotch, and Irish, into one British United Establishment, and appointed Dr. Walsh, rector of the Irish college at Paris, administrator-general. He proceeded to take possession of all the properties, St. Gregory's included (1806), and collected the rents and used them for the United Establishment, from which the English do not seem to have got the slightest benefit. The townspeople of Douai opposed this measure, for they contended, with truth, that St. Gregory's really belonged to St.

[1] *Dechriste*, p. 387.

Vedast. They appealed to the emperor, but with no effect; for Dr. Walsh pulled down the old monastery of St. Gregory's, sold the materials for 8350 francs, let out the recently built college in lodgings, and carried off all the money to the Irish college in Paris. His procurator was D. Parker of the Paris house, who, when Dr. Walsh was removed from his post in 1809, succeeded him as administrator-general. In 1811 the college of St. Gregory's was leased out at a rent of 1700 francs to a Monsieur Barruel, who used it as a factory for beetroot sugar. The beautiful church was left to go to ruins.

The agent for the administrator wrote, March 14, 1811, to D. Parker, that "The church of the benedictines is falling to pieces. A short while ago a great mass, ten feet high, from a buttress, fell down into the street. I had the stones carried into the court of the college. The commissionaire of the police came next day and closed the street to traffic. The church is still in the hands of the military, and is partly filled with gun-carriages and wood. If you think you can get possession of this church, as M. Walsh did of the old monastery, I think it will soon be time for you to act."

But it was proposed by the government to use the church, which was large enough to hold 1500 persons, as one of the parish churches for the use of the town. The report on the state of the building says that the roof, windows, gutters, and flooring are in a very bad way, and it will cost quite 3600 francs to put them in repair. But the people preferred to use the old English franciscan church,[1] and St. Gregory's gradually fell into ruins. In 1812 the town, claiming it as national property, took no heed of D. Parker's protests, and finally pulled the church down and sold the ground and the materials.

When Louis XVIII. came to the throne by the Treaty of Peace, signed May 30, 1814, restoration and compensation were secured for all that had been sequestrated since the year 1792. It was hoped by this that the English property, both secular and regular, would be saved from the clutches of the "United Establishment." The king was petitioned to this effect. But Mr. Ferris, an Irishman, who had had a great deal to do with the removal of Dr. Walsh and afterwards of D. Parker, was, since 1813, the administrator; and he kept a tight hold over all the property. He sent round a circular to all the bishops and clergy of the United Kingdom, and proposed that the money for ecclesiastical education should go to Maynooth, and the rest be spent in France.

As regards the property of the English benedictines, whom he affects to call "ex-religious," he asks the bishop (who had nothing whatever to do with the matter) whether this had not better be annexed to his establishment in Paris. Mr. Ferris had been too bold. The English clergy would

---

[1] The present St. Jacques.

not see their funds diverted to Maynooth, and the matter was taken up so thoroughly that on January 25, 1816, the king dissolved the United British Establishment, and the separate possession of their properties was restored to the superiors, who were acknowledged by name. By some strange oversight the English benedictines were omitted, and it was only after great trouble that, eight months afterward, D. Parker and D. Lawson were put in respective possession of the Paris and Douai properties. But it was only a nominal possession after all; for on September 17, 1817, the *Bureau Gratuit de Surveillance* was instituted, which undertook the whole administration of the property, and allowed the superiors what it was considered necessary for current expenses. The Board had the power of interfering in the internal discipline of the house, and to make what regulations it thought fit. The superiors were at the mercy of the minister of the interior, who could suspend, remove, and appoint at his pleasure.

It took nine years to get our English foundations rescued from this control; and in 1826 an arrangement was sanctioned by the king which remains in force to the present day. The English property, both secular and regular, is under the guardianship of the State, and is in the department of the minister of public instruction. An administrator, under the control of the minister, is appointed on the recommendation of the English bishops. He receives all the rents, but must pay them into the treasury, whence he gets such sums as are approved of by the minister, among other purposes, for the education *in France* of ecclesiastical students who are to be nominated by those whose property is thus administered.

We must now go back to Downside. When the prospect of a return to Douai seemed possible, some of the community wanted to go back to France, and this seems to have been the desire of the general chapter, though the greater part of the community preferred to remain in England, But still the older men were longing after the old house, and, in September 1814, an estimate had been prepared by an architect at Douai for the thorough repair of the college. In the February 1815, the president, D. Brewer, writes to D. Parker: "I am glad our confrères, late of Acton Burnell, have altered their minds and now seem willing to return." The next month the prior of St. Gregory's writes that the news from Douai is encouraging. The tenant is willing to give up his lease without any compensation, and to restore the house to the state he found it, and that possession might be had within two weeks. But the "Hundred Days" broke out, and all the arrangements came to a standstill. "Before Bonaparte's return," writes the president, D. Brewer, "all our young people at Downside appeared very desirous to return to Douai. It will now require some address to bring them back to the same way of thinking."

The general chapter was then almost entirely in the hands of the missionary part of the congregation, and it had no wish to have St. Gregory's monastery in England. So, as soon as peace was again proclaimed, D. Lawson, the prior, and D. Barber went to Douai and took possession of the property. But Mr. Ferris, the administrator, swooped down upon them, and, seizing 3000 francs in the hands of the agent, threatened to eject the prior. However, some terms were come to, and Mr. Ferris departed. The college itself was found to be in an excellent state of repair, and all that was needed were a few coats of paint. After having ordered the necessary repairs, D. Lawson returned to England; and a storm (they were twenty hours at sea) did not encourage him to return at once to Douai. On December 6, 1815, he writes from Downside:—

"As soon as I obtain news that our concerns are settled, and that the church is returned to us, and that there are satisfactory reasons to consider the French Government firmly established, I shall, if money, which is very difficult to find, can possibly be procured, order every necessary preparation to be made at Douai for our return. I hope all impediments will be removed against the spring."

The following August (1816) the president and definitors met at Downside and decided, in so far as in them lay, that the community should leave England. And in the November the prior went again to Douai, where he learnt he would be administrator only of the college; that he would be under the jurisdiction of the diocese of Cambrai; that there was no hope of regaining the country house at Esquerchin; that the "United Establishment" had a heavy claim against him; and, then, that the government had determined to build a prison on the site of the old monastery and church, and were going to take a part of the garden for the same purpose. It would be useless to attempt to return under these circumstances; and the prior returned to Downside in the December for advice. The community resolutely set their face once for all against any further attempt to force them to leave England; and the president had in the following April to rescind his order. The property at Douai is still recognised by the French Government as belonging to the benedictines: and its gregorian owners having resolved to settle in England, no better use could be made of the building than to place it at the disposal of those who were desirous of restoring the monastery of St. Edmund's of Paris.

At Downside, then, the gregorians were determined to stay; and it was decided to build. The old manor-house would serve fairly well as a makeshift monastery. But a church and college must be raised. The project was a favourable opportunity of fighting the battle of the styles. Persons of influence urged the merits of a classical building. Sir John Cox Hippesley, M.P., a protestant landowner close by, provided at his own expense plans for building a "classical academy." But the mind of the community was set all the other way; and this, be it remembered, was before the revival of Christian art by the illustrious Pugin. Gothic art is so largely bound up with the traditions of the English benedictines that the Downside monks, now that they had determined to remain in England, could not find heart to forsake it. After much discussion the old English style, dear to our forefathers, carried the day, and plans were prepared by a young architect of Bath, a Mr. Goodridge. The foundation-stone was laid with great ceremony, on 11th July 1820. D. Luke Barber was then the prior, and he had the satisfaction of seeing, in three years' time, the church solemnly opened by bishop Baines. The new building cost £6628, and was considered at the time a marvellous piece of workmanship. So it is, when we consider the low state of ecclesiastical art in those days. Here, then, at Downside the community of St. Gregory's took root, and attracted, as later history shows, able subjects.

It is not to our purpose to write a detailed history of St. Gregory's. But we must touch upon a subject which may be dealt with, we hope, without reviving old controversies, but which it would be unpardonable to pass over here; because the question raised involved not merely the existence of St. Gregory's in particular, but even that of the whole English congregation. We mentioned bishop

Baines as having opened the newly built chapel at Downside. He was a man of many parts, much brilliancy, full of zeal and of generosity, though this was quite forgotten, it must be added, when his will was thwarted. He was endowed with qualities which charmed, attracted, and fascinated, and it is no wonder that he exercised a singular power over his friends. His early years had been passed in the school at the abbey at Lambspring, which, it is to be remembered, though in the hands of English monks, had a petty principality attached to it, of which the abbat was sovereign lord. Here Baines imbibed a taste for splendour, for ecclesiastical magnificence, quite in keeping with the fortunes of the church in Germany before the great crash of which the outbreak of the French revolution was the beginning, but which sorted ill with the condition of catholics in England in the early years of the present century. Still an influx of new ideas is not in itself undesirable, provided that there is a proper ballast in the way of solid qualities and strong character. But, as time was to show, young Baines possessed neither the one nor the other.

From Lambspring, which was suppressed in 1802, he went to the laurentian community at Ampleforth, and in the year 1804 was professed in that monastery. In course of time he was sent out on the mission, and was appointed to Bath. That he possessed remarkable qualities is evident from his rapid advancement. In May 1823 he was consecrated coadjutor to bishop Collingridge, on whose death in 1829 he became vicar-apostolic of the western district. Years before, very early after his arrival in the west, he gave a specimen of his tastes and aspirations in the shape of a grand plan for the development or transfer of St. Gregory's, Downside, for the carrying out of which men, money, and other requisites were wanting. But now at length he had a free field for executing the scheme which had long been simmering in his imagination. He had already bought Prior Park, a large mansion in the neighbourhood of Bath, and his idea was to form there a grand catholic college or university. And with this undertaking, and the gradually accumulating miseries attendant on it, the rest of the life of this remarkable man was bound up.

He succeeded in inducing D. Burgess, the prior of Ampleforth, and some other monks[1] to leave their monastery and the English congregation, and put themselves under his obedience. He tried to do the same at Downside. His desire here seems to have been to make that house a seminary, and to have full jurisdiction over it. But the community, headed by their prior, D. Barber, a man of staunch principles, and not easily to be led away by the glittering appearance of the Prior Park scheme, resolutely refused to entertain the project. Foiled here,

[1] D. Burgess had no intention of leaving the order. He only wanted to found a house of stricter observance than was observed at Ampleforth.

the bishop then tried another plan; why should not St. Gregory's go to Ampleforth and St. Lawrence's come to Downside? But here, again, the gregorians refused to enter into the scheme, which in the execution probably would not have been found so easy as in the proposal, for many of the fathers of the laurentian community were as unwilling as the monks of Downside to give up their position, and to enter under the uncertain obedience of bishop Baines. It is unnecessary to pursue into detail the series of measures, extending over some years, adopted by the prelate to break down the opposition which he encountered in the carrying out of his grand scheme, and forcing those who were unwilling to enter it. On the main question Downside had to bear the brunt of the trouble; its prior gave an example of fidelity, and stood unmoved as a rock amidst all the storm and commotion; Ampleforth was only recovering from the exodus of its most capable members, and St. Edmund's was struggling with the difficulties of a new beginning. They, too, were at a distance. St. Gregory's was in the bishop's district, his near neighbour, and the vineyard he coveted.

The difficulties of maintaining so costly an establishment as Prior Park were beginning to press heavily. At length, in his straits, and as a last means to compass his end, the bishop raised questions involving the canonical existence of the monasteries in England at all—at best a legal quibble. The monks had no other remedy left but an appeal to

Rome; and accordingly the president, accompanied by Dom J. Browne, went in 1835 to lay their grievances at the feet of Peter. There they found the bishop had been beforehand with them, and they had immense difficulties to contend against. But by dint of unwearied toil and the inherent justice of their cause they won their case, and at length heard from cardinal Cappellaria, the prefect of the congregation, afterwards Gregory XVI., the memorable words, *Congregatio vestra nunquam peribit.* The main question settled, the minor difficulties were speedily disposed of by arbitration on the spot, and peace once more reigned. Sore feeling may doubtless have remained in some breasts, but no serious difficulty henceforth arose, and nowhere did the many good qualities of the bishop receive such generous and unstinted recognition as at Downside. Bishop Baines died in 1843, and was buried at Prior Park; and when in 1856 his estate was seized to meet his liabilities, the monks of Downside went over and removed the body of the bishop to their own cemetery, where he now lies amidst the monks of that order which was his first call.

In this slight sketch of bishop Baines we have only touched upon his difficulties with the English congregation, and some notice of them is demanded by our subject. To do justice to his great qualities, but justice to others as well, would require (as Dr. Oliver says of another able man) "a bold and impartial pen." It may be safely said that he was not happy in the epoch in which his life happened to fall. Had his lot been cast a hundred years earlier or a hundred years later, he might have been a great figure.

Fortunately such troubles as these, which must happen in this world (men, even the best intentioned, being what they are) did not occupy all attention or engross all energies. On the contrary, in their course there were not a few whose attention was absorbed in work and labours destined to bear abundant fruit in the near future. *In quietness and confidence shall your strength be* might well have been the motto of those men whom God was preparing to go out from their cloister, like the Winfrids and Willibrords of old, to rule the church in far-off lands. In 1831 D. Placid Morris was consecrated bishop and made visitor-apostolic of Mauritius, which then included a district now governed by nearly fifty prelates; D. Bede Polding, nominated first to Madras, soon followed as first bishop in Australia, and afterwards became the first archbishop of Sydney, and may be justly numbered as one of the greatest and most apostolic missionaries of modern days. D. Charles Davis was called out in 1848 as bishop of Maitland. He was cut off at the early age of thirty-nine, in the midst of a career full of promise, not only for his immediate ministry, but for the advancement of education in Australia. In 1840 D. Joseph Brown was consecrated vicar-apostolic of the Welsh district, and afterwards became the first bishop of Newport and Menevia; six years afterwards D. Bernard Ullathorne, on his return from Australia, where he went as ecclesiastical superior, was made vicar-apostolic of the western district, and afterwards nominated to the see of Birmingham. In the short space of fifteen years five were called to the mitre, and afterwards St. Gregory's saw a sixth, D. Bede Vaughan, succeed as second archbishop of Sydney, for whom higher honours were doubtlessly destined had not a premature death snatched him from us.

We must hurry on. D. Peter Wilson succeeded bishop Brown as prior, and set himself at once to build a large college, or rather to rebuild the whole establishment to meet the ever-increasing number of students. Pugin, then the great restorer of Christian architecture, was asked to make plans for the proposed new buildings, which are to be found in the *Dublin Review* of February 1842. His design is of great beauty and magnificence, but it was one which, even when modified, circumstances, that is, means, did not permit of being carried out. But as building had become a necessity, in 1853 a block of collegiate buildings was begun from the designs of Mr. Charles Hansom. D. Norbert Sweeney, who succeeded as prior in 1854, brought the buildings safely to completion.

Downside went on gradually expanding under its various priors,[1] until early in the seventies the *Alma*

---

[1] D. Sweeney was followed as prior by D. Cuthbert Smith, 1859; D. Alphonsus Morrall, now cathedral prior of Chester, 1866; and D. Ildephonsus Brown, 1868. In 1870 D. Bernard Murphy was called to

Mater of so many English catholics, to which all who have had the fortune to be educated there turn with such affection, renewed her youth and set to prepare herself for that future work for God which lies before her—a work of which her past records are an earnest. For nearly sixty years the community had put up with the old manor-house as a monastery, and only those who have lived in a cramped and confined lodging know how much monastic observance is thereby rendered difficult, if not impossible. The church, good as it was some fifty years ago, was now too small, and quite inadequate for the solemn celebration of those sacred offices which monks know so well how to carry out in all their dignity. Then, again, the benedictine system of education, appealing as it does so much to the English character, made St. Gregory's college in great request with parents who wanted to give their children all the advantages, without the drawbacks, of our traditional public-school life. The college was too small for the numbers that applied, and besides, it was necessary to make many changes. We think Downside was one of the first, if not the first, of our colleges to recognise the necessity of civilising school life.

the prior's chair, and he was succeeded in 1878 by D. Aidan Gasquet, who was obliged by ill-health to resign, a fortunate circumstance, as it has given to England a renowned historian. D. Edmund Ford was elected in 1884, and D. Clement Fowler at the general chapter of 1888. He held office until 1894, when, resigning, D. Edmund Ford, the present prior, was re-elected.

So on 1st October 1873 the foundation-stone of a great minster, built on the lines of the old churches of England, was laid by archbishop Manning. On the same day, the stone of a new monastery was set by the benedictine bishops, Brown and Collier, and that of new collegiate buildings by the ordinary of the diocese, bishop Clifford. Since then the works have been going on, and a new Downside has arisen which fills with astonishment those who remember the Downside of thirty or forty years ago. Under its succeeding priors there has been a vast progress, material and intellectual.

And meanwhile, not forgetting the claims of immediate needs, the monks of St. Gregory's were silently preparing themselves for work which, though it does not immediately appeal to the popular instinct, yet is the foundation which has to be laid slowly, patiently, and solidly before results easily to be admired can be reached. The first-fruits are the historical work done by D. Aidan Gasquet. And it is thus, too, that the monks of St. Gregory's have been the first to avail themselves of the opening of the national universities. Cambridge, hallowed by the memory of Blessed John Whiting, last abbat of Glaston, has now St. Benet's house as a residence for gregorian monks. Modest in its beginning, it is, we may hope, the promise of a future growth which will play the part Gloucester Hall at Oxford, and Monk's College at Cambridge, did for the benedictines of old. Nor were other matters, of less scope doubtlessly, though perhaps of more local interest, forgotten.

Strange it is to think that in this benedictine house, as at Glastonbury, the relics of one of God's great Irish servants should lie and be the monks' great treasure. For at Glaston, says the contemporary life of St. Dunstan,[1] were the relics of St. Patrick the younger, to whom in crowds came Irish pilgrims to venerate the tombs of the successor of their apostle; and here at Downside are the remains of the heroic Oliver Plunkett, another successor of St. Patrick, and the last to die for the faith in England. When in prison awaiting his martyr's crown, he left his body to English benedictines, who rescued it from a felon's grave and preserved it in honour, till the hand of the oppressor left the holy relics without their appointed guardians, and until other English benedictines, again mindful of the trust committed to them, went to seek those same holy relics of the just man and brought them close to the spot where[2] the Irish of old times had been wont to flock in pilgrimage to venerate one who was of their own race and kin: and where also they may see, to-day, rising a noble minster that will not be unworthy, God willing, of the

---

[1] *Stubbs' Memorials of St. Dunstan* (Roll Series), pp. 10, 11.

[2] Downside is, as it were, a shoot coming up from the very roots which the old, most venerable sanctuary of England struck down deep underground. Men thought by pulling down the walls of Glaston they were uprooting it for ever, and after three hundred years, it shoots up again hard by with a promise of a future strong and fair.

treasure deposed in it. For the church, built as many an old minster was built, by degrees, is of great beauty and dignity, and certainly seems to have caught more of the grand old catholic spirit than any work of modern times in England.

To-day the prior of Downside has added to his cares the solicitude of many churches scattered up and down the country.

In the well-nigh three centuries that have passed since its foundation, St. Gregory's can point to a past, taken all in all, such as many an ancient abbey might envy. Nor is the old spirit dead. Though it may have shown itself shy in embarking on showy ventures, its sons have abundantly proved that they have not feared to attempt great works for God; and it has kept well in view and taken to heart the needs of changed times and the calls of altered circumstances. Nor is it mere partiality of affection if those who know it best feel surest confidence that St. Gregory's, long tried in the school of affliction, will (raised soon, as we hope, together with its sister monasteries, to the dignity of an abbey) play such a part in the future as becomes an inheritor by descent of the great memories of Glaston, or the other ancient homes of St. Benedict in England.

CHAPTER XVII

ST. LAWRENCE'S MONASTERY

THE monastery of St. Lawrence was founded, as we have seen, in 1606 by the Spanish monks of Douai, and conventual life began there on 9th August 1608. D. Augustine Bradshaw and D. Gabriel Gifford were the principal promoters of this great work. For more than six years the Spanish fathers were in peaceful possession of the house; and, for a time, the latter of the above-named, it is said, exercised superiority over the new foundation.[1] Under the circumstances mentioned in chapter xiii., the owners, for the sake of peace, and to give "a local habitation and name" to the few men, then the sole representatives of the old English congregation, admitted them to a share in the house at Dieuleward (1612), and the "Union of the Four Articles" was drawn up to regulate this concession. The

---

[1] So says D. Maihew in his dedication to archbishop Gifford of the *Trophæa*. He says: "In hoc enim monasterio Illustrissima et Reverendissima Dominatio vestra mundo renuntiavit, habitum religionis assumpsit, vota monastica emisit ac primum Prioris officium obivit." As the two first statements are contradicted by facts, it makes the certainty of the last, D. Gifford's priorship, at least doubtful. D. Maihew was away on the mission during the short residence of D. Gifford at St. Lawrence's.

plan, however, could not, of course, be carried out till it had received the approbation of the Spanish general, who gave it, May 5, 1613. But before this was received, D. Maihew, the most active spirit of the English fathers, had already left the mission and came to Dieuleward, and, making his first essay of conventual life, took possession of the share bestowed on his congregation.

On his arrival, D. Paulinus Appleby, a professed monk of the Spanish congregation, was holding the prior's chair. Since its foundation, no less than eighteen monks, also of the Spanish congregation, had been professed for that particular house; and already St. Lawrence's had sent out off-shoots. D. Gabriel Gifford and D. John Barnes had been sent, in 1611, to Spain to ask for help for the new community, which had grown too large for its means of support, and was now threatened with an increase in numbers by the English fathers who were claiming a share. Tarrying at St. Malo for a ship, they were induced by the bishop of that town to settle there. D. Bradshaw, the vicar, finding in this a solution of his difficulties, consented, and sent for six others from Dieuleward to join them, three only of whom were professed of St. Lawrence's. Another opening that same year occurred at Chelles, and D. Francis Walgrave with several others were sent from St. Lawrence's to form a little community, and act as confessors and chaplains to the royal convent in that place. The abbess was anxious to reform her nunnery, and having heard from the prior of Cluny college in Paris of the wonderful abstemious life of the Dieuleward monks, begged for some to be sent to help her in her work. In 1612 D. Bradshaw himself went to Chelles and admitted some English youths to the habit.

Thus when D. Maihew came the community was greatly reduced. Almost all the Spanish monks who had been professed there since 1609 had been drawn off. This was useful to the end he had in view, which was practically to obtain entire possession of what he had already a part. He had strong "home rule" proclivities, and determined St. Lawrence's should be for the English, and for them alone. His policy succeeded. Upon his arrival in the February of 1613 he held a general chapter of the old English congregation, which was now set free from their dependence on the Cassinese, D. Anselm Beech. He began also to act as prior on behalf of D. F. Forster, who, though appointed prior, remained on the English mission.[1] Then he began to clear the house of the rest of the Spanish fathers. These went to Paris to start the monastery of St. Edmund. Among them was the future martyr, D. Alban Roe. During his presidency, which lasted till 1620, twelve novices made their profession. Having established himself at Dieuleward, he was in a better position as regards the questions then pending. As we have

[1] See *Downside Review*, vol. iii. p. 180; and Jas. Gillow's *St. Thomas' Priory*, pp. 34, 35.

seen, he now threw over the "Union of the Four Articles," under which he had entered into his share. How this all eventuated we have narrated in the account of the renewal of the English congregation.

We must now chronicle the chief events in the history of St. Lawrence's monastery; and here we lament a great dearth of materials upon which to work. Dieuleward, out of the way of any great centre of English activity, such as Douai then was, was also happily free from any of the vexations with which that house had to deal. The record of her sons is more to be found in England, where, in course of time, they did a great work on the mission, and bore their full share of toil and suffering. Missionary work has been from the days of D. Maihew the great object. He, himself a missioner, and unaccustomed to any other kind of work, would naturally impress that character on the house he practically refounded. The mission oath was first started at Dieuleward, at the general chapter held on February 28, 1613. To this oath, and under the same formula, was joined another in use among the fathers of the society, *de non ambiendo*, that is, not to aspire after ecclesiastical dignities. We think that the introduction of these oaths is due directly to D. Maihew, for they bear decided marks of his early training under the influence of jesuit ideas at Rome.

The house was to be one of strict observance, or, as D. Maihew was wont to say, *ad pedem literæ*.[1]

[1] *Cf.* document in *Downside Review*, vol. ii. p. 179.

For fifty years perpetual abstinence was kept up, and the monks arose at midnight for matins. The monastery got a great reputation, and attracted a number of postulants; so that we find, within the first twenty years, no less than fifty choir monks were professed. In 1621 a monk of this house, D. Clement Reyner, then at Chelles, was sent to the great abbey of St. Peter at Ghent, where St. Dunstan had stayed, to introduce the stricter observance practised by the monks of the restored English congregation; and so much was he loved there, that much importunity was used to induce him to accept the abbacy. But he refused, and returned to his own congregation. Together with this good reputation came a temporal increase. Considerable additions were made to the property by the purchase of farms, one of which, Marivaux, cost 31,000 francs of modern money. The monks also planted the hop, and established the first brewery (still standing) in those parts, thus establishing a new industry.

But the prosperity of St. Lawrence's was to be sadly shaken. The war of 1636 broke out, and St. Lawrence's was in the midst. For six years the monastery suffered greatly.

On the 8th January 1636 two of the religious, D. Anselm Williams and Br. Leander Neville, " being sent by their superiors to charitably assist a lady of quality in Lorraine, were met by certain soldiers belonging to the heretical army of Saxon

Weimar, near St. Mihel, and there by them cruelly murdered, and (as may be supposed) in hatred of their religion hanged on a tree in the wood in their religious habit."[1]

To war succeeded pestilence, and six monks died at Dieuleward. The prior, D. Laurence Reyner, sent off several to the other monasteries to escape the infection, but three of these bore the seeds of disease away with them and died. While the monks were thus suffering, they were not unmindful of the want which befell their poorer neighbours, and gave away land to help them in the distress.

In 1642 D. Alban Roe, a monk professed of St. Lawrence's, and one of the first to join the house at Paris, crowned seventeen long years of imprisonment with a glorious death for the faith on January 21st at Tyburn. His martyrdom is an undying glory to St. Lawrence's and St. Edmund's.

It took years for St. Lawrence's to recover from these and other losses, and during the next twenty years (till 1656) only four novices were professed. In 1669, in order to help St. Lawrence's and to procure members, St. Gregory's at Douai was made a common college of humanities, and four years after (1673) St. Lawrence's became a common novitiate. But judging from the profession lists,[2] it does not seem to have resulted beneficially to any of the

---

[1] Weldon, p. 172.
[2] See Weldon, Notes, *Appendix*, ix.

houses; and in a year or two the arrangement came to an end.

At the end of 1677, says Weldon, died D. Cuthbert Horsley, aged eighty, "whereof he had spent about fifty in regular duty, never quitting to go to the mission; and of this fifty he spent almost thirty in governing this house, as prior of which he had a sad time; for the country being involved in dismal wars, his house fared ill, which he bore like a Job, with a pleasant and gay countenance; and God gave him such grace with the generals commanding the soldiers, that though not a monastery in the country was more alarmed than Dieuleward, yet not one suffered less. All the time he had to spare after the Divine office and from his domestic affairs, he spent in holy meditations and writing them in a most delicate hand. His government was eminently in the spirit of meekness."[1]

Two days after him died another worthy, D. Thomas Fursden, who lived for sixty years at Dieuleward without going out on the mission. He had been one of D. Maihew's novices. In 1711, Lorraine having become a part of French territory, St. Lawrence's was threatened with extinction. It was discovered that it had been established without the royal letters-patent, although at the time of its foundation Lorraine was an independent principality. But the queen stood them in good stead,

[1] Weldon, p. 216.

and through her influence St. Lawrence's was preserved. But, alas, only for a few years. On October 12, 1717, a disastrous fire broke out, and the greater part of the monastery was destroyed. The community had been dwindling down, and now this last disaster nearly crushed them. However, they bravely set to work, and during the priorship of D. Francis Watmough (1721-1733) St. Lawrence's arose once more. But the main difficulty was men: and men meant money. An attempt to start a school for the Northern province in England, proposed in 1725, never came to anything, and the question of numbers became a serious one. About 1735 a few novices came—but during the next sixty years only forty-five choir monks were professed. This was a serious loss, and meant many difficulties. Although by 1750, under the careful management of D. Bernard Catteral, prior for twenty years, much had been done to recover the loss; yet in the succeeding priorships, the decline began again, and difficulties accumulated. Something must be done. So chapter, by that time consisting mainly of the missionary element, came again to the aid of St. Lawrence's with the same plan tried nearly a hundred years ago—a common house of studies and a common novitiate. At St. Lawrence's a school was started for aspirants to the order, and boys were sent from Douai and Paris; whilst St. Gregory's was made a common novitiate and juniorate. The arrangement was come to by the president in conjunction with D. Gregory Sharrock, prior of Douai.[1] But the French Revolution in a very few years put an end to the arrangement.

But before we turn to that event it will be pleasing to get an account of the internal life of the house from D. Fisher, who in 1790 writes to president Walker:—

"No one can have more at heart than I have the peace, concord, union, and regularity of the house, such as it was all the time I was resident in it during the space of eighteen years, when I left it forty-seven years ago in a flourishing condition in its finances, a number of promising youths, most of whom distinguished themselves afterwards in their own country."[2]

In 1786 a laurentian missioner, D. Anselm Bolton (professed 1751), was tried in England on the charge of high treason. His crime was converting a protestant young woman to catholicity. He was the last priest in England who had to stand for his life on account of his religion. The circumstances were these. He was chaplain to lord Fairfax of Gilling Castle, in Yorkshire; and when the latter died in 1773, his daughter and heiress, the hon. Anne Fairfax, entrusted D. Bolton with the management of the estate. One of the men about the place, Bently

---

[1] D. Sharrock had omitted in this matter to consult the members of his house; and was almost immediately afterwards raised to the episcopate.

[2] Allanson's *M.S. History*.

by name, was much indebted to her. He was a protestant, but had married a catholic, and had allowed his eldest daughter to be brought up in her mother's religion. But a younger daughter, Mary, had remained a protestant. In 1781 Mary entered Miss Fairfax's service, and expressed her great desire to become a catholic like her sister. After due instruction, she was received in 1783 by D. Bolton, and her father made no objection. Two years afterwards the young woman was discharged for misconduct. The father meanwhile had been an unsatisfactory tenant, and had got into arrears with his rent, and D. Bolton had to give him notice to quit his farm. In revenge he became a zealous protestant. He hied him to the magistrate, and there charged D. Bolton with converting his daughter. This being a charge of high treason, the monk was at once committed to York Castle, but subsequently was admitted to bail. He was tried at the Lent Assizes of 1786, and the grand jury returned a true bill :—

"For endeavouring to withdraw Mary Bently from her natural obedience to her sovereign, and from the religion happily established in this realm to the Roman religion, which was contrary to the statute of the 23 Eliz."

In the trial the girl admitted that her father had taken all her savings and was in want of money. Her brother swore to the identity of a certain bluepapered book, a catechism, which D. Bolton had given to his sister. He confessed he could not read, but staked his truth on the identity of the book produced in court. The book was handed to the judge, who found it to consist of blank leaves. The trial stopped at once, and the priest was acquitted. It turned out, however, that the lawyer for the defence had cleverly got up a book to represent the catechism, and had substituted the one for the other.

The first beginning of the revolutionary troubles at Dieuleward did not much affect the monks, for they were a long way out of reach of the capital. But when a constitutional priest was appointed to the parish, and the monks refused point-blank to take part in a public procession to the parish church, or in any way to recognise his schismatical authority, they knew that trouble was in store. The taking of Toulon excited a great deal of feeling against the English, and matters began to look very black. The prior of St. Lawrence's was now D. Richard Marsh, a man whose after career showed him to be gifted with abundant energy and determination. He foresaw it was only a question of time for the doom of his monastery to be pronounced, and therefore endeavoured to forestall the Government by realising some of the land belonging to his monastery. But the authorities got wind of this attempt, and orders were issued forbidding any one to purchase, and, furthermore, declaring any such sale void at law. It was also hinted that each individual member of the departmental government, in case the convention decided to lay hands upon the property, would be held responsible for everything missing. The prior, however, managed to remove the plate and some of the more valuable parts of the library. He then began to sell some of the movables; but the municipality, who were on the watch, immediately hastened to obtain power to stop the sale. As some had already been accused to the convention of being too favourable to the religious, the authorities for the district were determined not to expose themselves any longer to this reproach. The municipality received orders to set a guard of twenty-five men round the monastery to prevent anything being removed. The prior remonstrated energetically against this arbitrary proceeding; and although it was admittedly not in conformity with any existing law, he received answer that the measure was necessary on the plea of public safety. The vintage, however, was now at hand, and keeping guard over monks was, at the best of times, found to be but a sorry business. By degrees the guard dwindled away of their own accord; and the prior seized the opportunity to take down and break two of the church bells, and send them away with other things to be sold.

But the storm-clouds growing day by day more threatening, D. Marsh had to provide for the safety of his little flock. A decree, passed September 1793, allowed all foreign children in France for the sake of education to be sent back to their homes. Passports were applied for from Dieuleward; and as the decree had inserted the words "young students," the prior was able to get them for all the members of his community as well as for the boys of their school. But he himself was excluded. Although it was evident that the grown-up members of the house were not intended to take advantage of the decree, the municipal authorities put no obstacle in the way; for they were only too anxious to get the monks out of the way, and thus take possession of the estate of the monastery.

The day after the passports came, with the exception of the prior, D. Maurus Barret, an old and infirm priest, D. Oswald Talbot, D. John Dawber, and two lay brothers, the whole community and boys divided themselves into two parties and set out for England. Those who remained proceeded without delay to ask for "certificates of hospitality," in accordance with a decree of 22nd September; and in case these were refused, it was thought they could use their passports, which were available for a fortnight. After much difficulty the certificates were obtained; and the fathers considered themselves safe in remaining in the monastery. The prior took the further precaution of asking the mayor, an honest man, if he possibly could let him know privately, should any orders come for arresting his community. This was promised. But a few days were enough to show the monks their error in remaining in the midst of enemies sworn to destroy them.

On the evening of Saturday the 12th of October 1793, at about half-past nine, the monks had gone to their cells, and whilst praying for a quiet night they were disturbed by the roll of drums through the streets. This was the usual signal at that time for all townsmen, capable of bearing arms, to assemble before the house of the commandant. The prior was not much alarmed at the noise, for he thought he and his were secured by the lately obtained certificate of hospitality; and so concluded the people were only assembling to apprehend others suspected of designs against the republic. But he quietly withdrew to another cell, in which the window overlooked the town, to keep watch. The mayor, mindful of his promise, sent his sister to warn the prior that orders had been received that night to arrest him and his monks; but the poor woman, meeting so many people round about the monastery, got frightened and returned without fulfilling her errand. She, however, told the wife of one of the labourers employed in the monastery to get her husband, if he had a chance, to warn the prior. This woman happened to see the prior at the window, and made signals to him to come down to the door. There she told him the news. But he was partly incredulous; for he could not bring himself to believe the convention would deny the "letters of hospitality" so lately issued. So he hesitated for a while. At last, considering that he, as prior, would be the one mainly aimed at, and that the others, having passports, were safe at any rate from bodily harm, he quietly passed out of the monastery without giving the alarm to the rest. He told the porter he was going to a certain place in a neighbouring wood, and ordered him to come in an hour or two, and let him know what had been the meaning of all this assembly of the people.

We take the following account of the prior's escape from the narrative based on his own story, as given in D. Allanson's manuscript history:—

"The prior concealed himself for a time in a ravine not far from the convent, and soon satisfied himself, on hearing the rabble making towards his house, and then on hearing the convent bell ring, that the information he had received was too true; so he determined, in case patrols were sent out after him, to cross the Moselle that night. He reached the river-side as the great clocks were striking twelve, and on passing through the water, which was very low, he repaired to a village where the porter of the convent resided. Here he learned that upon the rabble breaking into the convent they ran directly to his room, but not finding him there, they broke down every door which was not open, under the pretence of seeking after him, and that one of the first places they went to was the church steeples, where, finding two of the bells missing, they broke into the most violent exclamation against him.

"A little above Dieuleward the Moselle divides, and, running some distance in separate channels, forms an island nearly two miles in circumference. The prior proceeded to pass the second part of the river in a boat, and reached, about three o'clock on Sunday morning, a small village, where he took up his quarters at the house of a person upon whom he could depend. At daybreak the man, at his request, proceeded to the convent under the pretence of seeing his brother who was there; and on his return he brought word back to him that Father Oswald Talbot and William Sharrock, a lay brother, had escaped; that Father John Dawber, Father Maurus Barret, James Johnson, a lay brother, and Charles Allan, a novice, had been conducted to the German college at Pont-à-Mousson, to be imprisoned there with all suspected persons; that the convent had been put into the keeping of the municipality, and that guards were placed at various stations about it.

"On hearing this sad news, the prior deliberated with himself whether to resign himself a prisoner or to attempt to effect his escape. In either case the most imminent dangers beset him. To resign himself a prisoner was almost certain death, as he was assured he would be brought to a capital trial on account of the bells, the church plate, and furniture which were missing. To attempt his escape without a passport, owing to his ignorance of the country and the position of the troops about the frontier and the distance he was from Germany, appeared almost impracticable. If he should happen to be taken by the military, immediate death would probably follow, or if a trial were allowed there was a plain decree which condemned all foreigners to the guillotine who were taken within two leagues of the frontiers. A third plan which suggested itself to his mind was to remain and attempt to conceal himself in the country. In this case he would probably perish from famine or from the revolutionary army or from the rage of the people. Besides, a decree had been recently passed which condemned all who should conceal a foreigner or any of his property to twenty years' confinement in chains, so he considered it would be impossible to conceal himself for any length of time, as no one would be willing to give him hospitality. After weighing the matter well in all its bearings, he came to the determination to attempt to effect his escape, and left the house where he had concealed himself at ten o'clock on Sunday night, and embarked on his hazardous enterprise.

"His great presence of mind, combined with natural shrewdness, enabled him to escape from the imminent perils which beset him on all sides. After a journey of some days he reached Trèves in safety. There he met his brethren, who had left the convent before with their passports, and Father Oswald Talbot and William Sharrock, the lay brother, who had effected their escape, and had joined the others two days before. After remaining with them for three days in order to settle his plans, the prior proceeded to Ostend, and left his community behind to await his further directions. Thence he sailed to Deal, which he reached with a joyful heart after having narrowly escaped imprisonment and death."

In the account of the return of St. Gregory's we spoke of Sir Edward Smythe's generous offer of hospitality to his old friends at Douai. As they then were not able to avail themselves of it, the prior and some of his monks being in prison at Doullens, the owner of Acton Burnell extended his hospitality for a time to the laurentians upon their arrival in England. To this refuge the homeless conventual members of St. Gregory's and St. Lawrence's had directions to repair; and as soon as could be, like good monks, they took care that conventual observance should be at once renewed. During the enforced absence of D. Jerome Sharrock, the prior of St. Gregory's, D. Richard Marsh took charge of both communities. There the two communities were residing when the general chapter of 1794 met; and the grateful thanks of the congregation were solemnly offered to Sir Edward for his charity in affording them an asylum in the day of their distress. The chapter decided that St. Lawrence's community should remain at Acton Burnell, and the wish was expressed that the two communities should amalgamate.

But after the return of the prior of St. Gregory's to England, at a meeting held on the 2nd April 1795, at Vernon Hall, Liverpool, by president Cowley, himself a laurentian, and which was attended by bishop Sharrock, D. Brewer, D. Michael Lacon, and the two priors, it was decided that the gregorians should remain at Acton Burnell and the laurentians go to Brindle in Lancashire. But the idea of carrying out the latter portion of the decision was afterwards altogether abandoned for a better plan which seemed to offer itself. In the September of that year the community of St. Lawrence's went to Birkenhead, where they remained till May 1796, whence they removed to Scoles, near Prescot. After a little more than a year they joined the president at Vernon Hall, and were residing there at the time of the next general chapter. The laurentian conventual fathers, having thus no fixed residence, had little hope under these circumstances of adding to their numbers by postulants, although the religious were anxious, and even in the midst of these perpetual changes made every effort to resume conventual life. A plan of leaving England and of going to Madeira was placed before the community, but happily this catastrophe was averted and St. Lawrence's remained to take its rightful place in St. Benedict's restored patrimony.

When the chapter of 1802 met, the small community were living at Parbold, whence they had moved from Vernon Hall in the May preceding.

Grave fears had been felt that it would be obliged to separate and give up conventual life altogether, as their losses had been so great both in men and money. Besides, there was no new blood coming in to reinvigorate the community, now almost worn out. It was indeed a trying time for superiors, and the fate of St. Lawrence's as a monastery seemed to be almost settled. And so it was. Happily not by the way of dissolution, but by a new gift of a new lease of life which in its present-day vigorous growth shows that it was God's mighty hand that was over His monks. President Brewer could not see his own monastic family dissolved; so he threw himself into the breach, and by his moral influence saved it when on the eve of extinction.

The future home of St. Lawrence's was being prepared for them by Providence in this wise.

A few years before her death, Miss Fairfax had determined to reward D. Anselm Bolton's long and faithful service by building a handsome home for him on the other side of the valley which lay opposite the castle. As soon as the house was finished she made him a present of it, together with about thirty-two acres of land. Besides this gift, she also settled upon him an annuity of some three hundred pounds. She also intended to endow the property, so that a priest might always be kept there. Little did she think how abundantly her charity was to be rewarded and her intentions carried out. She died in 1793, and left a sum of £2000 as the endowment;

but this money was claimed by a cousin as a legacy void at law, being left for "superstitious purposes." The money was lost and went to the heir, with what results we are not here concerned.

On the death of his benefactress, D. Anselm Bolton left the castle for his new home, which was then ready to receive him, and lived there for several years. This house was considered, from its beautiful situation and its own intrinsic value, together with the land attached to it, as a desirable home for the convent of St. Lawrence, if its owner could be induced to give it up for so praiseworthy a purpose. The old priest had received many acts of kindness from his benedictine brethren, and specially from president Fisher, during the period of his trial; and as age crept upon him, the old love for St. Lawrence's revived, so that when the project of handing over his house was broached by the president, he received the proposal as one worthy of consideration. After some little inward struggle he consented to relinquish the spot he loved so well; and by this sacrifice he had the satisfaction of rescuing his house from the extinction which apparently awaited it. Soon after the chapter of July 1802, he made over his property to the president on certain specified conditions. He was then well advanced in years, and had earned his rest from active missionary life. He went to live at Birtley, where in 1805 he died, rejoicing to have been the means of advancing the cause of religion by the sacrifice of some of the ease and comfort to which his long labours had given him a claim.

President Brewer took possession of the premises the day after the agreement was signed, and D. Appleton, the prior-elect of St. Lawrence's, repaired to Ampleforth to assist him in making the necessary changes. As soon as the house was prepared the prior-elect returned to Parbold, and was there installed on the 29th of November; and two weeks later, with D. Alexius Chew and William Sharrock, the lay brother, went to begin the new convent. In the following spring several promising young men from the recently dissolved abbey of Lambspring arrived at Ampleforth, and a novitiate was opened with D. Bede Slater as novice-master. Three novices, one of whom was the future bishop Baines, were clothed in May 1803, and another, an ex-naval surgeon, Brother Gregory Robinson, followed shortly afterwards. These four, duly professed after the year's novitiate, were the first-fruits of the new foundation amid the Yorkshire hills. The school was reopened on wider lines, and the community so increased that in 1814 the superiors had to enlarge the house by adding two wings to the original building. In 1819 a new refectory with rooms above it was erected. By 1822 the community had grown to thirteen members.

Passing rapidly over the years, we may note the silent and solid proof of the growth of St. Lawrence's by the buildings which here, as in the case of Downside, are landmarks in its history. In 1859 the first stone of the beautiful Gothic block of buildings which is now part of the college was laid, 11th July, by D. Wilfrid Cooper, the prior. Seen from the railway, Ampleforth looks like a dream of the past. It nestles on the slope of a hill which gives shelter from the north and east winds. Its long frontage of building and its graceful architecture are a pleasing sight in that lovely country. In the centre still stands the old house with its first additions; on one side spread the collegiate buildings opened in 1862, and admirably adapted to all modern requirements; and on the other is one of the most beautiful collegiate chapels in the land. Small if compared to the great minster at Downside, it is perfect in detail, and is finished in exquisite taste. Beyond the chapel, rising from the ground can be seen the new monastery, another proof of the fulness of the life which pervades Ampleforth. A handsome pile affording accommodation for twenty-four religious, it is the first portion of a plan which will eventually result in the rebuilding of St. Lawrence's. The present collegiate buildings will, we understand, remain; but the old house goes, and the present church in due time will give place to one more commensurate with the future dignity of St. Lawrence's abbey. The new buildings were begun July 1894, and the first stone of the new St. Lawrence's was laid by one of her sons, Bishop Hedley.

Thus, a hundred years after their arrival in England, the community of St. Lawrence, after having been on the point of extinction, is now a firmly established and flourishing community owning a college, whose name wakes loving remembrance in thousands of English hearts.

We must now note some of the foremost men who have been connected with Ampleforth, and to whose exertions St. Lawrence's owes to-day her proud and well-merited position. Of D. Richard Marsh, the last prior of Dieuleward, and the first prior of the community in England, we have already spoken. He held many of the highest offices in the congregation, such as provincial of York (1806-22), prior for the second time (1806-10), president (1822-26), procurator *in curia* (1829-31), and president again in 1837-42. His terms of office occurred in troublesome times, such as we have spoken of in our last chapter. But, in spite of all the cares those difficulties brought, he was able to devote himself for many years to the great work of restoring St. Edmund's monastery. He died in 1843, at Rishton, where he had built the chapel. He wrote the lives of the presidents of the English congregation, and also an account of his escape from France, from which we have taken extracts. Of D. Burgess, who was prior (1818-29), and the blow he gave to St. Lawrence's by leaving the congregation and drawing off some of the most able men to aid him in carrying out bishop Baines' scheme, we have already written.

One of his companions, D. Metcalfe, was a great linguist, and especially versed in oriental tongues. The translation into Welsh of "The Garden of the Soul" is his work. After having been with bishop Baines for some time, he petitioned to be received back into St. Lawrence's community, and, having gained his desire, he set out for his old home, but died on the way in 1847. Another notability of these early times was D. Athanasius Allanson, the annalist of the congregation. He left many bulky volumes of manuscripts, with unique and valuable information regarding the history of the Church in England after the days of the Revolt. He was a great friend of Dr. Lingard, and gave him material help in the compilation of his history. Among other notabilities who have come from Ampleforth monastery are bishop Slater, vicar-apostolic of Mauritius; bishop Hedley, the present bishop of Newport; and abbat Bury, probably one of the most learned Thomists of the present day. D. Adrian Towers, prior from 1836, was a well-known controversialist, and was one of the pioneers of "platform lectures." He had to gather up the fragments that remained after prior Burgess left. He was succeeded for the next four years by D. Bede Day, who, in 1838, gave way to D. Anthony Cockshutt. This prior's great ability as an administrator enabled him to restore the financial state of Ampleforth, which had been thrown into a great state of confusion by the flight to Prior Park. D. Ambrose Prest held office 1846–50, and was succeeded by D. Wilfrid Cooper, the great builder of St. Lawrence's, and to whose energy and taste its many beauties are due. D. Maurus Anderson (1863–66) followed, and in the priorship of D. Bede Prest (1866–74) a landslip nearly destroyed the college, and the structure had to be repaired. He added to the estate by the purchase of the adjoining farm—Sotheran's Farm—which had been for many years looked at with longing eyes. He was followed by D. Stephen Kearney, who in turn gave place to D. Placid Whittle. He, with the next prior, D. Basil Hurworth, did much to increase the community, and put the college upon its present satisfactory footing.

Of the work of the present prior, Dom Anselm Burge, who has held office for the last ten years, the time has fortunately not yet come when we may speak of the result of his priorship. To-day his mark is deeply set upon all belonging to St. Lawrence's. But, mindful of Holy Writ, which says, "*Before his death praise no man*," we will content ourselves with noting that under the present prior St. Lawrence's has advanced by leaps and bounds, so that it is in a more prosperous state than it has ever been. On him, too, has fallen the work of organising the missions, which passed under his care when the provincials ceased to hold office. The prior of St. Lawrence's now wields a jurisdiction such as is possessed by but a few abbats, and rules over some thirty missions in nine dioceses, and a house at Oxford, just opened for the higher studies of his community.

This, then, is the story in brief of St. Lawrence's and of its growth in our midst. As we think of the monastery up among the Yorkshire hills, in as fair a spot as man's heart could wish for, and we think of St. Benedict's sons carrying on their work manfully, in spite of difficulties which would have broken down men less devoted and earnest than they were, we see the visible signs to-day of their steadfastness. And now that the bull *Religiosus Ordo* has set each house free, St. Lawrence's will fulfil more adequately its right to carry out its own ideal without let or hindrance, and show a sturdy example of benedictinism as truly such as can be found anywhere. The name of their old home suggests the wish of all who, like the present writer, know and love Ampleforth. *Dieu-le-ward.* May God ward it!

CHAPTER XVIII

ST. EDMUND'S MONASTERY

FROM Dieuleward and Chelles was evolved the monastic family of St. Edmund's. The Spanish monks at Chelles gave so much edification to the abbess of that royal monastery, "that she resolved to procure for them a settlement in Paris, where, having finished their studies, they might better be sent into the English mission, or live at Chelles in the ministering of her community."[1]

It was, however, as subsequent events proved, that she was so pleased with the Spanish fathers she knew that she resolved to help their brethren; partly for their benefit and partly for her own.

In 1615 the abbess secured for the monks l'Hôtel de St. André in the Faubourg St. Jacques; but before this house was ready for them, six monks, one of whom was the future martyr, D. Alban Roe, had come to Paris, where a temporary shelter was found for them at Montacute College.[2] Besides paying the rent of the new house, the munificent abbess gave them a sum equal at least to £300 a year of modern money, besides frequently sending from her abbey

[1] Weldon, p. 90.   [2] *Gallia Christiana*, vii. 1071.

provisions of bread, wine, and meat. The object of the house at Paris was clearly that the monks might profit by the advantages which the great University of Paris had to offer in the way of higher studies. The house does not seem to have been at first intended to be an altogether independent foundation. It was under the jurisdiction of D. Francis Waldegrave, whom the Spanish general had, in 1614, appointed superior of the house at Chelles. But sometime in 1615 D. Bradshaw became its first prior; and in the following year, when he was summoned to reform the cluniac monastery of Longueville in Normandy,[1] D. Bernard Berington, likewise of the Spanish congregation, succeeded. In 1617 the house in Paris was the place of meeting for the nine definitors charged with the business of the Union. And as D. Waldegrave misliked that affair, the monks of St. Edmund's came in for a share of his opposition. The abbess, who sided with D. Waldegrave, began to give trouble; and it was found difficult to depend upon the vagaries of "a royal abbess." All connection was soon broken with Chelles, and the monks took a house in the Faubourg St. Germain. Weldon thus narrates the event: "D. Gabriel Gifford now become bishop, thinking it derogatory to the prosperity of the Union to have those who had engaged in it at Paris to depend any longer on Father Waldegrave and his

---

[1] He died there, May 4, 1618, having filled the post of sub-prior in that house.

at Chelles, he at his own expense placed them in another house, and the abbess she withdrew her pension and spent it on those she had at Chelles. This was the beginning of the convent at Paris which is now entitled to St. Edmund, king of the East Angles and martyr."[1]

This was in October 1618. In this house they lived for six years and a half, and when the land was bought over their heads, they moved in 1625 "near the carthusians in Hell Street," and in the March of 1632 they went back into the Faubourg St. Jacques and took possession of an old convent of Feuillantine nuns. But they had to look out for some permanent home of their own. They finally settled down in the Rue St. Jacques in 1642, close by the great convent of carmelite nuns with whom the community always entertained the most friendly relations. And also near the site of the famous benedictine nunnery of Val de Grace founded by Anne of Austria.

D. Waldegrave and his friends at last being dismissed from Chelles in 1627 by the abbess, they went to the college of Marmontier in Paris belonging to the congregation of Clugni, which they joined.

"The old monks got weary of them at the college, and therefore began to seek to get handsomely quit of them, but could find no better expedient than to put them at an old venerable monastery of above

[1] P. 136.

a thousand years' standing called La Celle, about a good English mile from the renowned nunnery of Faremontier in Brie. . . . It was (now) in a lamentable condition, and scarcely deserved the name of a monastery, (and was) attended but by three or four monks."[1]

This monastery of SS. Peter and Paul, when D. Waldegrave at last made his peace with the Paris house and with the congregation (about 1634), was made over to St. Edmund's, and was henceforth used as a novitiate for that house. The monastery of St. Edmund's being now firmly established, in 1650 the king granted letters-patent giving civil recognition, under the condition of a solemn annual mass for himself and his successors on the feast of St. Louis. The parliament of Paris registered these letters the following year (April 17, 1651). The royal favour went further; and on September 9, 1651, the king issued letters of naturalisation to all professed members of the monastery, and extended the favour to the other houses of the congregation should they send their subjects to Paris, to continue their studies as far as the Mastership of Arts. He also gave them a yearly pension of £25. In the year 1674 D. J. Shirebourne, the prior, began to pull down the old church, and the foundation of a larger one was laid with much solemnity by the princess Henriette Anne, sister of Charles II., who married Philip of Orleans, Louis XIV.'s brother. Abbat Montague,

[1] Weldon, 170.

first almoner to the queen of England, officiated, and gave £100 to the new church. The king also gave a handsome donation of 7000 livres. The benedictines were so favourably regarded by the clergy of Paris that the archbishop wrote a pastoral asking for alms for the new church of the English monks. On the completion of the work the new church was blessed, February 28, 1677, by M. l'Abbé de Noailles, who afterwards became archbishop and cardinal. The vaults under the church became later on a favourite place of burial for the adherents of the Stuart cause. When James II. abdicated, he used to come often to St. Edmund's, and made his retreats (1694 and 1696) in this monastery. Here also, by desire of Louis XIV., who knew that Westminster abbey had been the burial-place of English kings, when James died (1701) his funeral rites were solemnised. For forty days his obsequies were celebrated with great magnificence, and the church was hung with black from top to bottom. Weldon gives a full and characteristic account of his funeral; and also a curious story "of the extraordinary effects of the invocation of king James II. of holy memory."[1]

[1] "Anno 1702, the world taking alarm at miracles said to be wrought at king James' tomb, on the 18th of February, the princess of Condé came; on the 6th of April Madame de Maintenon; on the 17th of April the duchess of Burgundy made the jubilee stations at the church, and was some time in prayer in the chapel where the royal corpse reposed in state. A month after, to wit on the 17th of May, the archbishop of Paris, cardinal Noailles, did the same thing with the canons of his most illustrious cathedral in procession. And on the 15th of

It is now time to look at the inner history of the house. From the beginning abstinence was kept according to the strict letter of the Rule. This lasted from 1617 till the general chapter of 1666. This spirit of austerity went on till late; for D. Weldon, who was a monk of this house, bears witness in his own time (1688–1713) "that we keep here strict abstinence without touching anything of flesh all Advent and Christmas day, the like from Septuagesima till Easter Monday, and on Whitsunday we also keep abstinence in token that when it pleases God to re-establish us in England we must keep abstinence according to this rule, so that the pope dispenses with us but thrice a week—Sundays, Tuesdays, and Thursdays—during the rest of the year. But if on Tuesday or Thursday happen a fast, or Christmas day comes on a Sunday (as at Easter or Whitsuntide), we eat meat on a Monday, but never on Wednesday nor on Saturdays from Christmas to

June following his eminence issued out a commission to Joachim de la Chetardie (a person of great account, priest, bachelor of Sorbonne and curate of the great parish of St. Sulpice in the suburbs of St. Germain at Paris, a man of eminent learning and piety, who had refused a bishopric) to examine the king's miracles, which he did with great exactness and all the rigour used on such accounts, and has verified at least twenty. . . . Many other great persons publicly and privately have and do visit the royal tomb. Bishops say mass there and have masses said for them. Particularly the late famous bishop of Meaux, M. Bossuet, before his death had neuvaines celebrated for him; so likewise cardinal Collen, bishop of Orleans" (Weldon, p. 249). But by the express desire of the widowed queen the matter was allowed to drop; and the memory of James II. was hallowed only by the adherents of his cause.

Candlemas, so that we can only take Monday to make out the third day if any of the others be hindered."[1]

Besides this abstinence there was much fasting. From Pentecost till the middle of September the monks here, as in the other houses, fasted twice a week; and from the middle of September till Advent, and from Septuagesima till Lent, four times a week. The whole of Advent and Lent were fasting days. The novices were obliged by the constitution to keep perpetual abstinence during the year of probation, in order to teach them that when the monasteries were established in England they would be obliged to strict observances.[2] The discipline was taken, except during Paschal time, once a week, in Advent twice, and in Lent three times. The monks of St. Edmund's sang a high mass every day, and added the office of our Lady to their ordinary choir work. Three times each day mental prayer was made in common; and once a year a retreat was ordered for all the religious. At the time when king James II. frequented the monastery the community numbered twenty-four.

Being in the capital, the monks would come across many notabilities. St. Francis de Sales was a frequent visitor. He had been an intimate friend of archbishop Gifford, and shared in his love for this

---

[1] Vol. i. p. 936.
[2] It was evidently unknown that the law of perpetual abstinence was not generally observed in England.

house, and " much honoured the English fathers with his company when in Paris; one day as one of them was to sing the first vespers of his first high mass, to do him honour that holy apostolic bishop of Geneva stood on one side of him and R. F. Gabriel Gifford, then archbishop and duke of Rheims, stood on the other. . . ."[1]

Benjamin Franklin during his stay in Paris (1776-84) was a constant guest, and, it has been said, took from the constitutions of the English benedictines many features for those of the United States.

Another visitor was Samuel Johnson, during his memorable tour on the Continent. In his diary he makes mention of the great kindness the monks showed him. He enjoyed their hospitality on several occasions. Under the date of October 31, 1775, he writes:—

" I lived at the benedictines'; meagre day: soup *maigre*, herrings, eels, both with sauce; fried fish, lentils, tasteless in themselves."

But in spite of the meagre fare he evidently came again, for he tells us there was always a room for him in the monastery. " I am very kindly used by the English benedictine friars," says he in a letter; and closes the notes on his visit with these words: " I parted very tenderly from the prior and friar Wilkes." The friendship was kept up after the doctor's return, for " two of that college being sent to England on the mission some years after, spent

[1] Weldon, 163.

much of their time with him in Bolt Court I knew, and he was ever earnest to retain their friendship."[1] One of these two, or perhaps another one altogether, coming to England, unhappily fell away from the faith, and so convinced Johnson of his sincerity that in spite of the doctor's expressed opinions[2] of perverts from catholicity, he helped him to get a living in the protestant church.

During the priorship of D. Charles Walmesley (1749) the intellectual life of St. Edmund's was at its height. An "Academy" was founded, and the members used to meet regularly and discuss literary and scientific subjects. D. Walmesley himself was a great mathematician and astronomer, and his services were made use of by the British government in bringing about the reformation of the calendar. The sort of religious he was may be gathered from this trait. After he became bishop (1756) he gave up all his favourite scientific pursuits, because he found they caused too many distractions at his office and mass.

But St. Edmund's had its full share of difficulties, living in the midst of the court and in a pleasure-loving city like Paris. In a visitation made in 1786 the president said :—

---

[1] *Anecdotes of Dr. Samuel Johnson*, by Piozzi, p. 55.

[2] "Sir William Scott informs me that he heard Johnson say: 'A man who is converted from protestantism to popery may be sincere; he parts with nothing; he is only superadding to what he already had. But a convert from popery to protestantism gives up so much of what he has held as sacred as anything that he retains; there is so much *laceration of mind* in such a conversion that it can hardly be sincere and lasting'" (Boswell's *Johnson* (1769), p. 169).

"Every relaxation, therefore, which we may permit ourselves to take is more or less a breach of this vow (of stability); and though in obedience to superiors, and for the greater glory of God and the salvation of souls, we may sometimes be called off from some part of this practice, as when we are commanded to go upon the mission, yet our prior obligation certainly returns upon us in its original force as soon as we become incapable of serving God and our neighbour in that capacity."

Together with this, their financial position became so precarious that in the latter half of the last century it was seriously considered whether it would not be as well to disband the house altogether.

From the national archives [1] we can gather a few facts as to the state of the monastery on the eve of the Revolution. The prior was D. Henry Parker, and the president, D. Augustine Walker, was in residence at that time (1790). In a return furnished to the government officials the prior states the revenues of the house as 26,637 livres, 9 sols, 8 deniers. This was made up from various sources, from rents, from farming of lands, from the *mensa* of the priory of SS. Peter and Paul at La Celle-en-Brie, and from interest on capital otherwise invested. Their yearly liabilities amounted to 9264 livres, 4 sols, and this comprised taxation, &c., charges to the priors of Choisy and of La Celle, &c. It was most difficult with what remained to make both

[1] S. 3, 656, No. 1307.

ends meet. The community then consisted of fifteen religious. From some letters published in the *Downside Review*[1] we can trace some of the events of the gathering tempest.

D. Henry Parker, the prior, writes, August 15, 1790:—

"We jog on as to the rest so-so. You know the road is often rough; at best it is not easy nor pleasant. I know not how soon we shall be at the journey's end.... The decrees of our grand assembly fleece us daily more and more; we shall probably be starved out of house and home. But the prior of Douai is so good as to invite us to live with him, which I would immediately comply with if it were allowed to quit the hulk before the complete wreck." A month later: "The English monks and nuns are to be embarked I know not where; but this I know, that they remain in great uncertainty and uneasiness. Our habit is abolished by decree of the national assembly; the king has but his sanction to add, which he never refuses, to make our dress illegal, unconstitutional, lèse-national. The nuns are terribly afraid of being pensioners. I hope the English will escape that humiliation and injustice; but a long list of articles are ready to appear concerning those of France. This list is preceded by one as long concerning religious men, their going or staying, the payment of their pensions in January, the houses to be provided for those that stay, their

[1] *Among the Archives*, vol. ii.

future mode of monastic government, &c., &c. I heartily wish all at an end. . . . Fr. Walker, the president, stays at Cambrai, and purposes to assist the poor nuns whose circumstances do not allow them to pay a confessor. In the project of provision to be made for nuns there is no mention of supporting a confessor. I suppose they will be left to manage as they can in that respect."

Then the procurator, D. Kellet, takes up (September 23rd) his burden :—

"The hard fate of St. Edmund's will be determined very soon, and takes up most of my time. September 27th.—Our affairs give me an immense deal of trouble and hard labour. Nor have I here one single person in or out of doors whom I can depend upon for advice or assistance. In a few days I presume our inventory will be closed and sent to the National Assembly. What our lot may be afterwards God only knows."

Then the prior writes, October 30th, and speaks of the procurator : " He is working hard with a set of folks hard to manage. I am doubtful of his success. . . . We are in an alarming situation here, particularly as to church affairs ; a national schism seems unavoidable." Things now began to advance more rapidly. May 9, 1791, the prior writes : " I may not be superior here ten days more, as the Municipality persist in executing in our regard a decree which authorises our *confrères* to choose a superior and an *économe*, and to establish a new rule within the house such as may please their taste. I have fought hard this last week, but hitherto have only procured a delay of eight days."

Before the end of the next October the spoiling had begun. D. Shaw, the superior of La Celle, was arrested and imprisoned there. The priory, as belonging to the nation, was taken possession of, the farm sold, and preparations made for selling the house and the church. But still at Paris matters were in suspense, and this painful state lasted into the next year. "I have a great mind," writes the prior, July 12, 1792, "to take a run to Lancashire while the destiny of this kingdom, and with it perhaps of St. Edmund's, is depending: we may be sure that a few months will see great things decided."

In October he writes that "Citizen Shaw" had been made to take the oath; and "that we are not yet to expect perfect tranquillity in this capital of our new republic; there continue to be many agitators who know that the most fish are caught in troubled waters."

Suspense was not to last much longer. In the great outburst of 1793 St. Edmund's community was broken up, and such as had not escaped were sent to prison. The prior and community, now reduced to six monks and two lay brothers, were imprisoned in their own house, where they were kept all during the terrible time, which lasted for fourteen months. Two of the monks, D. Francis

Bewick (October 19, 1793) and D. Benedict Cawser (January 9, 1794), died from the rigours of their confinement.

When the decree of January 5, 1795, allowed the owners of British foundations to return to their houses and take possession of all the property remaining unsold, the edmundians became again masters of their own house. But the expiring Directory in 1799 once more stripped them of everything, and their house was ordered to be sold in the August of that year. They, however, kept possession of it till 1804, when the "United Establishment" under Dr. Walsh secured it, together with all other British property. Its sons were now scattered and homeless. After a history of one hundred and eighty-nine years, St. Edmund's monastery came to an end.

. . . . . .

We have seen the efforts made to recover the benedictine property in France, and the part D. Parker took. In 1815 he was again nominated prior of St. Edmund's, although with no community, in order to enable him to claim the property in Paris. This, after much trouble and expense, he succeeded in doing. He remained on in Paris, and died there 8th July 1817, without, however, having seen any hope of the restoration of his beloved monastery. He left D. Marsh, then provincial of York, a laurentian, as representative of St. Edmund's, his sole executor and heir to the French and English estates. He charged him to do his utmost to restore the edmundian house; and, failing this, his desire was for the property to go to benefit the laurentian community, which was then in great difficulties.

The question whether St. Edmund's should be restored as a monastery for a long time occupied the mind of the congregation. It seemed hopeless to attempt it; and we learn from Fr. Ryding, an edmundian himself, that chapter in 1816 decided that no house at Paris should be attempted. Then D. Marsh proposed that at least a school, under edmundian auspices, should be started at Douai in the buildings belonging to St. Gregory's, as that community had definitely refused to go back to France. He offered himself to go there and make the foundation. But the project was postponed until after the chapter of 1818, when, with the full concurrence of the president, D. Bede Brewer, he went to Douai for the purpose of establishing a scheme which, it was hoped, might ultimately end in the resuscitation of the monastery of St. Edmund's. This was the clear intention from the beginning. D. Allanson says: "To aid him in his laudable undertaking, Brother Charles Fairclough, who had been educated at Stonyhurst, and who had finished his noviceship at Ampleforth, was, with some reluctance of the prior, admitted to his profession, in order that he might repair to Douai to assist him in teaching a few scholars who were sent there to receive their education.

The college of St. Edmund's was now started, although the chapter had distinctly refused to countenance any such venture. Two years after, in 1820, two more laurentians, Brothers Basil Bretherton and Jerome Hampson, were professed and sent over to help. D. Marsh, on the death of president Brewer in April 1822, became president, and was re-elected to that post at the next general chapter, which was held at Ampleforth.

So in this scheme of the college of St. Edmund's the houses, independently of the chapter, took part. D. Marsh began it with the consent of the president; the gregorians allowed their property at Douai to be used for the purpose; the laurentians gave most valuable aid by sending men to help in the work; and, finally, although he had acted in the teeth of a prohibition, chapter seemingly sanctioned it all by re-electing D. Marsh to the presidentship. Nothing succeeds like success.

At the chapter the president brought forward the proposal that the welfare of the congregation demanded that an attempt should be made to restore, at least, a third house; and he asked for some mark of approbation to be passed in favour of the establishment at Douai. There was a strong opposition to the president's proposal, which does not seem to have been discussed on its own merits, but on side issues. When the proposal was brought to the vote, it was defeated by a majority of one. D. Augustine Baines, who was opposed to the plan of making the

Douai establishment a conventual residence, and therefore wanted chapter to forbid profession to be made there, tried to submit a proposition to this effect, which was almost carried. But, led by the monks of St. Gregory's, the chapter contented itself with passing, not a vote of censure as the adverse party wanted, but one of thanks " to the president for the labours he had undergone in establishing a school at Douai ; and he was earnestly entreated to devise the best means he could of preparing his subjects for holy orders, according to the powers granted to him by chapter."[1]

As it stands, this decision of chapter is really most unintelligible. On one side they refused to recognise it as a conventual establishment, and on the other the president was recognised to have subjects, and was left a free hand in devising means to promote them for holy orders. Again, another point, and that an important one, too, seems to be quite clear— chapter did not absolutely refuse to recognise the advisability of the restoration of St. Edmund's monastery. Indeed, their very action seems to have been devised for achieving the end D. Marsh had in view. At least no other would have so well served the purpose of leaving him free to do, without the interference of chapter, what he wanted ; for, as D. Allanson continues, " to have promoted his young men to holy orders without taking the religious vow, as intimated in the decision of chapter, was imprac-

[1] Allanson.

ticable, and showed its authors to be unversed in canon law on the subject; as any bishop in France would have incurred suspension by ordaining them without dimissorials from the vicar-apostolic in England in whose district they were born, and the bishops who granted these dimissorials would have immediately claimed them as their subjects."

The president, being commissioned by chapter to go to Rome on business, went there in 1823. Acting entirely upon his own responsibility, and against the deliberately expressed decree of the chapter (as far as St. Edmund's was concerned), he petitioned the holy see for the canonical establishment of the existing monasteries. In the escape from the Continent, no formal application had yet been made to Rome for the translation of the monasteries to England. The Sacred Congregation of Bishops and Regulars, by a rescript dated 15th June 1823, sanctioned the transfer of the gregorians to Downside, of the laurentians to Ampleforth, of the edmundians to Douai, of Lambspring to some other place not yet decided, and of the Cambrai nuns to Abbots Salford, "provided that the ordinary of those places sanctioned the establishment of those monasteries." It was on this occasion, too, that the pope gave power to the president to confer the doctorate upon a certain number of his subjects. This interpolation of the edmundian community, which no longer had any corporate existence, caused some to look upon the decree as surreptitious, and was one of the causes of the future troubles with bishop Baines, who, as a monk, had been the chief opponent.

The president, on his return to Douai, called the religious together and told them that, as there were already six postulating for the holy habit, the time had now come to constitute the monastery upon a canonical basis. He read letters from edmundians on the mission, praying that their house might be restored, even if it should have to be continued in another locality, as had been the case of the gregorians and the laurentians. He had "merely out of complaisance"[1] applied to the definitors for permission to admit his subjects to the habit and to their religious profession; but they, under plea of the chapter's action, refused their consent. But the state of affairs under which chapter had come to a decision had (thought the president) now changed; and, as the rescript in favour of canonical transfer of St. Edmunds to Douai had been obtained from the holy see, he considered himself to be acting within his legitimate rights in acting in direct opposition to the views of the definitors and chapter altogether. He at once proceeded on his own responsibility to clothe his novices. From this time the duty of choir and other cloistral observances were put in force. After the year of novitiate four out of the six were professed as members of the house of St. Edmund's. In the new community thus established was D. Cuthbert Wilkes, one of the old stock of Edmundians

[1] *Teste*, D. Baines.

(the friend from whom Samuel Johnson parted so tenderly), who had come back to link the new on to the old.

But the president had still to encounter much opposition to his new monastery; and in the disputes with bishop Baines, to which we already have referred, the canonical rights of St. Edmund's and the whole action of the president were seriously endangered. But suffice it to say, chapter veered round under the common danger and upheld the president. A rescript was obtained from Rome approving of the re-establishment of St. Edmund's monastery, and declaring null and void any attempts to disturb that establishment, and moreover decided that the profession of the novices was valid. This was an important decision in the way of independence, and confirmed the view held by the gregorians, as a body, that chapter could not interfere with the legitimate rights of a house.

Thus, then, all ended happily, and St. Edmund's was left to work out its own destiny. The college increased. In 1833 there were thirty-two students; six years after forty-three; two years more saw the number increased to sixty-six. The site of the old gregorian church and monastery had been taken by the government in March 1817, for the purpose of building a prison, for which compensation to the value of 8947 francs had been paid to the administrator. In 1840 permission was obtained to build a new chapel and refectory, with Pugin for architect, the result being a collegiate chapel unique in its simple beauty and elegant proportions.

The monks add to the ordinary work of a college that of educating boys for the secular mission. The settlement of the property belonging to English catholics brought this about. Hence, St. Edmund's, the only English establishment on the Continent, opened its doors to such subjects as the English catholic bishops send as ecclesiastical pupils.

Since its restoration St. Edmund's has been singularly gifted in its superiors, and two of its priors, D. Bernard Collier (1840) and D. Adrian Hankinson (1863), together with D. B. Scarisbrick, sometime prefect (1872), have been raised to the episcopate for the Mauritius. Its restorer, D. Marsh, two of its priors, abbat Burchall (1841) and abbat O'Gorman (1883), and one more of its community, abbat O'Neil (1888), just appointed bishop of Mauritius, have been called to exercise the high office of president-general of the whole congregation. Its present prior, D. Oswald O'Neil, a true edmundian, has held office for over ten years, and has carried out all the work of reorganisation thrown upon him by the changes recently brought about in the constitution of the congregation, and has done a great deal for the welfare of the college under his care. In order to facilitate business, and with an eye to a possible future necessity of leaving France (for no one knows from day to day what an atheistic government may do), the present prior, with wise forethought, bought a large house and grounds at Great Malvern, and opened it in 1891 as the Monastery of Our Lady and St. Edmund. A small community is in residence. The establishment was intended for a house of study for the juniors, and also to save the missioners belonging to St. Edmund's from having to cross the sea for the purpose of their yearly retreat. He has also bought at Planques a valuable property, which consists of an excellent country house and farm, most useful for the college.

St. Edmund's has been of immense service to the English catholics; and having the early training of a large number of secular priests, some of whom have risen to the very highest posts, the cordial relations which have always existed between the sons of St. Benedict and the clergy have been strengthened and made more lasting. This benedictine house has thus been an important connecting link; and one has only to ask an old Douai boy what his feelings are to find the spell St. Edmund's had woven round his heart. It has known how to imprint its own spirit of manly simplicity and open-hearted earnestness upon all who have been trained there.

CHAPTER XIX

ST. MALO, LAMBSPRING, AND CAMBRAI

THE circumstances under which the monastery of St. Benedict at St. Malo in Brittany was founded have been already mentioned. D. Gifford was appointed by the bishop his theologian, and attached to this position was a house which was made to serve as a monastery until such time as one could be built. Another house, with a chapel attached, was about the same time given to them at Clermont, just outside the town, where some of the monks were sent to live.

"Father Barnes taught casuistry in the cathedral, and the others sweated in the confessionals and pulpits; and as it began in drudgery, so it continued on, for the city of St. Malo's was scant of religious and needed such help; the cathedral itself was but a poor business, and the English benedictine monks formed two benedictine nunneries in the city besides, at the request of the bishop." [1]

But the foundation was not to take place without considerable difficulties. After five years the cathedral chapter awoke to the fact that these strangers were

[1] Weldon, p. 81.

doing the work they had neglected. They therefore began to look with unfriendly eyes upon the monks. The canons made an effort to force them to leave the town. "But the good bishop and the citizens stood by those they had called in, and who spared no pains to serve them."[1] D. Gifford, however, was not the man to give in to opposition of that kind. He had watched the struggle at Douai against opponents far more powerful and determined, and had witnessed its result. He, however, gave up the post of theologian and (November 1616) bought for his community a house and garden in the town, to which, two years after (1618), was added another house and garden. The bishop stood their good friend, and gave them leave to open a church. On November 21 (the *dies memorabilis*), 1621, they began a temporary church of wood, and it was used for the first time on the following feast of St. Thomas à Becket.

While D. Gifford was prior of this house he took a part in the reform of Fontevraud,[2] to which we

[1] Weldon, p. 127.
[2] Fontevraud in Poitou was founded at the end of the tenth century by blessed Robert d'Arbrissel. It was a double monastery, and the abbess governed both the monks and nuns. Foundations were made in other parts of France, in England (at Amesbury, Eaton, and Delagrave), and in Spain; and at a later date they were united into one congregation, with the abbess of Fontevraud as superior-general. The Hundred Years' War and the attacks of the calvinists brought about here, as elsewhere, a general decline of observance and material decay. These evils were met by the vigorous life which rose towards the beginning of the seventeenth century, and in which, as we see in the text, English benedictines took a prominent part.

must here allude. The capuchin, F. Joseph de Tremblay, the "grey cardinal" and confidant of Richelieu, had been called in by the coadjutrix of the abbess of Fontevraud to bring about a reform in that congregation. He was also provincial of his order. During one of his visitations he came across the English monks of St. Malo, and met D. Augustine Bradshaw (1613), who was on his way from Spain. These English monks so edified the capuchin by their holiness of life, their monastic observances, and strictness of the common life, that he saw in them the men who could successfully carry out the reform he had begun. D. Bradshaw, on his return to Douai, took in Paris on his way, and was introduced to the coadjutrix of Fontevraud, Mother Antoinette of Orleans. Chelles had already been started through him, and the good work the monks did there had spread to Remiremont and other houses in relation with Chelles. The abbess of Fontevraud and her coadjutrix heard of the good results at Chelles, and petitioned to have D. Bradshaw and some of the Spanish monks. The capuchin, F. Joseph, knew well that the first step in the reform must be to give new life to the monks of Fontevraud, who, in that double community, were the directors of the nuns. But belonging to another order, he felt it was impossible for him to undertake such a task. "These English benedictines were better able than any one else to give these monks a real monastic training. If they acquiesced in his views he could easily provide them with houses and means." [1]

D. Bradshaw went to Fontevraud (October 9, 1613), and was followed soon after by D. Gifford and D. Waldegrave. D. Leander, then the vicar, also paid a visit; and the matter was taken up in earnest on both sides, and a scheme of union was prepared by D. Bradshaw, whose enthusiasm outweighed his discretion.

"'The monks of Fontevraud were to accept the habit, the constitutions, and the ceremonial of Valladolid, modified according to the exigences of the place. They were to admit to the religious habit English catholics who should make application for it. The nuns were to do the same with young English girls. An experienced monk was to be sent to them, who should be the abbess' counsellor and her vicar-general in the government of the monastery and order; a master of novices also and two professors of philosophy and theology—all at least forty years of age—and they were to remain under the obedience of their own superiors. In exchange, Fontevraud offered endowed houses where the English monks might live under its protection. This scheme was signed on the 17th of December 1613. It was welcomed by Fr. Leander of St. Martin, by the best friends of the congregation, and in particular by the generous abbat of St. Vedast." [2]

The abbey of the Blessed Trinity at Poitiers, most

[1] *The Ampleforth Journal*, vol. ii. p. 31.   [2] *Ibid.* p. 32.

likely that also of St. Croix, came also under the care of D. Augustine Bradshaw; and he spent much time in helping on the movement towards a more observant life which was then beginning to affect so many houses of benedictines. But nothing could be done without the Spanish general's consent, and he took a long time in considering the question. Meanwhile D. Bradshaw, as we have seen, was also taking an active part in the work of the English Union in a direction not approved of by his superiors. This, together with a longer reflection, caused the vicar, D. Leander, to have misgivings about the whole affair of Fontevraud. He writes to the general (September 15, 1614): "The mission has nothing to gain from them;" and later on (October 4): "We shall have to give these nuns our best men. Chelles is already a burthen. It is Fr. Augustine who has prepared all this with Fr. Joseph, who lives out of his convent in a monastery of nuns, by virtue of apostolic bulls. He takes great care of his person. He has had recourse to the king to have himself named provincial in spite of the murmurs of his order."

D. Bradshaw was removed; but up to the last D. Gifford remained with them (December 5, 1614). The whole matter, and perhaps fortunately for the interests of the English monks, now dropped.

After this digression about the reform of Fontevraud, we must return to St. Benedict's. Weldon tells us: "The house of St. Malo, through the admission of French, being become a greater trouble to the congregation than it could manage in a foreign country where the fathers were unknown and had no friends to support them, they resolved (1661) to put it off the best way they could. The royal council of France was alarmed at the establishment of English bred up in Spain, fixed in such a seaport in France; and the parliament of Brittany was so contrary to them on the said account that when Louis XIII. had piously given his royal consent that the fathers might have the abbey of St. Jacat in the said province (the abbat and convent having agreed to it), they would never verify the agreement or transaction, whereby it had no effect."[1]

In 1659 Charles II. of England paid the monks a visit, and stayed eight days in their house at Clermont. In commemoration of this honour, a tablet bearing the following distich was put up in the guest-room:—

> ANGUSTÆ PAUPERTATEM NE SPREVERIS AULÆ.
> HOSPITIUM REX HIC REPPERIT ATQUE FIDEM.

In 1672 the monastery of St. Benedict at St. Malo, owing to the difficulties which beset them, ceased to belong to the English congregation. It was sold to the maurists, who undertook to pay to the English superiors a yearly rent of two hundred pistoles. During its uneventful history of sixty-one years, only fourteen choir monks were professed.

[1] Weldon, pp. 197, 198.

The English monks, some decades earlier, were offered the opportunities of settlement in the lutheran parts of Germany, and in monasteries which the Bursfeld congregation was unable to occupy. The conditions were that the English recovered them at their own costs from the lutherans, who then held them, and that eventually they should be returned to the German congregation. The English monks accepted the conditions, and the houses of Rintelen, Cismar, Dobran, Scharnabeck, Weine, together with Lambspring and Stoterlingburg for nuns, were made over to them. A small community, under D. Clement Reyner, was at Rintelen for a few years, and a seminary was started. But little, however, is known of this foundation, which did not last long. Under the date May 8, 1632, Weldon mentions the death there of D. Placid Frere, a monk of St. Gregory's, who was one of the first religious in the new house:—

"A most worthy, witty, and hopeful young man, and, for his time, an excellent scholar; being newly made priest, and having sung his first mass, died, to the great grief of all his brethren, at Rintelen, in Westphalia. This is remarkable, that he being an excellent violist, and having a bass viol hanging in his cell, the great string thereof broke asunder whilst he was in his agony, and his brethren reciting the litanies by his bedside, and soon after he expired."[1]

[1] P. 168.

The abbey of Cismar never was occupied by the English, though for some time an abbat was appointed and had a seat in the chapter. D. Leander was to have been the first English abbat, but untimely death prevented him. D. Maurus Corker held the same dignity. But the only one of these houses that proved any use to the English monks was Lambspring. Originally a monastery for nuns, the abbey of SS. Adrian and Denis, near Hildesheim, by desire of the elector of Cologne, was given over to English monks in 1643. But when it was first offered to them it was occupied by lutheran nuns, and it took thirteen years to get rid of them. It was not till 1644 that the monks could enter, and the church be reconciled. A reinforcement was sent, October 1645, three of whom were from Douai. One of the conditions upon which the house was lent by the Germans was that all the rights and privileges of the house should be preserved intact. It was therefore counted an abbey, and retained the rights of a house election. Its superior was a duly blessed abbat elected for life, and, as such, took precedence of all except the president. Soon it became an important house and attracted many members. From 1645 to 1802, one hundred and seventy-two professions took place, and eight abbats ruled.

D. Maurus Corker, a member of this house, was received publicly by James II., in full court, as envoy of the elector of Cologne. He came to a public audience as a benedictine monk, wearing his habit, and accompanied by six of his brethren. But his fame chiefly consists in his connection with the venerable servant of God, Oliver Plunket, archbishop of Armagh. He was confined in prison (Newgate) with that holy prelate, and prepared him for that martyrdom he himself was daily expecting. A beautiful correspondence passed between the two; and the archbishop conceived so much veneration for his companion in bonds that he left the priceless treasure of his body to English benedictines, to whom, it is said, he was joined in confraternity. Through D. Corker's care, the body of the martyr was saved from the usual fate reserved for those who died the felon's death, and it was secured by catholic hands. When he became abbat of Lambspring the relics were translated (1693) to the crypt of the new church, where they were religiously kept.[1]

Another monk of this same house, D. Placid Francis, played a part in James II.'s ill-advised and illegal proceedings at Cambridge. He obtained from the king letters to the university (February 7, 1687) commanding the authorities to admit him to the Master of Arts degree. Armed with this letter, D. Francis lost no time, but went to Cambridge (February 9) and produced the letter to the vice-chancellor, Dr. Peachell, who promptly summoned his council to decide how to resist this aggression. It met (February 21) and resolved that the applicant,

---

[1] They are once more in the keeping of English benedictines at Downside.

who had already received the degree in a foreign university, and had, therefore, shown his qualifications, should be admitted. But he must obey the general law and take the Oath of Allegiance. The senate petitioned the king to this effect. But this did not please D. Francis, who insisted upon the terms of the royal letter, which granted a dispensation from the requirements of the law. He returned to London and reported the result to James. An angry correspondence took place, the king insisting upon his right of dispensation, and the senate firmly refusing to break the law passed by parliament. The vice-chancellor, together with eight members of the senate, were summoned to Whitehall before the king's commissioners for ecclesiastical affairs, and he was (May 7) suspended from his office and from his headship of Magdalen College.

By the end of the century the abbey of Lambspring was upon a permanent footing. A noble church, with nine altars, and a large organ of forty-eight stops, was begun in 1670 and consecrated in 1691. The abbat was an important personage. He was prince of the neighbouring territory, and held his courts, in which he had power of life and death. For the needs of the people,[1] he had always some German monks in his community to attend to them. But this arrangement was attended with disadvantages, for upon the retire-

---

[1] When the monks went to Lambspring there were only two or three catholics. In 1696 there were at least three hundred.

ment of abbat Corker in 1696, he was succeeded by D. Maurus Knightley, "whose promotion was the work of the Germans, whereby great troubles rose in that abbey, which could not be ended of some years, the country maintaining him, and the monks not liking to be imposed on."[1]

Abbat Knightley's rule was not happy in any respect; nor was his zeal in procuring desirable vocations at all calculated to maintain the good name of his house and order. But it is pleasanter to turn to the picture of a later time. On the death of abbat Augustine Tempest (1708–30), a successor of abbat Knightley's, two monks of the house, D. Joseph Rokeby and D. Anselm Crathorne, fellow-novices, and both professed in 1703, were felt by the convent to have undisputed and almost equal claims to their esteem and respect. The choice of the monks, however, fell on D. Rokeby, and one of his first cares was to recall D. Crathorne from the mission, and obtain for him the titular abbacy of Cismar. To him abbat Rokeby committed the exterior ministration depending upon the monastery, together with the charge of his petty principality, while he reserved to himself the cares more immediately pertaining to his abbatial office. Thus did these two dwell in tenderest bonds of friendship, uniting their efforts for the common good until death separated them. The rule of abbat Rokeby (1730–61) was the most prosperous period in the annals of the abbey. The

[1] Weldon, p. 235.

monastery was entirely rebuilt by him almost as soon as he came into office. "If it had been completed," says one who had seen it when occupied by English monks, ". . . it must have been one of the first religious buildings in Germany."[1] "But of recent years," says another writer, "it is sad to see the neglect which is slowly reducing this extensive pile of buildings to premature decay. The grand hall, with its fading and damp-stained frescoes, is a pitiable sight; it now serves as a store-room for the apples and the onions of some thrifty housewives, and for the drying-room of the local laundries."[2]

Hardly a generation was to pass before the house of Lambspring came to an end. It was suppressed by the Prussian government in 1803. Some few of its members continued to live on in the neighbourhood in hopes of recovering their abbey, but were soon compelled to leave, and betake themselves to England.[3] Some small compensation was made to them by the Prussians, who assured those who chose

---

[1] Whitaker, T. D., *History of Whalley* (4th edit.), vol. ii. p. 528.
[2] *Downside Review*, vol. v. p. 216.
[3] At the priest's house at St. Godehard's in Hildersheim is an illuminated psalter of twelfth-century date, the work of the St. Alban's *Scriptorium*. It had belonged to the English monks of Lambspring. Mr. E. Bishop, in an article in the *Downside Review* (July 1896), suggests that it may have come to its present place through D. Anthony Meyer, a native of St. Godehard, who was the monastic parish-priest (1802–9). "In the midst of the upset caused by the suppression, it seems not unlikely that this manuscript found its way into his possession, and was by and by deposited in his old house, now secularised too, and was accordingly lost to its former possessors and its proper country."

to live in Germany of a regular pension from the government. A proposition was then made that they should amalgamate with the laurentians at Ampleforth; but it was not entertained, for the monks had hopes of re-establishing their monastery elsewhere. An attempt was made in 1832 at Broadway near Worcester; but six years later it was abandoned, and the Lambspring community died out.

St. Benedict has daughters as well as sons; and his English patrimony would not be complete unless there were houses of virgins consecrated in the holy habit to God's service. Already in 1588, about the same time when the movement from the seminaries began in Italy, a convent of English benedictine dames had been opened in Brussels, the history of which we will pursue in the next chapter. But this convent, though under the jurisdiction of the archbishop of Malines, was not at peace owing to the dissensions which existed in England between the jesuits and the clergy, and which dissensions unhappily found their way into the cloister. Another convent in Paris was attempted in 1612, under the auspices of the Italian fathers, but it was frustrated by the English ambassador, after a monastery had even been built by some English ladies.[1] It was now considered advisable by the monks of St. Gregory's of Douai to establish a monastery for nuns under

---

[1] See a letter of D. Augustine (Smithson), March 4, 1612, in the *Spicilegium Benedictinum*, No. 1, p. 16.

their own direction, where the difficulties met with at Brussels should find no place.

D. Benet Jones *or* Price was the superior of the benedictine missioners in the London district, and was on intimate terms with Mr. Cresacre More, great-grandson of Blessed Thomas More. This gentleman had one son, left motherless at an early age, and two daughters. The eldest daughter, Helen, had heard little or nothing about the monastic state before she had seen D. Price. But he soon discovered the rare qualities of soul possessed by the young girl, and broached the subject to her. She at first could not understand her aptness for this sort of life, and hesitated as to the reality of her vocation. But leaving it all to her father and to the monks, these after much deliberation settled that she should go abroad and make trial, at least, of her vocation. Brussels was out of the question, and the project of the new monastery under the care of the monks of St. Gregory's met with the approbation of Mr. More, who desired to be the founder of the house. The arrangements were put into the hands of D. Price. Helen was joined by six other young ladies, all of gentle birth, two of whom were her cousins. Her sister Bridget joined the little community afterwards (1629). These seven friends, with two others as lay sisters, were conducted by D. Benet to Douai in 1623, intending to settle there somewhere within reach of St. Gregory's. But no suitable place could be found for them in that town; and D. Rudisind Barlow, then president, hearing of a disused convent at Cambrai, went over to see it and to ask the bishop's leave to settle his nuns there. The bishop, Van der Burch, not only consented to the foundation, but freely and generously exempted the community from his jurisdiction and confided them to the care of the English fathers who had founded the house.

The house selected belonged to the abbey of Femy and was in a half unfinished state, and it cost the little community more than five hundred pounds to make it habitable.

"At first it was only lent to them, and they were, according to agreement, to leave it at six months' warning, and the money paid for the reparations to be reimbursed to them when they should be warned out of the house, which the workmen said could not stand past thirty years."[1]

In 1638 the abbat of St. Andrew's, to whom Femy was then annexed, made over the house altogether to the English dames, and the gift was confirmed by Urban VIII. Later on more houses and land were bought, and an establishment suitable for a monastery founded.

The nine ladies took possession of their new house on Christmas eve 1623, and at once began conventual life; and the bishop, always most fatherly to them, came to say the first mass in their chapel.

[1] Weldon, p. 143.

The house was dedicated to the Blessed Virgin under the title of "Our Lady of Comfort." Three religious from the English abbey at Brussels, at the request of D. Rudisind, were lent to train the postulants in the religious life, one of whom, dame Frances Gawen, became the first abbess. On the 31st of December the nine postulants were clothed, and solemnly professed on January 1, 1625. Their constitutions were given to them by the general chapter, and, like the monks, the abbess was appointed for a term of four years. The prior of St. Gregory's was the ordinary of the convent. As soon as the first four years of office were expired (1629), Dame Catherine Gascoigne, one of the original nine, was elected abbess in place of the nun who had come from Brussels. She held office until 1673, with the exception of one term of four years during which she was absent from her convent, employed by the archbishop in restoring religious observances in one of the other convents (St. Lazare) in the town. After Dame Frances Gawen, the ex-abbess, had finished her term of office, she and one of her companions remained by choice as simple religious in the new community. The third, according to the agreement made, returned some years later to the house of her profession at Brussels. The first chaplain or vicar, as he is called, seems to have been D. Maihew, who died there September 14, 1625.

But before any professions had taken place in

the new convent, Providence sent one who was to form the interior spirit of the young community, and lead many of them to a state of high perfection. D. Augustine Baker arrived at Cambrai in July 1624, and stayed there nearly nine years. All the novices at once put themselves under his direction, but as they did not yet understand him they soon left him, all excepting Dame Catherine Gascoigne. Under his wise and discreet teaching, she made such solid progress in virtue that D. Baker was ordered to remain to continue his good work. Among those who had left him in the beginning, and who was the last to come back, was Helen More, now known as Dame Gertrude. Young and ardent, she had chafed under the moderation D. Baker imposed upon his spiritual children. At last she, too, gave way, and came back to him; and eventually became, to quote Weldon, "singularly memorable for her holiness of life."[1]

She has left behind some papers, entitled her "Confessions," from which we are enabled to gather some further idea of D. Baker's system of spirituality. She speaks of the sound discretion he evinced, and of the difference between him and some other directors, who were inclined to demand too much at the beginning, and thus hurry on a frustrated vocation. God, as a rule, works slowly. D. Baker presupposes a scrupulous observance of all the com-

[1] P. 212.

mon practices of conventual life; and the affective prayer he recommends is the natural outcome of a love for the Divine office, which consists so much of the food for this simple kind of prayer. Indeed, we may say that those whose vocation is the *Opus Dei* must needs tend to affective prayer, rather than to the more discursive methods.

In all indifferent matters he taught her to act with complete liberty, and do or not do just as she found was good then and there for her soul. One point, however, he greatly insisted upon; and that was, liberty of spirit. He would not have his disciples fettered down by any dependence which savours too much of human nature. God's will made known by obedience is one thing, man's device another. The first binds, the other we can use or not use as we please. His instructions in the confessional were very brief, and he would not allow a constant inquiry on part of the penitent as to her growth in holiness. He set the soul once for all on the right path, and then urged her to persevere in that.

"In his treatise upon confession this discreet father is very earnest in showing the great evils of servile fear and self-will, scrupulosity and obscurity of soul, which come of unnecessary conferring with the confessor. The sacrament is made to be a human almost, rather than a Divine institution, and is distorted into a punishment rather than a relief of soul. Long and frequent conferences of this kind are mistaken for signs of piety and spirituality, and are allowed to take the time and place of mortification and prayer. . . . God is the great Master of perfection, and His light will never fail those who seek for it in simplicity and obedience."[1]

An interesting letter from D. Baker to Sir R. Cotton, preserved in the Cottonian MSS.[2] at the British Museum, may be here given as affording a glimpse of the life, spiritual and intellectual, of the dames of Cambrai :—

"I was glad to understand of your life and quality which the bearer, being lately in that part, made known to me. I shall pray to God that the prolonging of your days may be a means to dispose you to a better departure when it shall please God to call you out of this uncertain and short life.

"Ever since my being with you, I have lived in a city in these foreign parts called Cambrai, assisting a convent of certain religious women of the order of St. Benet newly erected. They are in number as yet but twenty-nine. They are inclosed, and never seen by us nor by any other, unless it be rarely upon an

---

[1] Abbat Sweeney, *Life of D. A. Baker*, p. 4.
[2] MS. Cott., Julius III., fol. 12. In this same volume are letters from D. Rudisind Barlow and D. Leander to Sir R. Cotton. Also one from D. Bradshaw, fol. 43, who, writing from Westminster (September 22, 1612), gives some information about a person Sir R. Cotton had inquired after. The letter from D. Leander is dated Douai, September 18, 1628, saying he intends going to England if possible, and will then call upon him. The letter from D. Rudisind from Douai, April 17, 1623, recommends D. Leander, about to visit England (this is, of course, for a visit previous to the one D. Leander refers to), and thanks him for the assistance he gave in the *Apostolatus*.

extraordinary occasion. But upon no occasion may they go forth, nor may any man or woman get in unto them, yet I have my diet from them, and upon occasions confer with them, but (we) see not one another; and live in a house adjoining to theirs.

"Their lives being contemplative, the common books of the world are not for their purpose, and little or nothing is in these days printed in English that is proper for them. They want many good English books in this time. They have some, yet they want many, and therefore I am in their behalf become a humble suitor unto you to bestow on them such books as you please, either manuscripts or printed, being in English, containing contemplation, saints' lives or other devotions. Hampole's[1] works are proper for them. I wish I had Hilton's *Scala perfectionis* in Latin, it would help the understanding of the English (and some of them understand Latin). The favour you shall do them will be had in memory both towards you and your posterity whenso it may please God to send some hither to be of the number, as there is always one of the name, if not of your kindred. The bearer will convey hither such books as it shall please you to single out and deliver to him. I desire my humble service to be remembered

---

[1] Richard Rolle of Hampole, whose works D. Baker refers to, was an English mystical writer of the age which produced S. Bernard, S. Bonaventure, and Thomas à Kempis. Rolle is in truth "an English father of the church." He was an anchorite in Yorkshire, and lived in the first half of the fourteenth century. His works are now being published for the first time in two volumes.

to my lady also, for whose soul, like your own and your posterity, myself and this convent will be glad to have such particular occasion as this will be to have you in (particular) recommendation, wherein we will not be wanting.—Your beadsman and servant in Christ, AUG. BAKER.

"CAMBRAYE, *the 3rd of June*, 1629."

It was while D. Baker was here that he was the object of attack and persecution. But D. Leander and D. Rudisind, after having put his methods to a rigorous examination, not only pronounced them to be conformable to the benedictine spirit, but procured the approbation of chapter and introduced them at their own convent at Douai, where they bore like fruit.

The community was growing largely. It was already twenty-nine in number when D. Baker wrote in 1629. But they were meeting with many losses owing to the civil war in England, which prevented their incomes being paid, and caused almost the total loss of their means. D. Benet, their procurator, was arrested in London, where he was attending to their affairs, and all their papers and money, which were on his person, were seized. In 1645 the community, numbering now fifty, were reduced to the verge of starvation and had no certain means of subsistence. The welfare of this house was always most dear to the fathers of the English congregation, and they made every effort to help their sisters in their distress. The nuns all suffered alike, for the common life had been from the beginning strictly followed, and "the use of particular pensions or anything savouring of propriety is unknown in the monastery, where all is in common and at the disposal of the superior, as the Rule and constitutions ordain."[1]

Relief was found partly by a new foundation to Paris in 1652, and by starting on a more permanent basis the small claustral school which seems to have existed from within the first ten years of the starting of the monastery. After this their life went on placidly till the times of the revolution. As soon as the Terror broke out, the president, D. Walker, hastened to their assistance; and he was with them when, late one night (October 18, 1793), a party of soldiers thundered at the door and demanded admittance. Everything was seized, and, amidst insults and all manner of barbarous usage, the helpless and terrified inmates, twenty-one in number, were hurried off in open carts to Compiègne. There they were imprisoned in the Visitation convent; and the following June they were joined by seventeen carmelite nuns. These, on July 17, 1794, were led out to execution, leaving the English dames in hourly expectation of the same fate. The poor nuns suffered terribly from want of bread and fuel; as to clothes, they had been hurried off from Cambrai without even a change. After the

[1] Weldon, 144.

carmelites were taken away to death the guards told the hapless English ladies that unless that "uniform," their habit, was put off they could not be answerable for their lives. As the nuns had no money to buy secular clothes, an official offered them the secular dresses which the carmelites had left behind. These they were glad to have, and wore them as a safeguard for the rest of the time in prison. Shortly after their arrival they had the consolation of the presence of D. Walker and another priest as fellow-prisoners. But the president and four of the nuns died early in 1794 under the hardships of that imprisonment.

At last they were released, and got passports on April 24, 1795, to leave France. They sailed from Calais on May 2nd, and arrived the same evening at Dover, where they remained for the next day, being a Sunday. On the 4th they went to London. As soon as their arrival was known, the marchioness of Buckingham procured a suitable house for them and afforded them every comfort in her power. D. Brewer, afterwards president, made over to them a house at Wolton, near Liverpool, where they continued a school for young ladies and recommenced conventual life as far as was possible. In 1807 they moved to Abbots Salford. But they found their final home thirty years afterwards at Stanbrook, some four miles out of Worcester.

Here, in the midst of a country redolent with memories of benedictine glories of bygone days, they have settled and prospered exceedingly. Of late years they have been developed on wise and broad foundations. A beautiful abbatial church in which the liturgy is carried out with loving exactness and splendour, monastic buildings of great dignity and suitableness, and a community of seventy full of intellectual life, show how God has blessed this house. The present abbess, lady Gertrude Dubois, who has held office since 1872, is now, by a return to benedictine tradition, chosen for life. She received the solemn blessing on November 21, 1895.

CHAPTER XX

OTHER BENEDICTINE HOUSES, DENIZEN AND ALIEN

THIS account of the restoration of St. Benedict's patrimony in England would not be complete without some notice of the other benedictine houses, which do not form part of the congregation. They are of two kinds; houses independent one of the other, but under English government (denizen, socalled); and houses in the same position as the alien priories formerly existing.

The honour of being the first benedictine house established for English subjects since the Reformation belongs to the abbey of the "Glorious Assumption of our Lady" now at East Bergholt in Suffolk. Its foundress, lady Mary Percy, daughter of blessed Thomas Percy, earl of Northumberland, after the death of her mother (1596) lived in Brussels. Her one great desire was to serve God in holy religion, and for years she had led a life of great fervour and devotion, waiting for God's will to be made known. Her director was Fr. Holt of the society, who was then living in Brussels, and had much influence at the archducal court. Flanders was the great place of refuge for English catholics; and the jesuit saw that a house of English religious women would meet a want. He encouraged lady

Mary Percy in her pious wish, and suggested that she should found a house of English nuns instead of joining a Flemish one. Her mind naturally turned to that great order in which so many ladies of rank had, in the happier days of England, found a home in which they could serve God. The way was soon made clear to her. Another English lady, mistress Dorothy Arundel of Lanherne, was passing through Brussels with her sister Gertrude, on their way to join the bridgettine nuns, just lately settled in Lisbon (1594).[1] While praying in the church of St. Gudule she received a supernatural intimation that she was to stay in Brussels and join lady Mary in founding a benedictine monastery. She obeyed, and her sister remained with her.

A brief authorising the foundation was obtained from pope Clement VIII., through the good offices of F. Parsons, whose niece later on entered the new monastery of English dames. The house, like almost every other English benedictine nunnery in former days, was to remain under the jurisdiction of the ordinary of the diocese, the archbishop of Malines, and was to be governed by an abbess elected for life by the free votes of the community. Early in 1598 a house was bought, into which they entered July 14 of that year. The archduke Albert granted all the legal privileges enjoyed by other convents, and the archduchess Isabella, being a per-

[1] These nuns, founded at Syon abbey by Henry V. in 1415, after three hundred years of exile have returned to England, and are now settled at Syon abbey, Chudleigh, Devon.

sonal friend of lady Mary Percy, wished to endow the new monastery. But she declined the generous offer lest this might interfere with the freedom of election she was determined to secure for her nuns.

In order that the foundation might be properly begun, lady Mary invited dame Joannna Berkeley, daughter of Sir John Berkeley of Beverston, a professed nun of St. Peter's abbey at Rheims, to come and preside over the new house as first abbess. A strange circumstance is connected with this lady. At her profession some seventeen years previously, the preacher predicted that she would be called to assist in the foundation of an English benedictine convent, which would be the first to return to England. On November 21, 1599,[1] dame Joanna Berkeley received the solemn blessing as abbess, and lady Mary Percy and seven other English ladies, together with four lay sisters, received the habit. The ceremony was attended by the whole court and the papal nuncio, and an eye-witness writes: "It was one of the most solemn things that was seen this hundred years; many ladies and others could not forbear weeping." The dinner was sent in from the royal kitchens, and the archduke and his wife on this occasion dined in the refectory.

"The lady Berkeley procured two religious from her convent at Rheims to assist in the beginning of the house, which, when they had charitably performed some years, (they) returned to their convent

---

[1] Again, the *dies memorabilis*.

much edified, being so humble (as) to say they had learnt themselves to be true religious, seeing with what fervour so many young tender ladies left their country, friends, and fortunes, to embrace with such cheerfulness a life of humility and mortification and live in so exact an observance of our holy rule." [1]

The following year, 1600, all the novices made their profession, and many others joined. Now that an English benedictine house was established, ladies were eager to cross the sea to join the new community. This was of course against the penal laws, then pressing so hardly upon catholics in England, and many were apprehended in the attempt, and suffered imprisonment for the crime of seeking in other lands the liberty denied them in their own. But by so doing they lost their property in England, and many of birth had to join the community in the humble capacity of lay sisters.

Under lady abbess Berkeley the convent grew

[1] From a MS. Relation by Lady Abbess Waldegrave of Ghent (1713-19), in the possession of the old English chapter, quoted by Tierney, vol. iv. pp. 102, 103. The abbess continues: "The Lady Berkeley procured our statutes to be composed by a consult of prelates, abbats, and divines well experienced in monastic discipline. They were confirmed by the pope, and delivered to the religious in the year 1612, by the right honourable archbishop, the Lord Matthias Hoven, on these conditions following: That we should be subject to the bishop of the diocese, and have for our spiritual directors the society who, at the beginning of our house, had much laboured in advancing the spiritual and temporal good of the monastery." But, at least in this last respect, the abbess is mistaken, for no such condition was ever appended to the constitutions of Brussels, as can be seen in the printed copy. It was precisely to secure jesuit direction that the new benedictine house at Ghent was founded, and that so much difficulty occurred.

apace, and new buildings were erected. In her successor's time a church was built. "There were then many English officers in the Low Country service who voluntarily out of their pay contributed to the beginning of our house. We have a list of their names and charities amongst our benefactors."[1] In addition to this, the soldiers of the English regiment then quartered in Brussels gave their labour, and worked as masons in building the house of God.

Lady Mary Percy succeeded as second abbess upon the death of lady Berkeley in 1616, and seven years after was asked by the monks of Douai to send three of her nuns to do for Cambrai what dame Joanna Berkeley of Rheims had done for Brussels. One of them became the first abbess, and after her term of office (four years) remained as a simple religious, together with one of her companions, the third returning to Brussels. Next year (1624) a colony went to Ghent to form a house, and the circumstances of its foundation will be noted in their proper place.

The relation of the nuns to the society, through the good offices of Fr. Holt, have been mentioned; and the kindness they received from the jesuits is borne in grateful remembrance to this day. But unfortunately the dissensions which existed in England between the jesuits and the clergy found their way into the cloister with new novices, who in England had been attached to one party or the other. It is difficult in these days to realise how strongly feeling

---

[1] M.S. Relation of Lady Abbess Waldegrave.

ran on what was the burning question of the hour. The main source of the difficulties was the question of confessors. Some would have only jesuits, and made it well-nigh impossible for any secular priest to hold this office.[1] Fr. Parson's niece, as may be imagined, was one of the leaders in this faction. For some years, although a secular had from the beginning been appointed the ordinary confessor to the nuns, yet for peace sake the abbess had allowed such, as particularly wished it, to have a jesuit in to hear their confessions and give them the direction they wished for. But this diversity of spirits thus introduced and fostered did not make for the peace of the community. Some went off to Ghent to be wholly under jesuit guidance, while those who remained deeply resented the action of the archbishop, who, acting according to their constitutions, nominated one confessor for the whole community. He appointed (1628) Dr. Champney, a secular priest, who was at first received with the greatest pleasure by all. He came highly recommended, among others, by D. Rudisind Barlow of Douai. But the hope of peace did not last long. A considerable faction in the convent insisted upon having a jesuit, although the archbishop of Mechlin, after appointing Dr. Champney as the ordinary con-

---

[1] "The nuns that were disobedient to their lady abbess *co ipso* that they saw any priest grateful to the lady abbess they presently endeavoured to avert him from that office, or to weary him being admitted, or through tedious wearisomeness to cause him to depart" (Add. MSS. 18,394, f. 2).

fessor, "condescended to the infirmity of those that were accustomed to the fathers of the society, (as to allow) that those that would might six times in the year be confessed unto them,"[1] and have a conference with them twice in the month. Advantage was taken of Dr. Champney having, twenty-five years ago, been one of the signers of the loyal address of the thirteen priests to queen Elizabeth, to suggest that he was unworthy to have the care of souls. The archbishop himself[2] sent the question to Louvain, and the theological faculty, while condemning the opinion of the signers as false, yet distinctly said it was not contrary to faith, nor did it make them unworthy to have the charge of souls.[3] In spite of all the means used, both from inside and outside the monastery, to exhaust his patience, the result was that Dr. Champney held his post till 1638, when at seventy years of age he resigned.[4] During the earlier part of these disturbances the archbishop,

[1] Add. MSS. 18,394, f. 5.

[2] In some most extraordinary way the name of D. Leander has got mixed up with this affair. One thing is most clear. It was the archbishop who sent the case to Louvain. To say that D. Leander was adverse to Dr. Champney, and opposed his appointment, is not only against all likelihood, all the circumstances of the case being considered, but is against such facts as we have. It was the jesuits who threatened "to indraw their labours from the nuns as long as Dr. Champney remained their confessor there" (*ibid.* f. 6).

[3] This, joined to the fact that another of the signers, Dr. William Bishop, had been appointed the first bishop, is only another proof that Rome herself is far more wide and tolerant than many of her officious defenders.

[4] The whole account from both sides is preserved in the British Museum, Harl. MSS. 4275, and Add. MSS. 18,393 and 18,394.

who displayed both prudence and patience, in 1636 proposed to get over the difficulty by putting the nuns under the jurisdiction of the English congregation. But he did not succeed in getting the approval of Rome for this course.

After these disputes, the Brussels house went on peacefully under its various abbesses; and from its foundation till the Revolution professed 137 choir nuns and 45 lay sisters. They were forced to leave Brussels, June 22, 1794, after nearly two hundred years, and made their way to England. Although other communities had set out before them, the Brussels nuns, the first to be founded, were the first to return (July 6th). After three days in London, bishop Douglas, the vicar-apostolic of the London District, found them a house at Winchester, in St. Peter's Street. They were welcomed by Dr. Milner, then the resident priest. He made every exertion to provide them with the necessary furniture, even giving up his own bed for their use. Two years after lady Austin Tancred was solemnly blessed in the church at Winchester, the first time that such a function had taken place since the reformation. The nuns were very poor, as almost everything had been lost in Brussels. Their papers and records had been confiscated, and their furniture destroyed.[1] To

---

[1] They were able, however, to bring over some church plate and vestments, among which is a set of black vestments made out of the pall used at the funeral of queen Elizabeth. After that ceremony, it became the perquisite of a member of the court whose daughter was a nun at Brussels.

help themselves they opened a school for young ladies, which in 1857 they transferred, together with the community, to East Bergholt, a beautiful village in Suffolk, where large conventual buildings were erected. Settled in their new home and their number increasing, the school no longer necessary as a means of support, by degrees a return was made to the simpler form of benedictine life. The school was closed in 1877, and now the community devote themselves to the Divine office and study. Their constitutions have been revised, and now that they can follow out to the full the life of their beautiful institute, God's blessing is visibly upon the community. Under the wise and kindly rule of lady Gertrude Lescher, the Abbey of the Glorious Assumption of our Lady has a flourishing and united community.

. . . . .

The origin of the Ghent house, now located at Oulton abbey, near Stone, has already been mentioned.[1] But to take up the story as it affected the new foundation. In 1611, soon after the profession of dame Lucy Knatchbull and dame Magdalen Digby, the jesuits persuaded them, with a few others (novices or postulants), to leave Brussels and found a new monastery at Liège or St. Omer. The reason given was that a report had reached them that the spiritual direction of the jesuits was to be wholly

---

[1] This account is taken from *The Annals of Oulton Abbey*, privately printed, 1894.

given up. The young ladies left Brussels, but every plan for the foundation failed. The jesuits then tried to persuade them to found a house of carmelites; but benedictines they were, and benedictines they would remain. There was no remedy but penitently to go back to Brussels, where they were kindly received back into the community. But the spirit of unrest had found entrance, and as Sir Toby Matthews[1] puts it, in his manuscript *Life of Lady Lucy Knatchbull:* " In multitudes, and especially of women, all like not easily to be of one dictamen or humour." Soon after, according to our judicious Toby :—

" Either upon certain rumours or else upon good reasons, they inclined and much more desired to procure a new plantation than to continue in the old. And I have heard (though I know not how true it was) that there grew to be a conceit, or at least a pretty loud kind of whisper, as if their superiors of that time had a mind to make themselves wiser (at least in their own opinion) than they had been before, and so to change the hand under which they had been happy till then, and this both in the temporal and in the spiritual way."

At this time (1622) Fr. John Norton, S.J., *alias* Knatchbull, dame Lucy's brother, heard the confes-

[1] Sir Toby Matthews was a son of the protestant archbishop of York. He became a catholic, and eventually a priest, although this latter fact was kept carefully concealed. If not himself a jesuit, he was the agent they employed as a "go between" with the government in the matter of Dr. Bishop and Dr. Smith.

sions of those of the nuns who were desirous of jesuit direction, and his hand is very evident in planning the new foundation. For two years the matter was talked over among themselves, but the abbess knew nothing about what was going on. Fr. Norton became very active on their behalf, and wrote letters to friends in England asking them to represent his views at Rome. In 1623 the archbishop came to the convent and conferred with the abbess about the expediency of making a new foundation, to which she assented, as it had been already in her mind, owing to the numbers then in the house, and one way, perhaps, out of the difficulties of the situation. After some demur as to the particular nuns to be sent, it was determined to make a foundation at Ghent. Some rich persons, through Fr. Norton's influence, were announced as ready to join the new house. So all leave being received from the proper authorities, four nuns with one novice and one lay sister, under the convoy of Fr. Norton, left Brussels (January 16, 1624) for Ghent, where a little house had been taken for them, and a temporary grille and choir arranged. They arrived on the 17th, and were met at the gates by a procession of townsfolk, who conducted them with every mark of respect and kindness to their temporary abode. The following Sunday Fr. Norton said mass, and the nuns settled down to community life. Two months after lady Lucy Knatchbull was blessed as abbess in the cathedral of St. Bavon, on the feast of St. Benedict. The constitutions of Brussels were observed, even the use of the Roman breviary, which had been introduced into the convent in place of St. Benedict's arrangement of the psalter.[1]

In the autumn of 1628 the community, now not far from twenty in number, moved into a newly built monastery hard by the great abbey of St. Peter, the abbat of which gave them leave to open a chapel, exacting as a tribute a wax candle of two pounds weight, together with a silver penny, to be presented each year at the high mass on the 29th of June. While here they must have seen a good deal of D. Clement Reyner, whom D. Leander, at the advice of abbat Caverel, had sent (1633) to St. Peter's in answer to the request of abbat Gerard Rym, to endeavour to restore the discipline of that abbey.[2] By 1635 the community numbered over forty. In 1650 king Charles II. honoured the convent with a visit, which is thus described from a MS. :—

"Upon the Annunciation eve, precedent to her last sickness, our young king, Charles II., a little after the beheading of his father, in his first passing through Ghent, was received into our monastery by this our reverend dear lady abbess (lady Mary Roper) and religiously entertained, her ladyship

---

[1] The present *Breviarium Monasticum* for the whole order only came out in 1612, but the various congregations had books formed upon St. Benedict's arrangement.

[2] D. C. Reyner was prior of this house, and was charged with the care of the novices and was the general confessor. When abbat Gerard died (1636) D. Reyner shortly afterwards left Ghent.

having a serious and private conference with his
majesty, she noting down what passed between
them; this was but a month before her happy
dissolution, and after her burial the paper was
found among her private writings in her oratory,
where she did not spare to speak plainly and most
piously in order to his eternal salvation and temporal good; who was so well pleased at her humble,
prudent, and cordial sincerity that then, and ever
since, his majesty showed himself upon all possible
occasions peculiarly and graciously affected to this
our community. After his departure he put us all in
mind of our dear Saviour, how He was deserted by
His own people, having this thought when we saw
the king in his purple coat mourning for his father,
which moved my lady and us all (at her ladyship's
precise ordain) to pray heartily for his conversion
and the good success of his bleeding affairs."

Charles II. never forgot the convent; and the nuns
in their turn were able to help him. The king sent
many of his letters to England enclosed in letters
of the abbess, all of which came safely to hand.
After the election of the new abbess he sent her a
donation of 1000 pistoles (£800), and settled an
annuity on the convent of £500. But, like all the
religious establishments on the continent, the dames
of Ghent had suffered great losses during the civil
wars. The community, moreover, lent money to
many of the king's adherents, who failed to pay
it back. A foundation to relieve the house was

determined upon; and at the beginning of 1652 five dames and one lay sister set out to make a foundation at Boulogne. After a great deal of difficulty, and through the good offices of "Monsieur Vincent" (St. Vincent de Paul), they got settled there in the April.

A pleasing letter from the king just before he embarked for England, and written in answer to one of congratulation, says :—

"I do assure you that as I have ever since being in these parts received many evidences of your good affection to me, so I shall never forget it, but shall always have a particular kindness for you and your community, and shall take all occasions to oblige you, of which you may assure your community. I have directed the chancellor to send you a little present of four hundred English pieces for the supply of your present necessities, and you shall find that I will do all I can to make your condition more easy, and that I am, your affectionate friend, CHARLES REX."

Nor was this all, for when in 1661 the abbess went over to England to see the king in person, he received her most graciously and gave her £3000 to help their necessities, which had become very pressing. A foundation was then made at Dunkirk in the year 1662, and another in 1665 at Ypres.[1]

---

[1] This convent still remains at Ypres.

James II., who had been reconciled to the church at Ghent (1669), shared in his brother's love for the English dames of this monastery. Soon after his accession he writes (January 20, 1686) to the abbess the following characteristic letter :—

"I would not have you imagine that I have been the less sensible of your letter and good prayers, because of my silence, for I am highly mindful both of them and your former signal service ; but as the Almighty by His prophet speaking to comfort His people useth this expression, '*He is silent in His love,*' so I, His vicegerent, use the same expression to you ; for till I have settled the affairs of my kingdom I will keep in silence and reserve what I intend ; which is to have your cloister, our darling monastery, the first in my kingdom. Then you shall find I will not only make good my brother's promises, but add new favours to show you how much I am, Madam, your affectionate friend,

"JAMES REX."

The king's benevolent intentions were never carried out. But in a little more than a hundred years the nuns were forced by the revolution to return to England. They went to Preston in 1794, and then to Caverswall Castle in Staffordshire (1811), where, by the advice of bishop Milner, the community made a return to the common life; for "the custom of the monastery at that time allowed (in accordance with a practice very common in France and Flanders) that individuals should have the disposal of a small annuity (seldom exceeding £5 in value), if given by their friends, in addition to the usual portion." In 1853 they moved to Oulton, near Stone, where St. Mary's abbey flourishes with its old bright and homely spirit which won the affections of the Stuart kings.

. . . .

St. Scholastica's abbey at Teignmouth is the old foundation made from Ghent at Dunkirk in 1662. This is counted a royal foundation, as the town was then an English possession, and Charles II., after making for expediency sake some public difficulties, not only gave his consent to the foundation, but contributed royally to the first expenses. In 1784 this community was joined by the dames from Pontoise, a former filiation from Ghent in 1652. They had settled first at Boulogne, and when Cromwell had taken Dunkirk removed for safety to Pontoise, near Paris. But the necessities of the convent became so pressing that it was considered expedient to break up the establishment and join their sisters at Dunkirk. This union of the two houses proved advantageous to both; and they remained a peaceful and happy community till the fatal year of 1793. Their church was seized for the meetings of the Jacobin club; and on October 13th the dames were turned out of the convent without time to make any preparations. They were first imprisoned with the poor clares in the town; but four days later both communities were sent off in a small boat, under a guard of fifty soldiers, to Gravelines. There they were imprisoned with the poor clares of that convent, suffering terrible privations, and wanting the bare necessities of life. For eighteen months they remained in this state, in terror and starvation, and ten of the benedictine dames sank under the imprisonment and died. When they got their liberty, they hastened to London, where they arrived on May 3, 1795, and went to their respective friends until a house could be found. The lady abbess Prujean, five days after, took a large house at Hammersmith,[1] but it was not till September 29th that the community were able to assemble and renew their religious life. Here they opened a school, and remained till they moved in 1863 to their present monastery at the beautiful seaside town of Teignmouth in Devonshire, given to them by the countess English. In 1870 the school was given up, and the nuns took up the work of perpetual adoration.

. . . . . .

The priory of our Lady of Good Hope and St. Benedict at Colwich, Staffordshire, is a foundation from the house at Cambrai. The circumstances which made the foundation necessary have been already

---

[1] The house was an old convent of "English virgins," three of whom alone remained. After the benedictines left, it became the seminary of St. Thomas of Canterbury for the diocese of Westminster. It was afterwards rebuilt by cardinal Manning, and has now passed into the hands of the nuns of the Sacred Heart.

told. Dame Clementia Cary, daughter of viscount Falkland, viceroy of Ireland, had joined the Cambrai community in 1638; and being personally known to the queen of Charles I., one of whose maids of honour she had been, went to Paris with her sister and another on account of her health, and to see what could be done towards founding a new house. Queen Henrietta received her with open arms and encouraged her to undertake the foundation, and inclined thereto the two queens of France, Anne of Austria and Marie Thérèse; "but the times were then dreadful even to the highest conditions. Also the honourable dames of the great Parisian convent of Mount Carmel and those of Port Royal, with their directors, were very charitable to them."[1] A house was hired (February 20, 1652), and four more choir nuns and a lay sister came from Cambrai to carry on conventual life. Dame Bridget More, a descendant of the martyred chancellor, was elected prioress and ruled the community till 1665.

"We continued in hired houses until March 12, 1664, when a gentleman, Monsieur de Touche,[2] waited upon us and conducted us in a coach, mother Clementia (Cary) and some of the community, to have our opinion of another residence he had been looking out for us. On our arrival we were wonder-

---

[1] Weldon, 199.
[2] Monsieur de Touche is most probably the Messire Paul le Pelletier, Seigneur des Touches, a layman, and sometime secretary to M. du Verger, abbé de S. Cyran. He is mentioned in the Port Royal necrology, p. 247, as dying June 22, 1703, aged 81 years.

fully surprised at meeting several of our friends there with lawyers, notaries, architects, and masons. We could not but express how pleased we were with the house and its situation, when the gentleman aforesaid led us into a private room and thus addressed us: 'My reverend mother, it is not without mystery that I made a particular choice of this day, the festival of St. Gregory the Great, by whose means the whole English nation was converted through the preaching of St. Augustine of the holy order of St. Benet. So I, though unworthy, am desirous on this day to be instrumental in beginning a monastery of the same holy order and nation, trusting it will prove a work much to the honour and glory of God, and that this place of solitude may become a dwelling for many souls and true spouses of Jesus Christ, who will seek and aspire after nothing but Him.'"

"We returned home transported with joy, blessing and praising God for His infinite goodness and providence towards us. This happening on St. Gregory's day much increased our devotion to this glorious saint, and conformably to the offering we make of ourselves, immediately after pronouncing our solemn vows, we add: 'I, sister N. N., do further, according to the vocation and holy institute of this convent, offer myself and all my actions for the conversion of England, for which this monastery was particularly instituted.'"[1]

[1] From a MS. Relation published by the Rev. G. Oliver of Exeter.

The community moved into their new house April 2, 1664, and lived there for 130 years. But this new foundation was not made without some sacrifice. The archbishop of Paris would not allow the nuns to found a convent unless they passed under his jurisdiction. The fathers of the English congregation consented to release them. "And yet gave them letters whereby they are still considered as sisters of the congregation, and ordered the convent of St. Edmund's (as the nearest to them) to treat them as such, and they were to have the same considerations for the congregation; which hath been so kind as to give them out of its bosom those for their confessors whom they have most desired, though necessary elsewhere." [1]

The archbishop gave them other constitutions, which were based mainly on those of Anne of Austria's convent of Val de Grace. Through this they have lost the old English custom of being called dames, and took instead, from the French, the terms "mother" and "sister." But the community itself remained exclusively English. Situated in Paris, they ran great risk of imbibing somewhat of the spirit of that time; the more so as many of their first friends and benefactors belonged to the Jansenist party. That the community entirely escaped infection is mainly due to the spirit they brought with them from Cambrai, and to the fact that their confessors were always English bene-

[1] Weldon, p. 200.

dictines. Their most cherished possession was the teaching of D. Baker, and this it was which preserved them in the time of danger. Looking to God and endeavouring to follow His guiding, they kept very closely to themselves and did not make use of outside help. Sermons, retreats, and long spiritual conferences were not in their line; so they escaped the snares into which other houses fell, and preserved their spirit in all its simple fervour. At the end of the eighteenth century they had l'Abbé Edgeworth as their special friend and counsellor.

When the revolution first broke out they were occasionally troubled with domiciliary visits from the democrats, but were still allowed to preserve their religious habit and life. But on October 3, 1793, they were put under arrest, and in the December their house was filled with prisoners of all sorts, several of whom were led out to be guillotined. Here they remained in much suffering and want till July 15, 1794, when they received the last domiciliary visit. The following day they were consigned to a dark dungeon, until coaches were made ready to take them off to the fortress of Vincennes, three leagues from Paris. They arrived about one in the morning, and were made to mount to the top of the tower, where four rooms were assigned to them. Living in hourly expectation of death, they were left here till August 7th, when they were removed in carts to the convent of the English austin nuns in the fosse St. Victor.

Here they were received by the sisters with great love. They had an allowance from the government of three livres a day. They were thus comparatively at ease, especially as they now had (January 17, 1795) the consolation of the sacraments. They were joined in their imprisonment by the English blue nuns, whose chaplain was incarcerated with them, and who managed to say mass from time to time. "Our bodily sustenance became very sparing; a pound of meat once in ten days, very little bread, and sometimes an egg. Salad was the only thing we could procure, of which we partook twice a day."

At length they had leave to return to England, where they landed, fifteen in number, 3rd July 1795. For about three months they took shelter in London; then, through the kind intervention of Lady Arundell of Wardour, Mr. Hussey let them his house at Marnhull, Dorset, where they remained till 1807. At the end of that time they removed to Court House, Cannington. After being there for twenty-nine years, the nuns at last, in 1836, found their permanent home at St. Benedict's priory, Colwich. This devout community in 1829 undertook the work of perpetual adoration, and since then the convent has never left our Lord in the Blessed Sacrament day or night without worshippers. Their community growing, in 1842 another house had to be founded for the same work of perpetual adoration at St. Scholastica's priory, Atherstone, which is quite an independent house.

At Princethorpe, near Rugby, is a large convent of nuns which came from France in 1792. They were thus the first to enter England. Founded from the royal abbey of Montmartre, the community had been since 1630 at Montargis. When the troubles first began in France, they came over thirty-four in number,[1] and landed at Shoreham. Mrs. Fitzherbert, the wife of the prince regent, had a relation in the community, and interested the prince on their behalf, and he received them very kindly. After a few days at Brighton, the community went to Bodney Hall in Norfolk; then, in 1811, to Heath Hall, Wakefield; and ten years after to Orrell Mount, near Wigan. They brought their wanderings to an end by settling at Princethorpe in 1855. Here they have erected large buildings, and have a flourishing and well-known school. The community, though of French origin, is now almost exclusively English.

There is also a monastery of Belgian benedictines in the Isle of Wight. They came from Liège, August 18, 1882, seven in number, and began choir that same day. In 1890 the nuns added to their house a chapel and other monastic buildings, and kept on their original dwelling as a school for young ladies. The community now numbers twelve. The mother house of this convent is the abbey "de la Paix" at Liège, which was founded from Namur in 1627.

A small monastery of nuns has been founded

---

[1] The community numbered thirty-eight, but three English sisters and a lay sister had come over some weeks previously.

at Tenby, and another at St. Mildred's Minster. These last, while keeping choir, do not profess the strict enclosure, in order to devote themselves more readily to active works. This return to the historic aspect of benedictine life is full of promise and interest.[1]

All these convents of women are denizen houses. Of the monasteries of men, the chief is that of Ramsgate, belonging to the new congregation of Cassinese of the Primitive Observance, founded by the abbat Casaretto in 1844. St. Augustine's monastery was founded in 1861 by Dr. Luck, whose sons all became priests, and who followed their example before his death. The church itself is the foundation of the famous Pugin, who built it entirely at his own cost. The convent, now almost entirely English, has a flourishing college attached to the monastery, which has been recently erected into an abbey.

The recent persecutions in France drew over some benedictine monks of Père Mouard's congregation, now the French province of the Cassinese of the Primitive Observance. They have settled at the old cistercian abbey of Buckfast in Devonshire, which they have restored as a house of God.

A small community of German monks of the Prussian congregation of Beuron, expelled from their home in Swabia, settled at Erdington through the charitable kindness of the late reverend Henry Haigh.

---

[1] In Rome, under lady abbess Pynsent, is a flourishing monastery of English benedictines with the modified enclosure.

He had built a beautiful church and endowed it, and when in his old age he bethought himself of retiring to Oscott, he was induced to let them have his foundation. They came in 1876. At a later date they built a small monastery, which has been recently enlarged, and has been created an abbey. To this they have also attached an alumnate for youths desirous of joining their institute.

A foundation of French monks of the congregation of Solesmes has been recently added to the list of alien houses. They are stationed at Farnborough in Hants, and have the custody of the tombs of the late emperor and prince imperial.

. . . .

This account of St. Benedict's patrimony in England cannot close without casting a wistful glance at other bodies of earnest souls outside who are striving after light, and seeking salvation under the patronage of the Holy Patriarch. May they too be brought in to join the great chorus of monastic praise which now goes up daily from so many English lips before the throne of God!

INDEX

A

ABBAT, deposition of, i. 45; leave for electing, 46; appointed for life, *ibid.*; as archdeacon, 57; relations with bishops, 118; high position of, 136, *note;* attainder of, 156; hanged, 158; on the, 267; election by compromise, 268; process of election, 269; elect, behaviour of, *ibid.;* royal assent to, 270; journey to Rome, 271; elect, confirmation of, *ibid.;* return from Rome, 272; installation feast, *ibid., note;* pontificating, 273; in choir, 274; his household, *ibid.;* his chaplains, 275; his chamberlains, *ibid.;* other officials, 276; servants of his household, 278; his relation with his community, 279; in bed, 280; obsequies, *ibid.;* his councillors, 300

ABBESS, privileges of, i. 106

ABBEYS, exemptions, i. 46; ii. 192, *note;* power of, i. 117; lands of, 173

ACTON BURNELL, chapter at, ii. 185; arrival at, 230; college at, *ibid.;* names connected with, *ibid.*

ÆDDE, life of St. Wilfrid, i. 7

AGAZZARI, FR., S.J., i. 232

AGGREGATION, deed of, ii. 82; ratification of, *ibid., note*

ALIEN PRIORIES, their origin, i. 129; kinds of, 130; number of, *ibid., note;* legislation against, *ibid.;* dissolution of, 182; to-day, ii. 324

ALDHELM, treatise on virginity, i. 103

ALLANSON, D., ii. 275

ALLEN, CARDINAL, i. 230; and Parsons, ii. 2, *note;* Agazzari on, 4, *note;* and jesuits, 4; on benedictine vocation, 5; disappointment of, 6

ALMONER, duties of, i. 291

ALMYR, BISHOP, and Fecknam, i. 207

ALTAR, linen, i. 286; breads, 287

AMERICA, and St. Gregory's, ii. 215

AMPLEFORTH, ii. 272; buildings at, 273

ANGLICAN BISHOPS, persecuting spirit of, i. 217

APPELLANTS, cause of, i. 252; go to Rome, 253; continuation of the contest, 254

APPROPRIATIONS, i. 55

ARCH-PRIEST, appointment of, i. 249; condemned, 253

ARRAS, college of, at Paris, ii. 68; abbey, spirit of, ii. 190

ARUNDEL OF WARDOUR, ii. 32

ASSOCIATION, THE, i. 248

AUTONOMY OF HOUSES, i. 34

B

BACON, FRANCIS, ii. 110, *note*
BAGSHAWE, D. SIGEBERT, ii. 99
BAINES, BISHOP, attacks of, ii. 187; his history, 241; and Ampleforth, 242; and Downside, *ibid.*; lies at Downside, 244
BAKER, D. AUGUSTINE, the historian, i. 163; and the common life, 115; biographical note, ii. 72, *note;* joins the Cassinese, 74; "discovers the congregation," *ibid.;* sees the value of D. Buckley, 75; goes to Italy, 77; professed by D. Buckley, 79; a conventual of St. Gregory's, 200; method of prayer, 202; meets with opposition, *ibid.;* at St. Gregory's, 203; inquiry into his method, *ibid.;* confirmation thereof, *ibid.;* and the clergy, 204; sent on the mission and dies, *ibid.;* his spirit, 205; on confession, 317; letter to Sir R. Cotton, 318
BALDWIN, FR., S.J., intrigues at Brussels, ii. 44
BALTIMORE, LORD, and the oath, ii. 154
BANCROFT, ARCHBISHOP, ii. 105.
BARBER, D., ii. 240
BARBO, ABBAT, i. 140
BARKING NUNNERY, i. 103, 106
BARKWORTH, VEN. MARK, his vocation, ii. 7; his martyrdom, 8
BARLOW, D. R., *Mandatum*, ii. 113; position of, 114; letter to Propaganda, 205; recommends Dr. Smith, 207
BARNES, D. JOHN, ii. 164, 300
BATH, the use of, i. 83, *note*, 303
BEC, in the time of Lanfranc, i. 21
BECCLES, school at, i. 152
BEDE, VENERABLE, i. 8, 100
BEDS AND BEDDING, i. 85; 303
BEECH, D. ANSELM, ii. 4, 23; defends the right, ii. 49; answers Parsons, 50; his further projects, 87-91; opposes the Union, 93
BEER, quality of, i. 288
BELLARMINE, CARDINAL, ii. 94
BELMONT, foundation of, ii. 187
BENEDICT XIV. and the mission, ii. 183
BENEDICTINE, the, debt of England to, i. 2; rule introduced, 6, *note;* constitution, 31; vows, 32; house, a home, *ibid.;* ideal, the family, *ibid.;* spirit, Lanfranc on, 33; monk, 39; work, 47; spirit, 48; secret of his life, 65, 76; bishops in Mary's reign, 171, *note;* mission, ii. 1; petitions for, 16; mission granted, 22; jesuit opposition to, 39; at university of Douai, 64; houses founded, 69; and Gothic art, 240
BENEDICTINISM, racy of the soil, i. 2; on the continent, 138
BENEFACTORS, book of, i. 286
BENTIVOGLIO, GUIDO, ii. 71, 93, 94, 123
BIRKET, GEORGE, ii. 109
BISHOPS, relation to cathedral monastery, i. 118; deprivations of, 191; endeavours for, 248; appointment of, ii. 109; question of, and the French prelates, 110
BISHOP, DR. WILLIAM, signs address to Elizabeth, ii. 105; made bishop, 110; treated as ordinary, 110
BLACK CANONS, i. 29
BLACK DEATH, THE, i. 64; effects of, 133
BLACKWELL, GEORGE, opinion of

Parsons, i. 242 ; made arch-priest, 249; and the oath, ii. 108, 109, *note;* deposed, 109.
BLESSED SACRAMENT, at the high altar, i. 76, *note*, 286
BLEEDING, practice of, i. 84 ; abuse of, 309
BOLTON, D., ii. 259 ; his trial, 260 ; estate at Ampleforth, 270 ; gives it to St. Lawrence's, 271
BONNER, BISHOP, at Westminster, i. 192 ; and Horne, 201
BOREMAN, ABBAT, i. 184
BOURNE, ABBAT, election of, i. 267
BRADLEY, MISS, i. 180, *note*, 194
BRADSHAW, D., his vocation, ii. 9 ; starts for England, 22 ; appointed vicar, 32 ; chaplain major, *ibid.;* attacked by jesuit colleague, 36 ; defends his order, 44 ; takes possession of Dieuleward, 46 ; and Caraffa, 48 ; and Arras college, 68 ; and the apostate monk, 76 ; action about the Union, 87, 88 ; and Fontevraud, 302, 303, 304 ; dies, 279
BREAD, i. 288
BRETT, CAPTAIN ARTHUR, ii. 158
BREVIARIUM MONASTICUM, ii. 335, *note*
BREVICULUM, i. 307
"BRIEF MEMORANDUM, A," ii. 217
BRITISH CHURCH, survivors of, i. 5
BRITISH UNITED ESTABLISHMENT, THE, ii. 233
BROUGHTON, D., ii. 53
BROWN, D. GEORGE, first prior of Dieuleward, ii. 56
BROWNE, D. JOSEPH, ii. 244, 245
BRUSSELS, CONVENT AT, ii. 312 ; its foundation, 324, 325 ; lady Mary Percy, *ibid.;* Fr. Parsons' niece, 325, 329 ; lady Joanna Berkley, first abbess, 326; statutes of, 327 ; growth of community, 328 ; its offshoot, *ibid.;* disturbances at, 329, 330 ; Dr. Champney and his trials, *ibid.;* at the revolution, 331 ; at Winchester, *ibid.;* at East Bergholt, 332 ; lady Gertrude Lescher, abbess, *ibid.*
BUCKFAST ABBEY, ii. 347
BUCCABELLA, MGR., ii. 151
BUCKLEY, D. SIGEBERT, i. 246 ; falls in with the Italian fathers, ii. 23 ; biographical note, 71, *note;* unique position of, 75 ; imprisonment, 77 ; aggregates two Cassinese, 78 ; goes blind, *ibid.;* professes D. Baker, 79 ; dies, 80 ; letter to D. Preston, 82
BULL, *Plantata*, ii. 167 ; *Romanos Pontifices*, 189 ; *Religiosus Ordo*, *ibid.*
BUREAU GRATUIT DE SURVEILLANCE, ii. 236
BURGE, D., prior of St. Lawrence's, ii. 276
BURGESS, D., ii. 242
BURSFELD, congregation of, i. 141 ; ii. 165
BURY ST. EDMUNDS, i. 290 ; ii. 175

C

CAJETAN, ABBAT, ii. 167
CAJETAN, CARDINAL, the protector, i. 249 ; secret instruction of, i. 250
CAMBRAI, CONVENT OF, foundation of, ii. 314 ; lady abbess Francis Gawen, 315 ; D. Maihew, vicar of, *ibid.;* lady abbess Francis Gascoigne, *ibid.;* D. Baker directs

the nuns, 316, 317; state of, 318; growth of community, 320; common life at, 321; school at, 321; offshoot, *ibid.*; during the revolution, *ibid.*; return to England, 322; St. Mary's abbey, Stanbrooke, *ibid.*; lady abbess Gertrude Dubois, 323

CAMBRIDGE, benedictine house at, i. 89; gregorian house at, ii. 248; D. Francis at, 308

CAMPION, VEN. EDMUND, character of, i. 236

CANTERBURY, a second Rome, i. 5

CANTOR, i. 283

CAPITULUM, meaning of, i. 299, *note.*

CARAFFA, nuncio, ii. 39; and D. Bradshaw, 48

CARROLL, BISHOP, ii. 216

CARYLL, D. A., ii. 211

CASSINESE CONGREGATION, origin of, i. 141; English members of, ii. 4; secures the old English congregation, 76, 77, 78, 79, 82, 83, 84; system, 96; opposition to the Union, 99

CATHEDRAL PRIORS, i. 79, *note;* ii. 167

CATHOLICS, STATE OF, ii. 117, 175.

CAVEREL, ABBAT, builds college at Arras for jesuits, ii. 33; befriends English monks, 38; founds St. Gregory's, 60; benevolence of, 62, 64, 65; and Fecknam, 65; protects St. Gregory's, 100; letter to Windebank, 147; death of, 159; care for St. Gregory's, 191; foundation for St. Gregory's, 192; his charter, 193; powers of visitation, 195

CECIL, SIR WILLIAM, i. 167

CELTIC MISSIONS, i. 6

CELLARER, i. 287; attendance at choir, *ibid.*

"CERTAINE BRIEFE NOTES," i. 250, *note*

CHAMPNEY, DR., ii. 329, 330

CHAPTER, rules of, i. 298; "voices" in, 299; proclamations, *ibid.*; decorum of, 300; penances, *ibid.*; petitions in, 302

CHARLES II., and benedictines, ii. 173; received on his death-bed, 210; and St. Malo, 305; and Ghent, 335, 336, 337

CHARNOCK, MR., i. 250

CHAUCER, and nuns, i. 110

CHEKE, SIR JOHN, i. 167

CHELLES, abbess of, ii. 278; foundation at, *ibid.*

CHILLINGWORTH, at St. Gregory's, ii. 208

CHOIR, lights in, i. 285

CHRIST CHURCH, CANTERBURY, foundation of, i. 5; in the time of Lanfranc, 22; rebuilt, 24; exempted from general chapter, 44; disputes at, 118; charge of forgery, 123; losses of, 134

CHRONICLES OF THE CONGREGATION, i. 117; ii. 162

CISMAR, abbey of, ii. 166; abbats of, 307

CISTERCIANS, origin of, i. 29, *note;* as wool-growers, 50

CLARENDON STATE PAPERS, ii. 117

CLAUSTRAL PRIOR, i. 282

CLEMENT VIII., i. 249

CLENOCK, DR., i. 231, 232

CLERGY, THE, obligations to monks, i. 59; envoys of, imprisoned, 251; looked down on, ii. 42

CLOISTER, THE, i. 81; garth, *ibid.*; furniture of, 82; laver in, *ibid.*, *note;* a workshop, 83; rules of,

INDEX

295; talking in, 296; order in, *ibid.*
CLOTHES, list of, i. 71; changing of, 303
CLUNI, origin of, i. 19; ideal of, 20; influence of, *ibid.*
CLUNIACS, introduction of, i. 27; relation to English abbeys, *ibid.*; grievances of, 131, *note*
COCKAYNE, MR., a mistake of, i. 14, *note*.
COLLATION, i. 84
COLLETON, MR., suspended, i. 252
COMING OF THE MONKS, i. 1
COMMENDAM, i. 138; effects of, 139
COMMON COLLEGE AND NOVITIATE, ii. 174, 185
COMMON LIFE, i. 115
COMMUNION, practice of, i. 41, 79, 308
CONCEPTION OF OUR LADY, feast of, i. 14, *note*
CONCLAVE OF PRIESTS, ii. 1
CONCORDIA REGULARIS, THE, i. 13; its author, 14
CONFESSION, place for, i. 82; rules for, 308
CONFESSORS, directions for, i. 307, 308
CONFIRMATION, sacrament of, i. 224; ii. 128
CONFRATERNITY, admission to, i. 61; effects of, *ibid.*
CONFRATRES, examples of, i. 62; privileges of, 307
CONIERS, Fr., S.J., ii. 33
CONGREGATION, numbers in, ii. 179, 185
CONQUEST, effects of, i. 18
CONSTITUTION OF CLEMENT XI., ii. 183
CONSTITUTIONS, the benedictine, i.
VOL. II.

31; changes advocated by the provinces, ii. 171; revision of, ii. 184
CONSOLANDI GRATIA, i. 289
CONSUETUDINARY OF ST. AUGUSTINE'S, CANTERBURY, i. *appendix*
CONVENT AT CLERKENWELL, A, ii. 174; destruction of, 179
CONVENTUS, THE, i. 293
COOKE, LEWIS, ii. 208
CORAL, ABBAT, ii. 21
CORBIE, influence of, i. 14, *note*
CORKER, D., ii. 176
CORPORAL AUSTERITIES, use of, i. 78, *note*
CORRODIES, i. 58, *note*
COTTON MS. *FAUSTINA*, C. XII., i. 259
COUNCIL OF LATERAN, i. 30
COURT OF AUGMENTATION, i. 152
COURTNEY, the book, ii. 124, 125; real author of, 125, *note*
Cox, to Burghley, i. 212, 216; and Fecknam, 209, 216, *note*
CRESSY, D., ii. 210
CRESSWELL, FR., S.J., and benedictines, ii. 18; his rancour, 20; leads the attack, 45
CROWDER, D., ii. 56
CROMWELL, policy of, i. 147; visitation, *ibid.*; object of, 149; commissioners' report. 150
CURIA, THE, i. 228

D

DANISH INVASION, THE, i. 8
DAVIS, D. CHARLES, ii. 245
DEAD, burial of, i. 306
DECLARATION OF THE CHAPTER, ii. 169
DEDEROTH, ABBAT, i. 141

Z

DEED OF AGGREGATION, ii. 80
DEFINITORS, number and power, ii. 97
DENIZEN HOUSES, ii. 324
DEPRIVATIONS, i. 223
DIES MEMORABILIS, THE, i. 176
DIEULEWARD, acquisition of, i. 46; arrival at, 55; building begins, *ibid.*; studies begin, 56
DISCIPLINE, i. 306; ii. 213
DISPENSATIONS, i. 309; ii. 287
DISPUTES, with vicars-apostolic, ii. 177
DIVINE OFFICE, i. 76, 77
DORTER, THE, i. 85; furniture of, *ibid.*, 303; rules of, 302
DOUAI, advantages of, for a foundation, ii. 26; siege of, 213, 214; and the revolution, 227; without the benedictines, 233
DOUAI MONASTERY, jesuit opposition to, ii. 40; papal decree in favour of, 57; and Dieuleward, ii. 25
DOUAI SEMINARY, i. 209; foundation of, 230; lowering of intellectual status, ii. 42; resumption of studies, 58; its battle fought by benedictines, 67
DOUBLE MONASTERIES, i. 104
DOWNFALL, THE, i. 143
DOWNSIDE, purchase of, ii. 231; buildings at, 239; a new Glaston, 249, *note*
DRINKING, manner of, i. 298
DUES, destination of, i. 58
DUNKIRK CONVENT, a royal foundation, ii. 339; during the revolution, *ibid.*; settles at Teignmouth, 340
DURHAM, cathedral chapter of, i. 28; recreation at, 87, *note*; house at Oxford, 90, *note*
DYING, attendance on, i. 95, 306

E

EDGAR, KING, i. 13
EDGEWORTH, L'ABBÉ, ii. 344
EDNER, D., ii. 209, *note*
EDWARD, D., "a merry wight," i. 86
EFFECTS OF EXCOMMUNICATION, i. 228
ELIZABETH, QUEEN, and Fecknam, i. 170, 186; at Westminster abbey, 186; and the clergy, ii. 105
ELY AND ST. ETHELREDA, i. 102
ELY, DR., and the envoys, i. 250, *note*
ELLIS, D., ii. 176, 180
ENCLOSURE, not binding on nuns, i. 108; result of, *ibid.*, *note*
ENGLAND, in St. Edmund's time, i. 120, *note*; without benedictines, 255
ENGLISH CATHOLICS, state of, i. 223; and the bull of Pius V., 229; factions among, 247; ii. 329
ENGLISH COLLEGE AT ROME, beginnings of, i. 231; disturbances at, *ibid.*
ENGLISH CONGREGATION, beginnings of, i. 37; renewal of, ii. 70; two currents in, 168
ENGLISH ECCLESIASTICAL PROPERTY IN FRANCE, ii. 236
ENGLISH HIERARCHY, state of, i. 187
ENGLISH MISSION, ii. 7.
ENGLISH REGIMENT, the fate of, ii. 87
EPISCOPAL POWER OVER ABBEYS, i. 45
ERDINGTON, Prussian congregation at, ii. 347, 348
EVESHAM, school at, i. 52; surrender of, 165
EXEMPTION, ii. 192, *note*
EXENNIUM, sending of, i. 288

INDEX

F

FAIRFAX, LORD, ii. 259
FAIRFAX, HON. MISS, ii. 259–270
FALKLAND, THE LADY, ii. 208
FARNBOROUGH, ii. 348
FECKNAM, ABBAT JOHN, i. 160; his birth, 161; parents' bequest, *ibid.*, *note*; age of, *ibid.*, *note*; early education of, 162; with Bonner, 165; rector of Solihull, *ibid.*; skill in controversy, 166; at Lambeth, *ibid.*; committed to the tower, *ibid.*; reasons for imprisonment, *ibid.*; and Horne, *ibid.*; "borrowed out of prison," 167; seven disputations, *ibid.*; and Hooper, 168, *note*; released, *ibid.*; preferments, *ibid.*; a popular preacher, 169, *note*; dean of St. Paul's, *ibid.*; gentle dealings with heretics, *ibid.*, 171, *note*; at Oxford, 169; and lady Jane Dudley, 170; and princess Elizabeth, *ibid.*; resumes his habit, 172; with others appears before the queen, *ibid.*; takes possession of Westminster, 175; installed, 176; his hospitality, 178; beautifies his church, *ibid.*; in parliament, 179; interview with Elizabeth, 186; speech on the religious changes, 187; opposition to all the bills, 188; public disputation, 189; refusal of the oath, 190; in his garden, 191; shelters Bonner, 192; tempted, *ibid.*; deprivation, 193; no pension, 194; committed to the Tower, 195; life in the Tower, *ibid.*; threats of death, 197; removed to Westminster, 198; to Winchester, *ibid.*; and the oath, 199; Horne's complaint, 200; leaves Winchester, 201; poem in honour of, *ibid.*, *note*; to Cecil, 202; pamphlet by, 204; removed to Marshalsea, 205; admiration of protestants for, *ibid.*; released on parole, *ibid.*; lives in Holborn, 206; his benevolence, *ibid.*, 220; goes to Bath, 207; and bishop Almyr, *ibid.*; and Walsingham, 208, 209, *note*; imprisoned with Cox of Ely, 209; rules for treatment of, 210; so-called confession, 213, *note*; closer imprisonment, *ibid.*; removed to Wisbeach, 218; death, 220; personal appearance, 221; benefactions, *ibid.*; literary remains, 222; compared with abbat Caverel, ii. 65.
FEET, washing of, i. 83, 296
FENWICK, D., his policy, ii. 179; his fate, 180
FERDINAND II., ii. 165
FERRIS, MR., ii. 235, 238
FINCHALL, life at, i. 87
FIRES, the use of, i. 87
FISH, quality of, i. 288
FISH DAY AT CHRIST CHURCH, A, i. 79
FITZJAMES, D. NICHOLAS, clothed, ii. 47; biographical note, *ibid.*, *note*; goes to Dieuleward, 54; the first superior there, 55
FLEURY, influence of, i. 14, *note*
FONTEVRAUD, ii. 301, *note*; project of reform, 303
FORGERY, causes for, i. 128, *note*
FORSTER, D., ii. 163, 253
FORT AUGUSTUS, ii. 188
FRANCIS, D., at Cambridge, ii. 308
FRANKLIN, BENJAMIN, ii. 285
FRENCH, the use of, i. 112, 296
FURSDEN, D., ii. 257
FYNDON, ABBAT, i. 267

G

GARNETT, FR., S.J., i. 245; and the clergy, 255, *note*
GASQUET, D., i. 149; ii. 247, 248
GENERAL CHAPTER, decree on, i. 35; of the southern province, 37; of the northern province, *ibid., note*; first united, 41; others held, 42; the power of, ii. 98; nominations of, 163
GERARD, FR., S.J., examination of, i. 245, *note*; converts Leander, ii. 9
GERMAN NUNS, not enclosed, i. 107
GHENT CONVENT, its origin, ii. 332; befriended by the jesuits, 334; a favoured convent, 335; and royalty, 335, 336, 337, 338; and St. Vincent de Paul, 337; its foundations, *ibid.*; returns to England, 338; settles at Oulton, 339
GIFFORD, JOHN, i. 89
GIFFORD, DR., biographical note, ii. 27, *note*; banished from Lille, 43, *note*; rector of Rheims, 45; obtains Dieuleward, 56; becomes a monk, 54; professed, 55; arrives at Dieuleward, *ibid.*; founds St. Malo, 300; and Fontevraud, 301;
GILBERT, D., his failure, i. 73
GILES OF SARUM, i. 45, *note*
GLASTON, and plain song, i. 26; petition for restoration, 181
GLOUCESTER HALL, i. 89
"GOOD FAT CAPON," A, i. 304
GRANGES, life at, i. 87
GRINDAL, BISHOP, to Cecil, i. 198
GROWTH, of ideas and knowledge, ii. 189
GUESTS, treatment of, i. 289; "consoling," 290

GUESTMASTER, i. 289
GUNPOWDER PLOT, ii. 35
GYROVAGUS, treatment of, i. 291

H

HARRISON, W., arch-priest, ii. 110
HART, MR., on benedictine agriculture, i. 50; on the downfall, 158
HAYWOOD, FR., S.J., i. 245
HEATH, ARCHBISHOP, speech, i. 188, *note*
HEDLEY, BISHOP, on the benedictine life, i. 47
HENRIETTA, MARIA, ii. 117, 275, 341
HENRY VIII., and benedictines, i. 155; accession, 244
HIPPESLEY, SIR JOHN COX, ii. 239
HOBB, SIR PHILIP, i. 167
HOLT, FR., S.J., i. 245; ii. 324
HOLTBY, FR., S.J., ii. 107
"HOLY THORN," THE, i. 183
HOODS, constantly worn, i. 296
HOOPER, BISHOP, i. 167
HORNE, and Fecknam, i. 198
HORSLEY, D., ii. 257
HOSPITALITY, i. 53
HOWARD, CARDINAL, ii. 211
HROSWITHA, i. 112
HUDDLESTON, D. J., ii. 209, 210
HULL, D., ii. 202

I

IL SCHIFANOYA, i. 189, 192, 193
IMPROPRIATIONS, i. 55, *note*
INFIRMARY, rules of, i. 304; music in, *ibid.*

INNOCENT IV., and English embroidery, i. 112
"INSTRUMENT OF PEACE AND CONCORD," THE, ii. 155, *note*
INTELLECTUAL LIFE, in nunneries, i. 103
IRELAND, RICHARD, and his legacy, ii. 68
ISHEL, JOHN, ii. 34
ITALIAN FATHERS, arrive in England, ii. 23; their care of D. Buckley, 24; small progress of, 70

J

JAMES I., and tolerance, ii. 102; care concerning oath, 107, *note*
James II., and benedictines, ii. 174; at St. Edmund's, 282; reported miracles of, *ibid., note;* at Ghent, 338; his conversion there, *ibid.*
JANSENISM, charge of, ii. 189
JESUITS, foundation of, i. 223; English members, 234; secret of the success, *ibid;* mission to England, 235; letter of St. Ignatius to Pole, *ibid., note;* arrival of, 238; reception by the clergy, *ibid.;* their instructions, 239; pretensions of, 243; number of, 246; position of, *ibid., note;* their plans as to the clergy, ii. 41; their opposition to the benedictines, 60, *note;* and bishops, 100; question of the succession, 102; and tolerance, 103; teaching affected by, 105; stirring up the pope, 106; opposed to episcopal superiors, 113, *note;* communicate the *Mandatum* to the government, 114; annoy D. Leander, 122, 123, 229, 150, 153; state of their mission, 139; ousting other missioners, 144; and the oath, 154; and the "Instrument of Peace and Concord," 156, *note;* witnesses of D. Leander's declaration, 160; and Brussels convent, 324, 325, 329, 330; and Ghent convent, 332, 333
JEWEL, BISHOP, i. 168; and Fecknam, 195, *note*
JOHNSON, DR., at St. Edmund's, ii. 285; and edmundians, 286; his opinion on converts, *ibid., note*

K

KELLISON, DR., ii. 204
KENNET, BISHOP, and Fecknam, i. 221, 222, *note*
KINGSTON, ST. MICHAEL'S, life at, i. 113
KNIGHTLY, ABBAT, ii. 310

L

LA CELLE, ii. 281
LAMBSPRING, abbat of, ii. 307, 309; abbats Rokeby and Crathorne, 310; abbat Knightly, *ibid.;* D. Francis and Cambridge, 308; ven. Oliver Plunket's relics, *ibid.;* D. Corker at court of James II., 307; D. Corker at the Savoy, 175, *note;* D. Corker at Clerkenwell, 174; abbey of, 166, 307, 309, 311; its suppression, 311; extinction of community, 312
LAUD, ARCHBISHOP, ii. 115; and Rome, 117
LEANDER, D., early years, ii. 115;

friendship with Laud, 116; conversion of, *ibid.*; his vocation, 9; at Rheims, 54; with the Lorraine congregation, *ibid.*; at Dieuleward, 56; return to Douai, *ibid.*; prior there, 64, 89; opposes D. Bradshaw's views, 88; proposes terms of union, 93; first precedent, 98; his mission, 101; questions before, *ibid.*; licensed to return to England, 118; precautions taken at Dover, 119; arrival, *ibid.*; begs for protection, 120; recommends Mr. William Price, 121; interview with Laud, *ibid.*; warns Windebank, 123; writes to Bentivoglio, *ibid.*; and the papal policy, 126, 133, 152; and bishops, 127; loved for his plain dealing, 129; writes to Barberini, 130; made prefect of the benedictine mission, 131; and the *via media*, 132; his attitude towards the oath, *ibid.*; and his conscience, 134; paper on the oath, *ibid.*; report on the apostolic mission, 135; on the Anglican (high) church, 136, 137; on Anglican orders, *ibid.*; on the puritans, 137; on the state of the mission, 138; on the Anglican controversy, *ibid.*; on clerical studies, *ibid.*, 142; on benedictine missioners, *ibid.*; on jesuit missioners, 139; on the clergy, 140; on the question of bishops, *ibid.*, 143; suggestions for the mission, 141; takes an oath, 144; asks for an accredited envoy, 145; Barberini on, 146; wants to return to Douai, *ibid.*; writes to Panzani, 147; his book against Courtney, 148; protestation of obedience, 150; and Courtney's book, *ibid.*, *note*, 151; instructions, 151; opinion as to terms of reunion, 152; attacked on all sorts of subjects, 153; his Apology, 154; his illness, *ibid.*; and the clergy, 155; and the apostate priest, 156; care for his brethren, 157; dying declaration, 159; death and burial, *ibid.*; care for his reputation, *ibid.*; Panzani's account, 160; and the jesuit provincial, *ibid.*; dislike to the Fontevraud scheme, 304; and Dr. Champney, 330

M

"MADAME EGLANTINE," i. 110
MAIHEW, D., joins the Cassinese, ii. 77; aggregated to Westminster, 78; a zealous missioner, 162; an impossible man, 162; goes to Dieuleward, 163, 252; holds a chapter there, *ibid.*, 253; becomes president of the old English congregation, *ibid.*; a "home ruler," 253; death, 315
MALMESBURY, i. 27
MARCHIENNE, abbat of, ii. 63; college of, 197
MARIAN PRIESTS, i. 224
MARLBOROUGH, and St. Gregory's, ii. 214
MARSH, D., and St. Edmund's, ii. 291, 297; his escape, 261-268; at Acton Burnell, 268
MARTIN, D. ANTHONY, ii. 4, 5, *note*
MARTYRS, ii. 59, 199, 256-308
MASTER OF THE CRYPTS, i. 291
MASTER KNIGHT'S HOUSE, ii. 32
MATINS, hour of, i. 75, *note;* rising for, 302

MATTHEW, SIR TOBY, and bishops, ii. 110, *note;* and the oath, 154; and Ghent, 333
MAYNE, VEN. CUTHBERT, i. 209
MEALS, number of, i. 79-81; punctuality of, 289; reading at, 81, 297; service of, 279, 288, 292, 297, 298
MEAT EATING, in Saxon times, i. 16, *note;* regulations for, 43, 307; ii. 255, 283
MICHIEL, GIOVANNI, i. 172, 174, 175, 177
MILES, FR., S.J., ii. 52
MISSION, petition for, ii. 7-16; renewed, 21; granted, 22
MISSIONARY WORK, of the English congregation, ii. 169
MINSTER, St. Mildred of, i. 101; convent at, ii. 347
MIXTUM, THE, i. 292
MONASTERIES, a home, i. 32; an example of domestic economy, 51; schools for the nobility, 60; hotels of the day, 62; visitations of, 146; visited by Cromwell, 147; articles of inquiry, 148; value of the dissolved, 154; exceptions to dissolution, 155; popular risings in favour of, *ibid.;* a dissolved monastery, 158
MONASTIC, names, i. 72, *note;* prayer, 77, *note;* vigour, 88, 138; reform, 128; vicars, 55; revenues used by the king, 63; wealth, responsibilities of, 64; pensions, 160, 194; cathedral chapters, 13; ii. 168, 188, *note;* disputes of, 118
MONASTICISM, the simple Gospel life, i. 31, 48; golden age of, 28
MONKS, in the world, i. 49; as landlords, 50; as educationalists, 52; caring for the sick, 53, 291; as parochial clergy, 55; and the clergy, 58; bestowing titles, 59; of aristocratic training, 60; inner life of, 65; studies of, 81; recreations of, 86, 308; holidays of, 128; parents and relations of, 91, 291; state of dispossessed, 153, *note;* new habits and clothes, 304
MORE, FR., S.J., on the mission, i. 243
MORE, MR. CRISACRE, ii. 313; his daughter, *ibid.*
MORIBUND SCHOOL, A, ii. 106, *note*
MORONE, CARDINAL, i. 225
MORRIS, FR., S.J., i. 232, 244, *note*
MORRIS, D. PLACID, ii. 245
MUSH, J., suspended, i. 252
"MYNCHYNS," i. 107

N

NAVAGERO, BERNARDO, i. 226, *note*
NEWMAN, CARDINAL, on St. Benedict's mission, i. 9; on St. Dunstan, 11
NEWPORT, monastic chapter of, ii. 180
NIGHT CLOTHES, i. 85, *note*, 137, *note*
NOVICES, outfit required at Ely, i. 71, *note;* at St. Augustine's, Canterbury, 280; admission of, 71; 293; education of, 73, 295, *note;* life of, 294; profession of, 75, 295
NOVITIATE, rules of, i. 293
NUNS, the Saxon, i. 9, *note*, 111; Columban, 98; going out allowed, 109; occupation of, 110; intellectual life of, 112; vanity of, 103; and Danish invasion, 105; of Norman foundation, 106, *note;* houses of education, 113; visita-

tions of, 114, *note*; influence of, 115; dissolution of, 157; restoration of, 324.

O

OATH OF ALLEGIANCE, text of, ii. 103, *note*; origin of, 104; condemned, 107; and Blackwell, 108; and D. Preston, *ibid.*; divisions among catholics, *ibid.*; and Rome, 109; benedictine martyrs for, 199
OBEDIENTIARIES, i. 93
ODO OF TOURS, i. 19
OFFICERS OF THE CONVENT, i. 280
OLD ENGLISH CONGREGATION, bound up in D. Buckley, ii. 75; discovered by D. Baker, 74; continuation of, 78, 79; numbers in, 84; under the Cassinese superior, 82; admitted to a share in Dieuleward, 90; general chapter of, 163, 253; united with the Spanish, 98
"OLD PRIESTS," THE, i. 224
OPUS ANGLICANUM, i. 112
"ORDER," meaning of the term, i. 48, *note*
ORDINATIONS in the diocese of York, i. 59
ORGAN, use of, i. 76
ORGANISATION, early attempts at, i. 29
OTHER RELIGIOUS ORDERS restored, i. 175, *note*
OTHO, LEGATE, decrees, i. 38, 127
OXFORD, house of studies, i. 89; ii. 276; age of students at, i. 162, *note*; religious schools at, *ibid.*, *note*
OWEN, BISHOP, i. 231
OUTSIDE THE FOLD, ii. 348

P

PAGET, CHARLES, ii. 4, *note*
PANZANI, mission, ii. 115, 145; correspondence, 118; arrives in England, 146; and the jesuits, 113; and the provincial, 157, 160
PAPAL POLICY, temporal, i. 227; ii. 116
PARIS CONVENT, foundation, ii. 341, 342; D. Clementia Cary, *ibid.*; Monsieur de Touche, *ibid.*; first prioress of, *ibid.*; vows made, 342; entire escape from a great danger, 343; its cause, 344; during the revolution, *ibid.*; settled at Colwich, 345; their work, *ibid.*
PARIS HOUSE, ii. 55, 276
PARKER, ARCHBISHOP, i. 200
PARLIAMENT, and the monasteries, i. 148, 151
PAROCHIAL SYSTEM, origin of, i. 54, *note*
PARPAGLIA, VINCENT, i. 226, *note*
PARSONS, FR., S.J., coming of, i. 235; biographical note, *ibid.*; character of, 236; declaration, 239; political intrigues, 240; his aim, *ibid.*; duped by the Spaniards, 241, *note*; flies out of England, *ibid.*; his activity, *ibid.*; founds seminaries, *ibid.*; directs English affairs, *ibid.*; result of his labours, 242; Blackwell's opinion of, *ibid.*; idea of the society, 243; his attempted monopoly, *ibid.*; his abusive language, 244; and the clergy, 248; and the question of bishops, 249; the device of archpriests, *ibid.*; his treatment of the envoys, 250; his reasons for so doing, 251; his ruinous tactics, 252; partial success in the appeal,

253; and the society, 254; master of catholic England, 255; at the conclave, ii. 2; change of policy, 4; and Fr. Creswell, 19; an ally in Dr. Worthington, 41; his policy toward the college at Douai, 41; opposes the benedictines, 48; consistent with himself, 49; his diplomacy, 51; his Spanish intrigues, 102; letter to James I., *ibid.*, *note;* his death, 67, *note;* his niece, 325. 329
PASTORAL OBLIGATION, *ibid.*
PAUL IV., irritation against, i. 185, 188, *note*
PAUL V., ii. 107; appeal to, 108; James I.'s rebuke to, *ibid.*, *note*
PERCY, LADY MARY, ii. 324-326
PERKINS, SIR CHRISTOPHER, ii. 105
PERNE, DEAN, to Burghley, i. 213, *note*
PICKERING, VEN. THOMAS, ii. 174
PIERSON, DIDACUS, ii. 55
PITANCE, i. 58, *note*, 288
PITTS, ARTHUR, dean of Liverdun, ii. 46; his benefaction, 55
PIUS IV., and ELIZABETH, i. 226
PIUS V., ST., his policy, i. 226; bull of, i. 245
PLUNKET, VEN. OLIVER, ii. 249, 308
POLDING, D., ii. 245
POLE, CARDINAL, protector of the Cassinese congregation, i. 173; wishes to restore a Canterbury house, 180; death of, 184, *note*
POLITICS, in seminaries, ii. 1
POPE, THE, between two fires, ii. 106.
PONTIFICALIA, use of, i. 78, 273; ii. 188
POSTULANT, i. 293
POWELL, VEN. PHILIP, ii. 201
PREACHERS, and monasteries, i. 152
PRECENTOR, duties of, i. 92, 283

PREE, the prioress of, i. 109
PRESIDENT, his power, ii. 97; dispensed from residence, 172
PRESTON, D., ii. 3, 23; and the oath, 108, *note*
PRINCETHORPE CONVENT, ii. 346
PRIOR, THE, his duty, 286; his power of dispensing, 281; third and fourth, 283
PRIOR PARK, ii. 242-244
PRISONERS, treatment of, i. 211
PROCESSIONS, i. 84, 308
PROCLAMATION, i. 299, 301
PROPOSED SCHOOLS, ii. 180
PROVINCES, of Canterbury and York, i. 37; ii. 97, 137
PROVINCIALS, institution of, ii. 97; abrogation of, 189
PROVINCIAL CHAPTER, of Canterbury, ii. 171
PRUSSIAN CONGREGATION, of Beuron, ii. 347
PSALTER, of St. Alban, ii. 311, *note*
PUGIN, MR., ii. 246

Q

QUEEN ELIZABETH, her religious policy, i. 184, 185, *note;* at Westminster abbey, 186; wishes to keep monks there, 192; on Anglican bishops persecuting, 218; excommunication of, 228; plots against, 229, *note;* and the appellants, 252; ii. 105; her death, *ibid.*
QUEEN ETHELBURGHA, i. 100
QUEEN MARY, restores abbey lands, i. 173; reinstates the monks, 174; visits Westminster, 177; her death, 184
QUEEN SEXBURGH, i. 100

R

RAMSGATE, ii. 347
RASTURA, i. 293
READER, i. 297
RECREATION, times of, i. 86; ii. 213; forbidden, 308
RECTORIAL DUES, i. 57
REFECTORY, service in, i. 292; behaviour in, 297; order of serving in, *ibid.*; rules of, *ibid.*
REFECTORY MASTER, his duties, i. 291
REFORMATIONCULA, i. 307
RELICS, care of, i. 286
RESTORATION OF ABBEY LANDS, i. 180
RESULT OF DISPUTES AT SEMINARIES, ii. 2
REVESTIARIUS, i. 285
REYNER, D. CLEMENT, clothed, ii. 54; at Ghent, 255; 335
REYNER, D. LAWRENCE, his views, ii. 169, 171, 182
REVOLUTION, the French, ii. 185, 178
RICHARD OF WALLINGFORD, i. 163, *note*
RICHELIEU, CARDINAL, ii. 13
RIGHTS OF PRESENTATION, i. 57
RINGWODE, D. AUSTIN, i. 183, *note*
RINTELEN, ii. 166, 306
ROBERTS, VEN. JOHN, biographical note, ii. 10, *note*; his vocation, 10; leaves the seminary, 11; defamed by the jesuits, 12; excuses himself, 13; foils them, 14; received as a monk, 15; arrives in England, 22; popularity in London; 25; is successful, 26; arrested, 29; released, *ibid.*; visits Douai, *ibid.*; goes to Spain, *ibid.*; returns to England, *ibid.*; arrested, 30; released and goes to Spain, *ibid.*; returns to England, 32; arrested, 33; released, *ibid.*; founds the house at Donai, *ibid.*; prior there, *ibid.*; returns to England, 37; arrested and released, *ibid.*; remains in London, 38; banished, *ibid.*; guards the interests of Douai, *ibid.*; returns to England, 51; again arrested, 52; escapes from prison, *ibid.*; lives in London, 53; exiled, *ibid.*; goes to Spain, 57; defends his house, 58; is successful, *ibid.*; returns to Douai, 59; goes to England, *ibid.*; arrested and dies, *ibid.*
ROE, VEN. ALBAN, ii. 253, 256
ROLLE OF HAMPOLE, ii. 319, *note*
ROME, reproduced at Canterbury, i. 5; and the Oath, ii. 109
ROOKS, the searcher, ii. 120, *note*
ROYAL MONASTERY, at St. James's, ii. 174
ROYAL SUPREMACY, i. 190
RULE OF ST. BENEDICT, in Anglo-Saxon, i. 13; earliest known copy, 14
"RUNNING REGISTER," THE, ii. 10

S

SACRIST, i. 92, 284
SADLER, D., joins the Cassinese, ii. 77; aggregated to Westminster, 78; death of, 163
Saint AIDAN, i. 8
—— AUGUSTINE, and his companions, i. 3; his foundations, 5
—— BENEDICT, his vision, i. 1; "father of many nations," 1; mission of, 9
—— BENET BISCOP, i. 7

INDEX

Saint COLUMBANUS, i. 6, *note*
—— CUTHBERT, i. 102
—— DUNSTAN, i. 11
—— EANSWITH, i. 99
—— EBBA, i. 102
—— EDMUND, and monks of Christ Church, i. 118; character of, 119; his claim, 120; goes to Rome, 122; worsted there, 125; excommunicates the monks, *ibid.*; death of, 126
—— EDWARD, translation of, i. 178
—— ETHELWOLD, i. 13
—— ETHELBURGHA, i. 103
—— FRANCIS DE SALES, ii. 284
—— GREGORY, Book of Dialogues, i. 1; sends St. Augustine, 3; advice to him, 4
—— HILDA, i. 6, 99
—— MILDRED, i. 101
—— OSWALD, i. 13
—— SCHOLASTICA, i. 97
—— WILFRID, i. 7
—— ALBAN's abbey, i. 25
—— AUGUSTINE, abbey of, i. 4; public school of, 52
—— BENITO, abbey of, ii. 8
—— JAMES's, chapter held at, ii. 176
—— JUSTINA OF PADUA, abbey of, i. 140
—— MAUR, congregation of, i. 141
—— VANNES, congregation of, *ibid.*
—— EDMUND, MONASTERY OF, origin of, ii. 270; foundation of, 279; royal favour, 281; building at, *ibid.*; and king James II., 282; life at, 283; and Benjamin Franklin, 285; and Dr. Johnson, *ibid.*; and St. Francis de Sales, *ibid.*; and Dr. Gifford, *ibid.*; D. Charles Walmesley, 286; "The Academy," *ibid.*; financial difficulties, 287; spirit of, *ibid.*; on the eve of the revolution, *ibid.*; D. Parker's correspondence, 287-290; "Citizen" Shaw, 290; suppression of, 290; extinction of, 291; recovery of the property, 291; a school started, 292; and president Marsh, 291-297; refusals of chapter, 292-294; formal reconstruction at Douai, 296; growth of the college, 297; its gifted sons, 298; D. Oswald O'Neil, prior, *ibid.*; its work, *ibid.*; and the clergy, 299.

Saint GREGORY's MONASTERY, ii. 190; the spirit of, 190, 200, 213, 250; foundation of, 192; election of priors, 192-194; tributes to St. Vedast's, 193; charter of, *ibid.*; under Caverel's visitation, 195; confirmation of charter, 196; deed of acceptance, *ibid.*; obligations of, *ibid.*; funds of, *ibid.*; and college of St. Vedast's, 197; origin of the college, 198; list of martyrs, 199; and D. Baker, 200, 201, 203; numbers at, 204, 218; and Chillingworth, 208; visited by cardinal Howard, 211; daily life at, *ibid.*; liturgical spirit of, 213; and duke of Marlborough, 214; visited by Louis XIV., *ibid.*; rebuilding of the school, 215; and America, 215; proposed foundation, 216; and the French revolution, 217; suppression of, 219; plan of escape, 220; return to Douai, *ibid.*; imprisoned at Doullens, 221; life at Doullens, 220, 223, *note*; Doullens and Wisbeach, 223; mass at Doullens, 224, *note*; search for buried treasure, 226, *note*; return to Douai, 227; return to England, 228; at Acton Burnell, 230; purchase of Downside, 231; possession taken, *ibid.;* destruction of monastery and church, 234, 235; possession recovered of property at Douai, 236; proposed return to Douai, 237, 238; resolution to remain at Downside, 239; new college and church, 240; the struggle with bishop Baines, 241, 245; sends out bishops, 245; new buildings, 246; succession of priors, 246, *note;* renews her youth, 247; building of the minster, 248, 249; new monastery and collegiate buildings, *ibid.;* intellectual life, *ibid.;* hours of studies at Cambridge, *ibid.;* and ven. Oliver Plunket, 249; the future of, 250

Saint LAWRENCE'S MONASTERY, ii. 251; old English congregation admitted to a share, 251; D. Appleby, prior, 252; offshoots from, 252; D. Maihew arrives, *ibid.;* his mode of procedure, 253; missionary spirit of, 254; want of history, 254; starts the mission oath, *ibid.; de non ambiendo, ibid.;* a house of strict observance, *ibid.;* growth at Dieuleward, 255; martyrdom of two monks, *ibid.;* ven. Alban Roe, 256; pestilence at, *ibid.;* reduced state of, *ibid.;* threatened extinction, *ibid.;* difficulties at, 257; fire at, 258; D. Watmough, prior, *ibid.;* D. Catteral, prior, *ibid.;* an alumnate started, *ibid.;* internal state, 259; D. Bolton tried, *ibid.;* D. Marsh, prior, 261; certificates of hospitality, 263; suppression of, 264; the prior's escape, 265; at Acton Burnell, 268; proposed amalgamation with St. Gregory's, *ibid.;* wanderings of the community, 269; Miss Fairfax's generosity, 270; D. Bolton gains Ampleforth, 271; settles at Ampleforth, 272; the growth, 273; its famous men, 274; D. Anselm Burge, prior, 276; its future, 277; *Dieu-le-ward, ibid.*

ST. MALO'S, monastery at, ii. 300; and Charles II., 305; difficulties with the French, *ibid.;* given up to the maurists, *ibid.*

SALAMANCA, theological faculty of, ii. 58

SAXON MONKS, daily life of, i. 15; missions, 9

SAXON NUNS' ILLUMINATIONS, i. 111, *note*

SAXON PRINCESSES, i. 102

SAYER, D., ii. 3

SCRUTATORES ORDINIS, i. 281, 282

SEMINARISTS, unprepared, ii. 42

SERVERS, in the refectory, i. 292; treatment of, 298

SHAFTESBURY, nunnery of, i. 106; abbess of, 107, *note;* 109

SHARROCK, D., ii. 229, *note,* 230

SHAVING, i. 84, 296

SICK, care of, i. 305; visitation of, 53; 305

SIESTA, i. 85; 303

SIMON LANGTON, i. 119

SINGING-SCHOOL, i. 67

SKILLA, i. 290, 972

SLATER, D., ii. 186

SMITH, DR., inquires into faculties, ii. 12; obliged to fly into France, *ibid.*

INDEX

SMYTHE, SIR EDWARD, ii. 229
SOME GENERAL RULES, i. 307
SOMERS, VEN. THOMAS, ii. 59
SOMERSET HOUSE, ii. 173
SOUTHCOTT, D., ii. 181
SPANISH FATHERS, start on the mission, ii. 22; arrive in England, 23; success of, 25, 70; on the look-out for a house, 26; Douai and Dieuleward, 25–69
SPANISH GENERAL, THE, ii. 21; subjection to, revoked, 99
SPANISH MONKS, English vocations, ii. 7, 15, 17; jesuits try to hinder, 17; denounced to the Inquisition, *ibid.*; and to the nuncio, 18; indignation of, 45
STABILITY, i. 47
STAPLETON, BISHOP, i. 108
STAPLETON, D., ii. 173
STAPLETON'S "COUNTERBLAST," i. 166
STOWE'S *MEMORANDA*, i. 197
STUART D'AUBIGNY, ii. 173
SUB-PRIOR, i. 282
SUCCENTOR, i. 284
SUPERIOR OF HOUSES, appointment of, ii. 166
SUSPENSION OF BULL OF PIUS V., i. 245
SWEENY, D., ii. 246
SYON ABBEY, ii. 325, *note*

T

TABULA, i. 284, 299
TE DEUM, ring bells at, i. 285; ii. 212
TEMPEST, ABBAT, ii. 181
TENBY CONVENT, ii. 347
TETTA, ABBESS, i. 104

THORNE, ABBAT, i. 307
THORNTON, BISHOP, i. 171
THOUGHT, development of, ii. 106
THURSTAN AND GLASTON, i. 26
TICHBORNE, FR., S.J., on tolerance, ii. 103
TITHES, i. 56
TITULAR ABBACIES, ii. 186
TREMBLAY, FR. JOSEPH, ii. 131, *note*, 302
TRUTANNUS, treatment of, i. 291
TWO CONGREGATIONS UNITE, ii. 94

U

ULLATHORNE, D., ii. 113, 246
UNION, THE, projects for, ii. 84, 86, 87; meeting at Rheims, 85; Union of the Four Articles, 90; holy see intervenes, 92; letter of gregorians, 93; election of definitors, 94; problem before them, *ibid.*; solution of the problem, 97; opposition to, 99; confirmed by the pope, 100
UNION OF THE TWO PROVINCES, i. 38
UNIVERSITY EDUCATION, i. 40; ii. 248, 276
URBAN VIII., wiser policy of, ii. 114; and the congregation, 167
"USE" OF BEC, THE, i. 22

V

VACANT SEES, filling the, i. 225
VALLADOLID, congregation of, i. 141; seminary of, i. 241; ii. 8
VAUGHAN, D. BEDE, ii. 246
VENTNOR CONVENT, ii. 346

VICARS, origin of, i. 55 ; complaints of, 56 ; civil legislation for, *ibid.*; the tenets of, 59 ; relations with the monks, *ibid.*
VICARS APOSTOLIC, not asked for, ii. 111 ; disputes with, ii. 113, 177
VINEYARDS OF CHRIST CHURCH, i. 80
VISITATIONS, reports of, i. 44, 114
VOYAGE LITTERAIRE, ii. 197, 211, 212

W

WALKER, D., letter, ii. 177 ; his address, 287 ; at Cambrai, 289 ; his death, 322
WALLACE, D., *Life of St. Edmund*, i. 126, *note*
WALSGRAVE, D., clothed, ii. 54 ; opposition of, 99, 164 ; history of, 279, 280, 281
WALSH, DR., ii. 233
WALSINGHAM, SIR F., and Fecknam, i. 208, 209, *note*
WARIN, MASTER, i. 52
WARNER, SIR EDWARD, i. 196
WASHING OF FEET, i. 83
WEGG-PROSSER, MR., ii. 187
WELDON, on the foundation at Douai, ii. 35 ; remarks on, 36
WESTMINSTER, conference at, i. 134 ; reforms of, 136 ; restored, 172 ; with Cassinese ideas, 173 ; secular canons of, *ibid.*; Cassinese visitors for, 174 ; the monks in possession, 175 ; material state of, *ibid.*; numbers at restoration, 176 ; monks of, *ibid.*; 178 ; visit of queen Mary, 177 ; rights of sanctuary, *ibid.*, 179 ; making the paschal candle, 179 ; queen Elizabeth at, 186 ; approaching fate of, 190 ; again dissolved, 193 ; no pensions, 194
WESTON, D. JOHN, an imaginary monk, i. 67 ; his oblation, *ibid.*; growth of his vocation, 68 ; education as a boy, *ibid.*; not a "prig," 69 ; how the call came, 70 ; a novice, 71 ; his training as such, 72 ; a fellow-novice, 73 ; his profession, 75 ; his daily life, 76 ; at choir, *ibid.*; at chapter, 77 ; at mass, 78 ; at meals, 79 ; use of meat, 80 ; use of wine and other drink, *ibid.*; in the cloister, 81 ; in the dormitory ; 85 ; duties of the day, 86 ; at recreation, *ibid.*; during vacation, 87 ; at Oxford, 90 ; ordained, 91 ; an obedientiary, 92 ; as prior, 94 ; his illness, *ibid.*; his death, 95 ; his memory, 96
WESTON, FR., S.J., i. 219, 245 ; his plan, 246 ; his procedure, 247
WHITE MONKS, i. 29
WILFORD, D., clothed, ii. 54 ; D. Leander, 128, 129, 150, 153, *note*; and Buccabella, 151
WILLIAM OF MALMESBURY, i. 22
WILTON NUNNERY, i. 106
WIMBORNE NUNNERY, i. 104
WINCHESTER, the assertion of a monk of, i. 12 ; the centre of the Saxon revival, 13
WINDEBANK, the secretary, ii. 118 ; to Caverel, 147
WISBEACH, Fecknam at, i. 218 ; description of, *ibid.*; charity reigning at, 219 ; life at, *ibid.*; Fr. Weston at, 245 ; troubles at, 246 ; the schism, 247
WOLSEY, CARDINAL, his character, i. 144 ; his reforms, 145 ; his

foundations, *ibid.;* suppresses monasteries, *ibid.;* his fall, 146

WOMEN under the rule, i. 97; early monasteries for, 98

WOODHOUSE, MR., ii. 23

WORCESTER, cathedral monastery, i. 119, *note*

WORTHINGTON, his vow of obedience to Parsons, i. 255; a tool in his hands, ii. 41; delated to Rome, 57, *note;* tries to give up the seminary to the jesuits, 67, *note*

Y

YORK, ordination for the diocese of, i. 59; St. Mary's abbey, ii. 175

THE END

Printed by BALLANTYNE, HANSON & CO.
Edinburgh & London

www.ingramcontent.com/pod-product-compliance
Lightning Source LLC
Chambersburg PA
CBHW030406230426
43664CB00007BB/768